MW00799397

THE BATTLE FOR YOU

Also by Gordon Kainer:
The Other Side of Orion: Unveiling the Mysteries of Heaven

To order additional copies of *The Battle for You,* by Gordon Kainer,
call **1-800-765-6955** or visit **www.adventistbookcenter.com**.

Visit us at **www.reviewandherald.com** for information
on other Review and Herald® products.

GORDON ★ KAINER

THE BATTLE FOR YOU

THE LIFE-AND-DEATH STRUGGLE FOR CONTROL OF YOUR SOUL

REVIEW AND HERALD® PUBLISHING ASSOCIATION
Since 1861 | www.reviewandherald.com

Copyright © 2014 by Review and Herald® Publishing Association

All rights reserved. No portion of this book may be reproduced, stored in a retrieval system, or transmitted in any form or by any means (electronic, mechanical, photocopy, recording, scanning, or other), except for brief quotations in critical reviews or articles, without the prior written permission of the publisher.

The Review and Herald® Publishing Association publishes biblically based materials for spiritual, physical, and mental growth and Christian discipleship.

Review and Herald® books may be purchased in bulk for educational, business, fund-raising, or sales promotional use. For information, e-mail specialmarkets@reviewandherald.com.

Unless otherwise noted, Bible texts are from the *Holy Bible, New International Version.* Copyright © 1973, 1978, 1984, 2011 by Biblica, Inc. Used by permission. All rights reserved worldwide.

Texts credited to ASV are from *The Holy Bible*, edited by the American Revision Committee, Standard Edition, Thomas Nelson & Sons, 1901.

Scripture quotations identified CEV are from the Contemporary English Version. Copyright © American Bible Society 1991, 1995. Used by permission.

Texts credited to Clear Word are from *The Clear Word*, copyright © 1994, 2000, 2003, 2004, 2006 by Review and Herald Publishing Association. All rights reserved.

Scripture quotations marked ESV are from *The Holy Bible*, English Standard Version, copyright © 2001 by Crossway Bibles, a division of Good News Publishers. Used by permission. All rights reserved.

Texts marked KJV are from the King James Version.

Texts credited to Message are from *The Message*. Copyright © 1993, 1994, 1995, 1996, 2000, 2001, 2002. Used by permission of NavPress Publishing Group.

Bible texts credited to NIrV are from the *Holy Bible, New International Reader's Version.* Copyright © 1985, 1996, 1998 by International Bible Society. Used by permission of Zondervan. All rights reserved.

Texts credited to NKJV are from the New King James Version. Copyright © 1979, 1980, 1982 by Thomas Nelson, Inc. Used by permission. All rights reserved.

Scripture quotations marked NLT are taken from the *Holy Bible,* New Living Translation, copyright © 1996, 2004, 2007 by Tyndale House Foundation. Used by permission of Tyndale House Publishers, Inc., Carol Stream, Illinois 60188. All rights reserved.

Bible texts credited to NRSV are from the New Revised Standard Version of the Bible, copyright © 1989 by the Division of Christian Education of the National Council of the Churches of Christ in the U.S.A. Used by permission.

Bible texts credited to Phillips are from J. B. Phillips: *The New Testament in Modern English,* Revised Edition. © J. B. Phillips 1958, 1960, 1972. Used by permission of Macmillan Publishing Co.

Bible texts credited to RSV are from the Revised Standard Version of the Bible, copyright © 1946, 1952, 1971, by the Division of Christian Education of the National Council of the Churches of Christ in the U.S.A. Used by permission.

Bible texts credited to TEV are from the *Good News Bible*—Old Testament: Copyright © American Bible Society 1976, 1992; New Testament: Copyright © American Bible Society 1966, 1971, 1976, 1992.

Statements in this volume attributed to other speakers/writers are included for the value of the individual statements only. No endorsement of those speakers'/writers' other works or statements is intended or implied.

Edited by Vesna Mirkovich
Copyedited by Delma Miller
Cover design by Daniel Anez/Review and Herald Design Center
Interior designed by Derek Knecht/Review and Herald Design Center
Typeset: Minion Pro 11/13

PRINTED IN U.S.A.
18 17 16 15 14   5 4 3 2 1

Library of Congress Cataloging-in-Publication Data
Kainer, Gordon.
  The battle for you / Gordon Kainer.
    pages cm
  Includes bibliographical references.
  ISBN 978-0-8280-2723-6
  1. Seventh-Day Adventists--Doctrines. 2. Church history. 3. Bible--Criticism, interpretation, etc. 4. Eschatology. I. Title.
  BX6154.K35 2014
  230'.6732--dc23
                          2013015350ISBN

978-0-8280-2723-6

Dedication

To all my students in my
academy Bible classes from 1961 to 2001.

Contents

Introduction: God's Story

I t was one of those aha moments! A third-grade teacher pointed to a city on the globe on her desk and asked her students, "How do you know that such a city exists, when you've never been there?" After a few moments a girl raised her hand and said, "If I turn the globe to the place where I live and I see it is right about that, then I know that the globe is right about all the other places." What a simple but insightful answer, one that we can also apply to the way we view the Bible.

Wouldn't it be refreshing if we found the Bible uncomplicated and easy to understand? If we turned each page and found a nice, flowing, continuous story? Perhaps our hope for a "one story" scenario is unrealistic, considering the books of the Bible were written by at least 40 authors over a period of 1,500 years, reflecting a variety of different settings, languages, occupations, and localities. Amazingly, the Bible represents diverse collections of writers, such as kings, fishermen, shepherds, prophets, historians, a tax collector, and even a doctor. Could this be the reason that God's special book has such a wide array of genre and rhetorical forms? With this in mind, what's the chance that we can find any kind of discernible as well as meaningful continuity in the Bible?

As a Bible teacher for many years, I often wondered, *Is there an ideal method of study by which we can accomplish this objective?* Would it help if we studied with others rather than by ourselves? Is it realistic to assume that there's an underlying theme that should be our focus? Our struggle to understand the Bible is not isolated. In a recent issue of *Christianity Today,* the noted American theologian and ethicist Stanley Hauerwas, professor of theological ethics at Duke Divinity School, "recalls asking a classroom of theology students, most of whom had grown up in the church, 'What is the story of the Bible?' He was met by blank stares. Michael Goheen, professor of religious studies at Trinity Western University, found that his students could neither relate the story of the Bible nor explain why it was important."[1]

What is the key to unlocking the Bible's primary theme? Does it have to do with those who study the Bible or, perhaps, with the biblical record of the events themselves? A brief look at the Bible's arrangement obliges us to concede that most of the books seem to be placed in some kind of time sequence. In other words, the Bible starts with Genesis, the book of "beginnings," and more than 1,000 pages later it concludes with Revelation, a book that focuses on "last things." What may throw us awry are the thousands of pages in between that contain chapters relating to history, poetry, prophecies, epistles, exhortations, and genealogies. They seem to lack continuity and connectedness. The idea that the Bible is basically "one story" is not readily apparent. It forces us to admit that understanding the biblical narrative is not a simple matter that is neatly packaged and ready for the marketplace.

In our quest to understand the Bible in its current form we may be wise to look at the sacred writings of other world religions. By examining the insides of these books, you may appreciate the Bible's consistent, coherent flow and the interrelationship of its parts.

There are literally thousands of religions around the world, but let's take a look at the sacred books of Islam and Hinduism. These two religions seem to closely follow Christianity in terms of their numerical size. It is estimated that there are 2.1 billion Christians, 1.5 billion Muslims, and nearly a billion Hindus. These three religions comprise roughly two thirds of the world's population.

The Islamic Koran

The sacred book of Islam is the *Koran*. Contrary to popular Muslim belief, the Koran read by Muslims today is not the same Koran that was spoken (not written) by their prophet Muhammad.[2] When Muhammad died, it was unexpected and without warning, thus no concerted effort had been made to collect the inspired teachings he had dictated to others. This presented a problem to Islam, explains Arthur Jeffery, professor of Semitic languages at Cairo Oriental Studies, Columbia University, and Union Theological Seminary: "To begin with, it is quite certain that when the Prophet died, there was no collected, collated, arranged body of material of his revelations. What we have is what could be gathered together somewhat later by the leaders of the community when they began to feel the need of a collection of the Prophet's proclamations, and *by that time much of it was lost, and other portions could only be recorded in fragmentary form.*"[3]

In Islamic tradition the original copies of the Koran were probably written on anything handy, such as stones, palm leaves, tree bark, animal ribs, wooden boards, or even a variety of human body parts. What was not written down was memorized by the *qurra'*—Muslims who specialized in memorizing and reciting certain suras (i.e., chapters) spoken by Muhammad. According to the Muslim caliphs (religious leader of Islam), the reason that none of the suras were gathered and collated was that Muhammad had never ordered such a thing to be done. However, the loss of some of the *qurra'* at the Battle of Yamama in the year 12 A.H.[4] awakened some of the Islamic leaders to the realization that with a few more battles, a great portion of the revelation material would be irretrievably lost.

This led to the next stage of getting the material assembled and written down in a more fixed and durable form. When the Koran was put together, it was arranged in 114 suras, each with its own title taken from a key word in the text. For some unknown reason, instead of arranging the suras in chronological order and historical sequence, they were arbitrarily placed according to size from the smallest to the largest. The result was a book that was evidently without any logical order of thought, either as a whole or in its parts. Consequently, the reader of the Koran may at one moment read about a Meccan sura and then flip the page to a Medinan sura, and then read further on to another Meccan sura.[5]

Robert Morey, in his book *The Islamic Invasion*, explains, "You are, as it were, left hanging after each Sura because there is no logical connection from one to the other. For example, one Sura will deal with some pedestrian matter such as Allah wanting Muhammad's wives to stop arguing and bickering in his presence, while the next Sura attacks the idols of the Arabians. Thus, you are left with a feeling of incompleteness and dissatisfaction that you are not getting the whole story."[6]

This peculiar structure of the Koran creates yet another serious complication. When it comes to rightly interpreting Islam's holy book, the Muslim believer must abide by *naskh*, the rule that the suras that were written later *overrule*, or *abrogate*, the suras written earlier.[7] This means that some suras actually have little value or significance, based on their time of origin. As Sura 2:107 says: "If We abrogate any verse or cause it to be forgotten, We will replace it by a better one or one similar. Do you not know that Allah has power over all things?"

Let's illustrate this with another sura: "Let there be no compulsion in religion; truth stands out clear from error" (Sura 2:256). Defenders of Islam often quote this verse, but most non-Muslim contemporaries unfamiliar with the Koran imagine that it has the same theological logic as the Christian Bible; thus they assume that Islamic scripture presently teaches religious tolerance toward non-Muslims. But this is an inaccurate assumption, since it is abrogated by verses written later.[8] As a general rule, abrogated verses remain in the Koran, and thus Western readers may mistakenly view them as still representing current Islamic beliefs.

Just a brief overview makes it abundantly clear that the Koran not only lacks systematic coherence but also does not form a unified story.

The Hindu Gita

Hinduism is not only one of the oldest religions known to humankind but also one of the most complex. It is actually a synthesis of the world's religions—always changing, always accommodating the beliefs and practices of other spiritual systems. Hinduism's tolerance of almost all religious viewpoints is based on the pantheistic concept of *monism*—that all things are bound together by a common oneness.

"Hinduism is a religion of great variety, with six major schools and plenty of theological disagreements."[9] Being a pluralistic religion, Hinduism has, understandably, a large array of sacred books. The one most prominent among Hindus is affectionately named *The Song of God*, known as the *Bhagavad Gita*. It is the most sacred, the best known, and the most beloved and read of all Hindu works. Simply referred to as the Gita, this Hindu holy book is 700 verses long and part of the ancient Sanskrit epic *The Mahabharata*.

The context of the Gita is a conversation between two people sitting in a chariot: Lord Krishna and the Pandava prince Arjuna, a practitioner of yoga. It takes place in the middle of a battlefield, with armies on both sides ready to go to war in the climactic battle at Kurukshetra (located in the northern district of Haryana in India). In the midst of Arjuna's confusion and moral uncertainty about fighting, he turns to his charioteer and guide, Lord Krishna (the Master of Yoga), for advice.

In reality, the Gita is a story within a story. Vyasa, an ancient sage, poet, and historian enfolds the story of Arjuna's overt perplexity and Krishna's teaching into the epic poem, *The Mahabharata*, which is centered on a large battle between two factions of the royal clan of the Kurus. It is a classic story of good versus evil, with plots, subplots, twists, and turns, culminating in a great battle scene. The bad guys are part of the "one hundred sons of Dhritarashtra." The good side focuses on the five sons of Pandu, the Pandavas, one of whom is Arjuna.

As the Gita begins, the armies are squared off against each other and waiting for the battle to begin. Krishna, referred to as "the Divine One" overseeing the battle, cannot take sides, so he offers a deal to the leaders of the two armies—one can have his vast army, and the other can have him as a charioteer, even though he will not fight. Arjuna chooses to have Krishna, and Duryodhana, eldest of the 100 sons, is delighted to have Krishna's army. Arjuna asks Krishna to take his chariot to a place where he can see those he will be fighting. As he recognizes some relatives and revered teachers among the enemy army, Arjuna falls into great despair. What should his attitude and perspective be at this moment?

As already stated, in Arjuna's moral dilemma about fighting, he turns to his charioteer and guide, Krishna, for much needed counsel. It is at this point that Krishna's teachings begin. This is no time for empty words. Krishna explains to Arjuna his duties as a warrior and prince. Then in a brief discourse, which later turns into several hundred Sanskrit verses by the sage Vyasa, Krishna outlines to Arjuna the way to live one's life in order to gain perfect self-knowledge and self-mastery—a definitive guide to self-realization. Krishna proceeds to expound on a variety of heavy topics, such as Jnana yoga (path of knowledge), Samkhya (Hindu philosophy), reincarnation, moksha, and karma.[10]

Hindu scholars are divided as to whether the Gita should be regarded as a factual story or an allegory. While the Gita has many inspirational and deeply spiritual insights woven through, it is difficult for the reader to piece together its complexity of thought and teaching. It should be noted that in sharp contrast to the underlying theme of the Bible, in the Gita the Divine One "cannot take sides" in the conflict. This fact greatly hampers or even negates any possibility of a controversy that actively involves human and cosmic forces.

What we have just outlined regarding the scriptural foundations of Islam and Hinduism is also a fitting description of other contemporary religions such as Taoism, Buddhism, Shinto, and Chinese folk religions. This holds true also for the ancient polytheistic and pantheistic belief systems of the Mayan, Egyptian, Babylonian, Arabic, and Greco-Roman civilizations. All of these religions of the past and the present offer a variety of spiritual truths and moral philosophies, but none are recognized for making known a cohesive doctrine of salvation or a unified narrative promoting a universal controversy. Clearly, non-Christian religions do not provide front-row seats for observing the cosmic clash between antithetical worldviews.

The Christian Bible

In *Christianity Today* Leslie Leyland Fields, in her article "The Gospel Is More Than a Story," affirms that "the Christian faith is first, last, and always a story," but she warns that in the pursuit of this story, we may be tempted to abridge or reshape the Bible. We tend to do this, she suggests, by either putting ourselves into the narrative in such a way that we rewrite the biblical story in order to fit our own story or by selectively reading the narrative in a way that simply underlines—and corroborates—our convictions. Keep in mind that we are not the main focus of the Bible. Christ is! The Bible's primary meaning is the story of how Jesus came to save us. If the first question we ask about a Bible text is how it applies to our lives, then we are leaping over meaning and going directly to application. In so doing we place ourselves at the center of the biblical story. We should keep in mind that the Bible is not a safe or simple story. In its pages appear unlikely heroes, terrifying battles, wayward saints, a bloodied God on a cross, as well as wrath and judgment, and therefore we may be enticed to gut the Bible of its offensive side.[11]

In light of the above warning, the Bible, in contrast to the Koran and the Gita, presents an "unabridged" story, "a coherent and powerful narrative."[12] Its many writers speak with one voice. The narrative has one central, all-encompassing thought—a unique plot, predicament, and resolution—whose paramount focus is the entrance of sin into this world and the atonement of Jesus.[13] It leads the reader to a theistic worldview that consistently shapes, at every stage, the stories and statements that make up the biblical narrative. For this reason the Bible, for me as an educator, is without rival.

The central theme of human evil and divine redemption is intertwined, running through the biblical story like a distinct thread. It can be said that this cosmic tension in reality boils down to *God's story versus Satan's story* and the question of whom we should believe. This epic drama involves the entire universe and is generally referred to by Seventh-day Adventists as the great controversy. As this powerful spectacle surges through Scripture, the reason for its existence, its effects on our planet, and God's ultimate solution are clearly set forth. Thankfully, it has a truly satisfying ending.

Ellen White amplifies this underlying theme of God's Word. She says: "The student should learn to view the word as a whole, and to see the relation of its parts. He should gain a knowledge of its grand central theme, of God's original purpose for the world, of the rise of the great controversy, and of the work of redemption. He should understand the nature of the two principles that are contending for supremacy, and should learn to trace their working through the records of history and prophecy, to the great consummation. He should see how this controversy enters into every phase of human experience; how in every act of life he himself reveals the one or the other of the two antagonistic motives; and how, whether he will or not, he is even now deciding upon which side of the controversy he will be found."[14]

Revealed From Above

The familiar old fable of the blind men and the elephant is widely believed to have originated in India and was translated into an English poem, "The Blind Men and the Elephant," by John Godfrey Saxe, in the nineteenth century. Here's a summary of the story: Several blind men from Indostan are led into the king's courtyard, where they encounter an elephant. One feels the tusk and concludes an elephant is like a spear. Another touches a leg and thinks the elephant is like a tree. Yet another bumps into the side of the animal and believes it's like a wall. The one who touches the ear believes the animal to be a soft and flexible creature. Because of each man's ignorance about the whole elephant, a noisy argument ensues. The king hears the commotion, steps out on the balcony, and informs the blind men that each of them encountered only a small part of the entire whole. (Strangely enough, the creator of this story portrays all the religions of the world as blind men.)

The moral of the story is that each religion stumbled upon one particular aspect of ultimate reality but is unaware of the total picture. In light of the fact that every religion makes exclusive claims for its particular view or understanding of truth, the story suggests, there seems to be no logical reason for conflict or quarrel.

However, traditional interpretations overlook the elements that may be the most important part of the story. How do the blind men discover the all-encompassing truth about their encounter with the elephant? I like the way the *Apologetics Study Bible* puts it: it was revealed to them *from above!* When the all-knowing observer, the king, steps out on the balcony, he has a transcendent view that sees all, which enables him to reveal to those below the truth that is not accessible from their limited perspective.[15]

Without divine revelation, finite minds cannot grasp the infinite. While human discovery is always incomplete, divine disclosure, also known as special revelation, offers a much more unabridged picture. What is received from the divine realm amplifies and sharpens our perception of reality. It provides wisdom and insight not only about the innermost sanctum of our lives but also about the world that surrounds us.

Suppose we had the possibility of being seated next to God, to climb up high and get near the throne so we could see things as He sees them. On that level our judgment and discernment would broaden and become comprehensive. However, instead of climbing up to where we can see as God sees, let's think of God coming down to us from above and giving us His ideas, His conclusions, His wisdom, and His view of things. This is what God has done in the Bible, His Word.

Three Steps at a Time

God's special revelation of the big picture, the great controversy theme, can be portrayed in many different ways. This book will employ a simple approach—telling a series of chronicles. The chronicles are just different parts of the same story, and each involves a three-step sequence. This approach will not only allow for a better understanding and easy outline but also identify the key events in this universal narrative. As you become more familiar with the *dry bones* rendition through study and contemplation, God's Spirit, as in Ezekiel 37, will make it come alive with flesh, blood, and sinew, giving the entire story beauty and fullness. Beyond that, studying God's Word in this unique way (three-step sequence) validates the Bible as one amazing story of controversy.

Listed below are the six biblical events we will focus on in this book:

Event 1: Three Steps in Rebellion
    The origin of the great controversy in the angelic uprising in heaven

Event 2: Three Temptations in Eden
    Lucifer's quest to deceive Adam and Eve to join him in rebellion against God

Event 3: Three Temptations of Jesus
The confrontation between Jesus and Satan highlighted in heaven's redemptive plan

Event 4: Three Prophetic Directions
The kings of the north, south, and east in Daniel and how they represent three primary religious worldviews

Event 5: Three Angels' Messages
Heaven's last appeal to the world's inhabitants in the conflict that climaxes the great controversy

Event 6: Three Evil Spirits
Final display of demonic activity and proclamation against God and His people at the end-times.

---

[1] Leslie Leyland Fields, "The Gospel Is More Than a Story," *Christianity Today,* July/August 2012, p. 40.

[2] Muhammad was illiterate and thus simply recited to others what he believed he had verbally received from the angel Gabriel. Thus these revelations became known as the Koran, meaning "the recitation."

[3] Arthur Jeffery, "The Textual History of the Qur'an," *Answering Islam*, accessed Aug. 31, 2012, www.answering-islam.org/Books/Jeffery/thq.htm. (Italics supplied.)

[4] A.H. means "After Hijrah," the time of the withdrawal of Muhammad and his followers from the city of Medina to Mecca in A.D. 622; this marks the beginning of the first year of the Islamic calendar.

[5] Muhammad was born in Mecca around 570 and lived there until he fled to Medina in 622, a migration that became known as the "Hijrah," meaning "flight."

[6] Robert Morey, *The Islamic Invasion: Confronting the World's Fastest Growning Religion* (Las Vegas, Nev.: Christian Scholars Press, 1992), p. 114.

[7] "Abrogation (Naskh)," *WikiIslam*, July 13, 2013; http://wikiislam.net/wiki/Abrogation_%28Naskh%29. See also "Naskh (tafsir)," *Wikipedia*, http://en.wikipedia.org/wiki/Naskh_%28tafsir%29.

[8] In his book *Christian Apologetics: A Comprehensive Case for Biblical Faith* (Downers Grove, Ill.: IVP Academic, 2011) Douglas Groothuis says, "Historic Islam cannot support a Western doctrine of religious and political tolerance" (p. 601).

[9] *Ibid.,* p. 571.

[10] *Reincarnation* is the idea of a continual cycle of rebirths until the soul dissolves into a blissful oneness with the Divine, called enlightenment. *Moksha* is escaping the cycle of rebirths, accomplished by good works or mystical experiences carried out over thousands of lifetimes. *Karma* is the law of cause and effect that determines what condition a person is born into in each succeeding lifetime.

[11] *Christianity Today,* July/August 2012, pp. 41, 43.

[12] Jan Barna, "The Grand Story," *Ministry*, March 2012, p. 21.

[13] "The sacrifice of Christ as an atonement for sin is the great truth around which all other truths cluster. In order to be rightly understood and appreciated, every truth in the Word of God, from Genesis to Revelation, must be studied in the light that streams from the cross of Calvary" (Ellen G. White, *Gospel Workers* [Washington, D.C.: Review and Herald Pub. Assn., 1915], p. 315).

[14] Ellen G. White, *Education* (Mountain View, Calif.: Pacific Press Pub. Assn., 1903), p. 190.

[15] Ted Cabal, ed., *The Apologetics Study Bible* (Nashville: Holman Bible Publishers, 2007), p. 566.

★ 1 ★
The Power of Three

A preacher was pointing out to a group of coal miners how God had so bountifully endowed the earth. "Look at your own occupation," he said. "Isn't it wonderful how God has enabled you to get fuel and power from the earth's resources?"

"That's quite right, sir," replied one of the miners, "but I wish He had put it closer to the top."

I've never stepped into a coal mine or been close to one, but I have seen coal miners coming out of mines that were thousands of feet underground. These men would emerge covered with layers of coal dust and sweat, hardly recognizable as human beings. Far too often, mine explosions and other tragedies have kept miners from surviving a tedious and dangerous job. The lyrics of Loretta Lynn's 1970 country song "Coal Miner's Daughter" display a passionate, true-to-life account of the hardships she endured while living in a coal miner's home in Butcher Hollow, Kentucky. From her perspective, the only thing that kept her father working in the coal mine every night was the love for his family.

Do you see any similarity between coal mining and studying the Bible? Perhaps the connection isn't obvious. Just like miners, students of the Bible are searching for valuable discoveries, the kind that makes them shout *Eureka!*—similar to what miners do when they uncover a lode brimming with coal. Granted, believers are saved by grace through faith alone, *without works*, but this doesn't mean that rewarding, effective Bible study comes without a great deal of digging and hard work.

Biblical truth, like coal, doesn't lie on the surface.[1] It's not readily accessible like dust that's easily blown about. Far below the exterior are facts, concepts, and unfathomable knowledge that need to be dug up, examined, evaluated, and prayerfully applied. Wisdom and real understanding never come without concerted toil and effort. Like Loretta Lynn's father in the coal mine, if we are going to be successful in our mining of the Bible, we too must be driven by love.

Discerning Bible Study

I pointed out in the introduction that the grand underlying theme of the Bible is commonly referred to by Seventh-day Adventists as *the great controversy.* Our goal is to continually discover new and broader dimensions to this ongoing story. It will also be our privilege to discern more fully how to apply the deeper things of God's Word to our own lives.

Although some may declare otherwise, the key issue in the great controversy is not whether God exists. You don't have to look any further than the first verse in the Bible, which states, "In the beginning, God . . ." He was already there! His existence is a given. For many people this an uncontested, foregone conclusion. The controversy seems to be centered, rather, on the nature and character of God. What is God really like?

A youth pastor talking to a classful of children illustrated the practical significance of this when he asked the children to raise their hands if they were willing to follow God and obey Him. All the children eagerly raised their hands, except for one boy. When the pastor looked his way, the youngster quickly defended himself: "I don't want to give my life to God when I don't know what He's like," he said. A very thoughtful response, wouldn't you say? Our concept of God is the most fundamental issue of life. This is because the question "Who am I?" can be understood or answered only in light of the question "Who is He?"

This is impressively demonstrated by Deirdre Sullivan's book titled *What Do We Mean When We Say God?* Is He someone we can love and trust, someone we can be friends with, someone we can obey and be loyal to? It is within this setting that it's been said, "The Bible is all about God." [2]

In our study we are going to see that the way God reveals Himself is in the expansive context of His relationship with people. It is in the Bible that God makes known His will and love through dynamic interaction with the human race, and in real-life stories rather than in mere doctrinal statements. For this reason, we need to make our Bible study personal, practical, and progressive. We need to see God not only as someone who helps us solve the nitty-gritty problems of everyday life but also as someone who expands our perception of the volatile issues that pervade all of reality. Indeed, God desires to comfort us as well as confront us.

An optional assignment I gave to my religion classes involved each student calling five people whose names they randomly selected from the telephone directory. That aspect of their task always elicited a gasp from the students. When the person answered the phone, the students would say that they are doing a survey for a high school class and would appreciate their input. If they got an affirmative response, the students then asked the question "What is your life philosophy?" Most listeners were startled, sometimes to the point of total silence, or reduced to stammering queries as to what the question meant. The students quickly discovered that the majority of people had not really given this question much thought. Can you imagine what the response would have been had the question about life philosophy been replaced with "the great controversy"? It seems that behind the bright lights and outward façade of our everyday culture lurk some haunting questions that many people choose to simply ignore.

Since some of the biblical narrative depicts outlandish, immoral, and violent behavior, we should not assume that the people who act this way are out of the ordinary or radically different from us. The truth is, it's exactly the opposite. They are not exceptions but, rather, typical examples like you and me. Unfortunately, our high opinion of ourselves makes it difficult for us to recognize this similitude. It is instinctive on our part to simply ignore rather than take to heart the warnings and incriminations throughout the Bible. Our natural tendency to see ourselves wiser than our forebears has been insightfully referred to as chronological snobbery. After all, we're far too intelligent to do the stupid things others have done, right? With such rationalization, however, we may miss out on how patient, loving, and just God is when He deals with sinful people like you and me. Pogo the comic strip character seems to be right when he says that someday, sooner or later, we will meet the enemy and discover—*it is us* (see Matt. 23:10). When we carefully peruse Bible stories, all the characters at some point experience this confrontation.

Rather than focusing on our differences, we need to ask ourselves "In what way is their life and experience similar to mine?" Get used to asking the rhetorical but challenging question "You surely can't mean me?" If we fail do this, then such people as Rahab, Jonah, Samson, Lot, or perhaps the Pharisees will come across as having very little to say about God or about us. While we may start out reading biblical narratives as curious spectators, it is essential that we eventually see ourselves as active participants.[3] This will open us to all kinds of new discoveries and practical lessons. Paul expresses it this way: "Now these things which happened to our ancestors are illustrations of the way in which God works" (1 Cor. 10:11, Phillips).

Finally, challenge yourself to discover new truths in old Bible stories or in passages that you are familiar with. It's been said, "Woe to the person who opens God's Word expecting to learn nothing new." As a Bible teacher I discovered that the most difficult lessons to teach were the ones the students were already acquainted with. Too often they saw themselves as saturated Adventists; they had heard it all, or at least they thought they had. They were somewhat like the rich young ruler, who, when he encountered Jesus, declared, "I know all that stuff already."

Studying the Bible is a great pleasure as well as one of the major responsibilities of every Christian. It's exciting to share newly discovered truths and yet, at the same time, humbly acknowledge our ignorance and our self-serving pride. We need to recognize that each of us brings to our study certain prepackaged data, such as cultural blinders that can negatively influence our learning. I am reminded of a cartoon in which a prospective buyer confronted a salesperson in the bookstore with this request: "I want an unbiased history of the Civil War from a Southern point of view." In the study of the Bible, our biases, our preconceived ideas, our social and cultural influences, as well as our limited knowledge of the original time, place, and purpose of the text will affect our discernment.

Instead of skipping over difficult words when we read the Bible, we should look up the definition of the word and do the same with unfamiliar terms, concepts, and ideas. Increase your knowledge about biblical people, places, and locations. When reading a passage or story, become familiar with biblical geography, history, and cultural settings.

In your research, analysis, and prayerful contemplation, avail yourself of such simple tools as a concordance, Bible dictionaries, and books by Ellen White. Discriminate use of technology such as a computer can also be helpful. What can also be beneficial is using a variety of translations of the Bible. Each translation will stimulate new thoughts, broaden your interpretations, and enhance your understanding.

Some of us may have developed an inaccurate or inadequate understanding of the setting or context of biblical events or key texts. This can easily happen if our study tends to be superficial, or we're using (and thus abusing) only the proof-text method of Bible study. Such study involves stringing together biblical passages in a sequence designed to teach predetermined doctrines or points of view. While this method of study has the advantage of having a collection of texts that generally deals with the same topic, it can readily ignore the contextual setting that determines the precise meaning of each text and its proper application. It can also diminish an ongoing awareness of the broad, underlying themes of the Bible.

As you can see, intensive, intelligent Bible study cannot be done easily or quickly, but the payoff is worth it. Your divine teacher, the Holy Spirit, will continually help you to experience the joy of uncovering something that is fresh, enlightening, and useful (see John 14:26; 16:13). It will leave you wondering how you could have known a story or a text of Scripture for so long and not seen what now appears to be obvious to you. Thankfully, aha moments will occur for you when sparkling new wine is poured out even from old wineskins.

Discovering Biblical Continuity
Closely akin to studying the Bible without discernment is the failure to connect Bible stories or texts that may initially appear totally unrelated. This frequently occurs when we specialize in trivia instead of dealing with integration and unity. Rather than wrestling with the big picture, we're busy dabbling with little ones. We've failed to grasp how all the pieces fit together, and thus we miss out on a sense of the ebb and flow of biblical revelation. In our study we're often guilty of not taking time to discern underlying themes, to detect continuity of thought, or to assemble a picture of the whole.

There's great joy in discovering that every piece of the biblical puzzle will ultimately fit together just like the picture on the top of the box. Our problem may be that too often we don't see the connection between some biblical stories or passages and the underlying themes of Scripture. In our view the Bible appears disjointed because we would like it to be one continuous story, a book with one primary message. There's nothing wrong with that view. For this reason, some describe the Bible as an account of Eden lost to Eden restored, while others see it as the ABCs of revelation:

Creation—How did it all begin?
Calamity—What went wrong?
Calvary—Here's the answer!

A good example of biblical unity can also be found in the story of Christ's life. Every aspect of His life and teachings has its seed in the Old Testament. He came to testify to truth already existing. In His sermons recorded in the Gospels, in His conversations with the disciples, in the parables shared with the multitudes, there is scarcely a thought that is not in some way connected with the Old Testament.

In conversing with the two disciples on the road to Emmaus, Jesus let it be known that the Messiah was the unifying theme of Scripture. For these two men everything that had happened the past few days in Jerusalem didn't make any sense. Christ's death had shattered their fondest dreams and dismantled their most cherished hopes. But then Jesus, unrecognized by them, came along, and Luke 24:27 says, "And beginning with Moses and all the Prophets, he explained to them what was said in all the Scriptures concerning himself." Looking back on what they had learned, they could hardly contain their excitement: "Didn't our hearts burn within us as he talked with us on the road and explained the Scriptures to us?" (verse 32, NLT). Why were their hearts ablaze with unbridled enthusiasm? Because Jesus had tied together the entire Old Testament into one exciting story, pointing out how it all focused on the story of the self-sacrificing Messiah.

At the Billy Graham library, a 40,000-square-foot barnlike building near Charlotte, North Carolina, the individual bricks that people walk on were put together in such a way that they form a magnificent cross. But they can be recognized as such only when looked at as a whole. With careful planning and precision, the bricks were joined together so that they would highlight what the designer believed to be the unifying theme of the Bible—the cross of Jesus.

When we look at the Bible, we see many individual stories. These stories relate to one another in the same way as the individual bricks at the library—they have a grand central purpose in mind. They were not randomly scattered bricks on the library walkways. The stories in God's Word are carefully arranged to highlight its central message.

Old and New Testament

One could say that Jesus Himself saw the Old Testament in an altogether different light than that commonly seen by the Jewish leaders of His time. This held true in numerous ways; the most notable was their different views regarding the Messiah. Though those Jews had access to the entire Old Testament, they anticipated His coming as a conquering king rather than a suffering servant. This eventually became the decisive dividing line between Jews and Christians, between unbelievers and believers. If we read the Old Testament without gaining the believer's concept of Christ, then we will be reading the Old Testament as though we reject Jesus as did the nonbelievers of His time.

But beyond that, since the time of Jesus, Christians themselves have been in conflict over the relationship between the Old and New Testament. For many it seems that these two halves of Scripture are practically unrelated to each other. For example, the stern, demanding God of the Old Testament seems very different than the compassionate, loving Jesus of the New Testament. People in the Old Testament appeared to be saved in a way that's unlike the way in the New Testament. God's law is seen as being the focal point of the first half of the Book, while grace seems to be the obvious highlight of the second half. The list goes on. So what's happening here?

The truth is that both Testaments are intimately dependent on each other. Rather than competing with each other, they complement each other. The Old Testament gives us the historical and theological foundation for the New Testament. Thus, we cannot hope to understand and apply the New Testament without a solid acquaintance with and appreciation of the Old. It was never the intent for the Old Testament to be seen as an end in and of itself. It was designed to point us to something—to *Someone*—beyond itself.

The Old Testament has been appropriately likened to a land of symbols and shadows. We are not to settle down there like the Jews of old and fail to see that those shadows and symbols point to Christ. The New Testament is the land of fulfillment. And that fulfillment is embodied in Jesus. While the Old Testament promises, "For behold, the day is coming" (Mal. 4:1, ESV), the New Testament declares, "Today this Scripture is fulfilled in your hearing" (Luke 4:21). Thus, Malachi, the last book of the Old Testament, concludes with a prophecy of Christ's first advent (Mal. 4:5, 6), and Matthew, the first book of the New Testament, ushers it in (Matt. 1:18).

Seventh-day Adventists believe that a right understanding of the Bible enables them to incorporate both Testaments into a single coherent whole. It's been said that the Old Testament is the New Testament *concealed* and the New Testament is the Old Testament *revealed*. Any one text of interest must be seen as part of the larger stream of revelation, a revelation that progressively flows from the Old into the New Testament. As a Bible teacher, I had the privilege of helping students see the intimate relationship between the two Testaments. It was essential for them to recognize that all of the underlying themes of the Bible flowed equally from both the Old Testament and the New Testament.

Let me give you an example. Jesus confirmed the Ten Commandments (as given in the Old Testament) as a *perfect* expression of God's will and then uttered the Lord's Prayer (in the New Testament) as the *ideal* response to it.

The Ten Command-ments	The Lord's Prayer	Their common message
1. No other gods	Our Father	We have only one Father
2. No graven image	Which art in heaven	God has no earthly representation
3. Don't take God's name in vain	Hallowed be Thy name	We are to be reverent with God's name
4. Remember the Sabbath	Thy kingdom come	The sign of God's kingdom
5. Honor your parents	Thy will be done	Parents stand in the place of God
6. You shall not kill	Give us our daily bread	We are not to shorten or take life
7–9. No adultery, stealing, or lying	Forgive us our debts	Sin violates God's law of love
10. Do not covet	Lead us not into temptation	Coveting is the very root of evil

Here we see God's law, as written down on Mount Sinai, and the Lord's Prayer, as spoken on a mountain in Galilee, equally revealing the kind of obedience that identifies those who are saved by grace. In innumerable ways the theme of law and grace is illustrated and reinforced throughout the Bible, sometimes in graphic, unmistakable ways; at other times, in a subtle or mysterious fashion.

Three Steps at a Time

Numbers play an important role throughout Scripture. The most common examples are the numbers 40, 12, 7, and 3. While often used in a literal sense, numbers often convey a symbolic value and call attention to other critical events in the Bible. However, we need to be sure that we make a clear distinction between studying numbers for their numerical or symbolic value, and numerology, where the focus is on the occult use or mystical significance of numbers.

By using a simple numerical device, this book will demonstrate the intimate connection between the Old and New Testament. It will show that the events that connect the Testaments are the foundation for the underlying theme of the Bible. Many of these particular events are unique in that they are associated with the number 3, a number commonly used in Scripture to connect events of great significance. There are scores of examples, as already given in the previous chapter.

In using the "three steps at a time" approach, we are going to explore several major events in the Old and New Testament in order to discover their contributions to the underlying theme of the Bible—the great controversy.

---

[1] "The most valuable teaching of the Bible is not to be gained by occasional or disconnected study. Its great system of truth is not so presented as to be discerned by the hasty or careless reader. Many of its treasures lie far beneath the surface, and can be obtained only by diligent research and continuous effort" (E. G. White, *Education*, p. 123).

[2] Marva Dawn, *In the Beginning, God: Creation, Culture, and the Spiritual Life* (Downers Grove, Ill.: InterVarsity Press, 2009), p. 9.

[3] "Stories are the most prominent biblical way of helping us see ourselves in 'the God story,' which always gets around to the story of God making and saving us. Stories, in contrast to abstract statements of truth, tease us into becoming participants in what is being said. We find ourselves involved in the action. We may even start out as spectators or critics, but if the story is good (and the biblical stories are very good), we find ourselves no longer just listening to but inhabiting the story" (Eugene H. Peterson, "Introduction: Jonah," *The Message Remix: the Bible in Contemporary Language* [Colorado Springs: NavPress, 2006], p. 1352).

★ 2 ★
Walks, Stands, and Sits

Blessed is the man who walks not in the counsel of the ungodly, nor stands in the path of sinners, nor sits in the seat of the scornful; but his delight is in the law of the Lord, and in His law he meditates day and night . . . and whatever he does shall prosper. The ungodly are not so, But are like the chaff which the wind drives away. Therefore the ungodly shall not stand in the judgment, nor sinners in the congregation of the righteous. For the Lord knows the way of the righteous, but the way of the ungodly shall perish.
—Ps. 1:1-6, NKJV

Walk, stand, sit. These three words portray in order the steps of a righteous life or an evil one. The righteous life is blessed; like a tree planted by the water, it will prosper. The evil life is cursed; unstable like the chaff that the wind blows away, it will perish. As is clearly illustrated throughout the Bible, every one of us is going in one of two directions: either climbing the steep ascent to heaven or descending down a pathway away from God to certain destruction.

The Downward Path

The road to apostasy and unbelief is not one of swift action or a sudden downward plunge. At times we may be caught off guard by a serious blunder by someone we know, making us wonder how he or she could have fallen so far so quickly. But the truth is that deterioration of character is gradual, taking place in such small increments that it's nearly imperceptible to us or to others. Many times as a teacher I had the opportunity to observe firsthand how students at school changed slowly through the years in such a way that they were often unaware they had become entirely different persons.

The psalmist tells us that the downward path is highlighted by three choices. The first is *walking* in the counsel of the ungodly. The ungodly could be classified as respectable sinners, people who seem to be relatively good, whose true colors (motives) are carefully hidden. There are no overt signs that something is terribly wrong, so their advice is still sought and valued. However, those who associate with the skeptical at heart will slowly but surely become skeptical themselves.

Walking with the ungodly makes taking the second step easy: *standing* with sinners. Standing, or hanging around, indicates that one has found agreement with the opposition. He or she feels at home with that kind of surrounding. It indicates a growing insensitivity to sin—losing one's antagonism toward evil and being brought under its spell.

Walking naturally leads to the final step: *sitting* with the scornful. This suggests an act that is deliberate and defiant—no misgivings or apologies. Sitting indicates that one has settled into a lifestyle that's hardened and confirmed in sin.

So then, sin generally occurs in three simple steps: gradual, decisive, and final. Someone once described it like this: "An evil thought passes your door, first as a stranger; next, it enters your room as a guest; and finally, it installs itself as lord and master."

The anatomy of a gradual shift in one's spiritual perspective is visually illustrated in Zechariah 7:11, 12: "But they refused to heed, shrugged their shoulders, and stopped their ears so that they could not hear. Yes, they made their hearts like flint, refusing to hear the law and the words which the Lord of hosts had sent by His Spirit" (NKJV).

These are the words the prophet uses to describe Israel's disheartening response to God's loving exhortations. It's essential for us to see that Scripture portrays the progressive change of a person's attitude by likening it to three expressions of body language. First, they shrug their shoulders; second, they stop their ears; third, they harden their hearts. Once rebellion is initiated, it gradually but relentlessly becomes more inward and intense. While shrugging one's shoulders suggests a lackadaisical attitude, closing one's ears is a deliberate choice that finally infects the heart, hardening it like flint—the hardest of all stones. It reminds us of Jeremiah's statement, "The sin of Judah is written with a pen of iron; with the point of a diamond it is engraved on the tablet of their heart" (Jer. 17:1, NKJV).

The Original Rebellion

These three steps of evil, while a visual portrayal of human behavior, also highlight the angels' rebellion. Our world has endured all kinds of strife, revolutions, world wars, as well as personal struggles and tragedies, but only the Bible makes us aware of the warfare that underlies all other conflicts—*the controversy that began in heaven.*

To understand that controversy, let's take a step back and consider that each one of us is individually etched in the mind of God because He is the ultimate center of all reality. It is only as we come to know Him and His Word that we can correctly interpret the significance of everything else. This holds true whether we are dealing with the reality of goodness and truth or the existence of sin and conflict. It is God's Word alone that makes us aware of the warfare that undergirds all discord and hostility—what we've come to know as *the great controversy.* While its breadth encompasses the universe, its depths reach the innermost recesses of the human heart. There are no exemptions in this war; everyone is a participant in the struggle of life and death, whether they like it or not.

The "great controversy" motif is a biblical, comprehensive framework through which Christians, especially Seventh-day Adventists, view and understand the entire span of human history.[1] According to this paradigm, the entire universe is focused on and affected by an unrelenting conflict between the forces of good and evil, both seen and unseen, which had its beginning even before creation (see 1 Cor. 4:9).

Revelation 12 describes the initial outbreak of this conflict in a very concise and straightforward manner: "Then war broke out in heaven. Michael and his angels fought against the dragon, and the dragon and his angels fought back . . . and *they lost* their place in heaven" (verses 7, 8). This brief summary of an extremely unusual war contains no basic explanations or commentary. Thus it raises some intriguing questions: Why an insurrection—an arrogant challenge to God's rulership in the holiest of all places? How could such a devastating event occur in a perfect environment?

To understand why Lucifer chose to rebel against God and establish a rival kingdom, we need to know what he was rebelling against.

God reveals to us in His Word that since the beginning of time the universe has been ruled by a government based on love. There was no aggression, no selfishness, no striving for mastery, no lack of communication, and no competitive rivalry—only loving cooperation between God and His creation. Nothing that was needed was missing. Yet at some point in eternity a revolutionary idea was introduced. God has never been opposed to new ideas, but this one emerged as the deadly seed of a rival power system.

Reading Lucifer's personal manifesto against God helps us to get a better handle on the underlying nature of his allegations: "You said in your heart, 'I will ascend to the heavens; I will raise my throne above the stars of God; I will sit enthroned on the mount of assembly, on the utmost heights of Mount Zaphon'" (Isa. 14:13). Or as *The Message* puts it: "You said to yourself, 'I'll climb to heaven. I'll set my throne over the stars of God. I'll run the assembly of angels that meets on sacred Mount Zaphon. I'll climb to the top of the clouds. I'll take over as King of the Universe!'" Sounds very much as though Lucifer had become an unhappy camper, a disgruntled angel.

Lucifer's self-serving aspiration reminds me of an insightful study done several years ago. It revealed that in a normal environment the personal pronoun "I" is used once in every 30 words. In a psychiatric institution, "I" is spoken every 15 words. In Satan's declaration recorded in Isaiah, "I" occurs every nine words. But in the Sermon on the Mount, "I" appears every 94 words. In the Lord's Prayer, "I" is never used at all. This insight highlights the contrast between the evil one and those with the mind of Christ, doesn't it?

In the book of Isaiah we discover the core idea in Lucifer's rival system: love for God gets twisted around into love of self. Such a frame of mind occurs when one's desires and thoughts are defiantly and scornfully turned inward. Love of self is an egocentric clamor for the most power, the highest place, and the greatest honor for oneself. Whenever self takes over, it always aspires to God's level. God's unique position of not having to take orders from a superior is exactly what self desires for itself. It wants to rule; it wants to give the orders; it wants to make the laws. Self is not content until it has usurped the power of God.

All of this raises some far-reaching questions: How could someone who already was "the model of perfection" (Eze. 28:12, NLT) have such unbelievably egotistical ambitions? How could such feelings and thoughts arise in one who was the most exalted and gifted angel in heaven, one described as God's "anointed" (verse 14)?

The inception of sin is a perplexity that baffles all explanations; hence, the Bible calls it the "mystery of iniquity" (2 Thess. 2:7, KJV). Could Jean-Paul Sartre have been describing Lucifer's particular vanity when he wrote, "Life has no meaning the moment you lose the illusion of being eternal"?

Ezekiel gives us some additional details as to what was going on in Lucifer's troubled mind: "Your heart became proud on account of your beauty, and you corrupted your wisdom because of your splendor" (Eze.

28:17). *The Message* puts it very succinctly: "Your beauty went to your head." The awakening of the original sin was definitely an inside job. In becoming enamored with his own beauty and brilliance, this "angel of light" (2 Cor. 11:14) turned himself into a demon of darkness—a liar and a deceiver. And the first one to be deceived was Lucifer himself. The Bible maintains that his rebellion had no legitimate or rightful cause; it was based entirely on his deception and pride. Jesus made this clear when He called Satan "a liar and the father of lies" (John 8:44).

This is affirmed in Revelation 12:4, where we learn that in the angelic uprising "Its [the dragon's or Satan's] tail swept a third of the stars out of the sky and flung them to the earth." This tells us not only the number of angels that were deceived but also how their deception came about. Isaiah gives us a clue: "The prophet who teaches lies, he is the tail" (Isa. 9:15, NKJV). In other words, it was the lies of Satan—his deceptive allegations against God, his verbal suspicions hurled against God's character, government, and laws—that proved to be the deciding factor for those who chose to rebel.

Lucifer's pride, egotism, and self-interest so twisted the thoughts and desire of his own heart that he began to view God as nothing more than a rival to heaven's throne. What blatant arrogance! Slowly but surely his jealousy of God's position, his mounting desire for supremacy, and his ability to make his clamor for greatness sound right and reasonable led to a restless, contentious fervor among the angels. In a mysterious, cunning way he was able to excite a spirit of opposition to God and diffuse a spirit of disaffection among the angelic host. It set the stage for vigorous discontent to spread throughout heaven. Suspicion, alienation, accusations, and disruptive violence eventually began to reverberate throughout heaven's corridors.

Ellen White states that Satan deceptively claimed that he simply wanted to improve God's government—His governing framework.[2] In reality, his purpose was to "dethrone" God and rule the universe himself.[3] All along he had no intention of making his real ambition fully known to the angels. Many of them did not discern his double-edged attitude, depicted so clearly by the psalmist: "The words of his mouth were smoother than butter, but war was in his heart: his words were softer than oil, yet they were drawn swords" (Ps. 55:21, NKJV).

Lucifer did not fully understand at first where he was drifting, but slowly and imperceptibly his feelings of jealousy and envy turned into full-fledged defiance and discontent. In line with his carefully crafted "false assertions,"[4] he began to "insinuate doubts concerning the laws that governed heavenly beings."[5] Interestingly, when Lucifer began to criticize the law of God, "the thought that there was a law came to the angels almost as an awakening to something unthought of."[6] He presented God as being selfish and arbitrary, forcing His will upon them and reducing their freedom. He spoke of God's laws as "an unnecessary restraint,"[7] promoting instead the alluring idea of "unrestricted freedom."[8] He had become heaven's first advocate of "deregulation." He reasoned that holy, sinless beings were capable, in and of themselves, of making the right choices. Lucifer, "anointed as a guardian cherub" (Eze. 28:14), the one especially ordained as the defender and protector of God's law, had himself become the first "lawless one" (2 Thess. 2:8).

Lucifer claimed that his only desire was that heaven's occupants experience a higher level of existence—one of absolute freedom—a life immune from all divine restrictions and authority. He contended that law and freedom could not exist together, blatantly equating total freedom with total happiness. His desire for Godlike autonomy was persuasively presented as an enticing alternative to the inhabitants of heaven, capped by his concluding argument, as John T. Anderson demonstrates, that the angels had unwittingly become God's slaves.[9] This so inflamed the passions of the angels that one third of them erupted in open rebellion against God.

While it's nigh unto impossible to understand Lucifer's rebellion, it's equally mind-boggling to think that one third of the angels chose to follow his example! Who would have thought that holy angels would come to defy a loving God and actually go to war against Him? One wonders how any of the intelligentsia of heaven could have been attracted to or had any faith in Lucifer's unproven proposals. What were they thinking? Did he confuse them with his sophistry, manipulate them with his charm, or distort the controversy to blur the primary issues and obscure the ultimate consequences? Did the self-aggrandizements that he insinuated actually blind some of the angels to potential pitfalls? Was he such a gifted spokesperson that the angels believed his misrepresentations of God—that the Father was arbitrarily harsh and manipulative—and thus perceived their Creator as their adversary? Were they deceived into thinking that Lucifer's ideas would ultimately improve heaven's government?

God could have immediately destroyed the archrebel along with his combative cohorts, but this would have only expanded the insurgency.

Nothing would have been resolved by arbitrary destruction. Swift retaliation on God's part would certainly have created new fears and suspicions among His creatures. In His infinite wisdom and patience, God gave Satan the opportunity to demonstrate more fully his proposals so that the real nature of sin would become evident to angels and the universe.

God knew that He could not refute Lucifer's charge by merely displaying superior strength; it had to be by demonstrating the depths of His love and the rightness of His ways. What this cosmic conflict required was a revelation of God's character so vivid and compelling that it would forever silence all critics about the underlying essence of His government.

No doubt God could have, in a relatively simple, easy manner, removed the rebellious angels from heaven. But instead He chose the loyal angels as His partners in casting out Satan and his angels. Now, that's a thought that always amazes me. How significant it is that the restoration of heaven to its original purity occurred through a *war* that embraced all of heaven's inhabitants. Apparently, the angels who remained faithful to God were to be decisively tested by their active involvement in casting out their former comrades who had chosen to rebel. The breakup of angelic friendships defies our imagination. What an excruciating, painful experience that must have been. But only with the departure of the rebellious ones could heaven be restored to its former state of love and harmony.

We may be tempted to think this wasn't war as we know it; the Bible simply says both sides "fought" and that the rebellious beings "lost their place" in heaven. But this is the language of a real war. Ellen White says that even today, "the battles waging between the two [heavenly] armies are as real as those fought by the armies of this world." [10]

Lucifer's Claims Examined

Lucifer's subversive objectives must be seen in light of the fact that God is the ultimate wellspring of *life* and *love* (John 1:4; 1 John 4:8) as well as the universal administrator of *law* and *justice* (Ps. 19:7). These unique attributes are the very heart of His nature and character and serve as the infrastructure of His government. Lucifer's declaration was not only self-serving and defiant but was also an inflammatory accusation regarding God's rightful position as the Creator, the ultimate Authority, Lawgiver, and Judge. It was a direct challenge to the person, power, and position of God, an open accusation of His being unfit to rule the universe.

Lucifer's attack on God as Creator may come as a surprise to many, but from the very beginning it played an important role in his defection. In his declaration of war, he made no distinction between himself, a created being, and God the Creator—as though they were vying for the same position. In Lucifer's flagrant disregard of this essential difference, he was attempting to negate the necessity of the creature being totally dependent upon the Creator. It seems that it was within Lucifer's heart that the beginning traces of evolutionary thinking first sprouted into existence. After all, according to the principles and discourse we find in the Bible, the theory of evolution is not based on scientific evidence but rather on the desire to be one's own god.

Ellen White adds another dimension to all of this as she explains that when the Godhead planned the creation of this world, Lucifer's disappointment in not being part of the planning committee turned into bitterness.[11] He was disgusted at being left out. This was probably encouraged by the fact that he saw himself as "a favorite in heaven among the angels."[12] His anger was fueled by his self-serving pride. His jealousy of Jesus' position of equality with the Father festered in his mind until love and loyalty for his Creator was unilaterally transferred to himself. Lucifer's affections had taken an unjustified and ill-fated turn.

In God's preordained structure of the universe, divine love plays a paramount role. Created beings are designed to live within loving relationships. The outgoing love of the Creator serves as the model for all other relationships. This divine pattern not only keeps the union between God and the created beings intact but also ensures peace and harmony throughout the universe. For this to happen, human beings are to depend upon their Creator for guidance as to how life is to be lived. They need to understand that the moral framework of the divine law—a law that is to be freely chosen and obeyed by all, safeguards love. But Lucifer failed to accept God's law as a revelation of divine wisdom and love, even though it reveals the truth about life and how it ought to be lived.

A delicate and essential relationship exists between law and love. The *principles* of divine love are found within the *parameters* of God's law. It is God's Word that gives love its content and direction; it provides a flawless explanation of how real love works. In other words, love's role is to *inspire,* to motivate us to obey God and serve others, while the role of law is to *instruct,* to define for us what obedience to God and serving others really means. From heaven's perspective, love and law are complementary, each playing an important role in maintaining order and stability while upholding the spirit of unselfishness.

Three Steps Downward

So what have we established? The road to apostasy and unbelief is not one of swift action or sudden plunge. You could say that there are three basic steps in the spawning of evil in the establishment of a rival kingdom. Lucifer's first step was to initiate *doubt* regarding the character of God and the authority of His law. Lucifer's doubts were not so much an honest intellectual questioning of the mind owing to a lack of knowledge, but rather unbelief of the heart that springs from pride and jealousy. His doubts regarding God's way of doing things increased in proportion to his desire for a higher position. His doubts eventually led him to challenge reality as it existed and then questioning God's fairness and justice as a ruler.

Lucifer's next step was *presumption,* an act or attitude of believing that something is true for which there is no proof or evidence. He presumed he had a better idea, a better way of governing the universe—one that set aside God's law. His arrogance incited him to create an alternative, assuming that his self-seeking proposals would improve God's government.

Lucifer claimed that he simply wanted to give the divine government a well-deserved face-lift. He went about his work, however, in "so deceptive a way that many of the angels were won to his allegiance before his purposes were fully known." [13] With extreme subtlety and mysterious secrecy, he made it appear to heaven's inhabitants "that he was seeking the good of the universe." [14]

His final step was choosing *independence.* Lucifer's pride led him to issue the very first declaration of independence, breaking his relationship with his Creator. He chose separation, demanding complete freedom from God's sovereign rulership and establishing for himself a self-centered existence. He chose to become his own god—something that could be accurately labeled as the ultimate fantasy. Lucifer, the brightest of all creation had slowly, but decisively, become Satan, the adversary. By transferring his trust, loyalty, and allegiance from the Creator to the creature, the disastrous notion we now know as sin became a reality in a once-perfect universe.

Biblical History: Not Make-Believe

Many years ago I came across an interesting story in the July 22, 1967, issue of the *Saturday Review.* In the Trade Winds section, the editor wrote on August 5, 1961, that as a joke he had written about Alexander the Great having invented the first wristwatch. Supposedly the renowned Grecian ruler had worn a chemically treated cloth under his left forearm and from the heat of the sun the cloth changed colors each hour. With tongue in cheek the editor referred to it as "Alexander's Rag Time Band."

The 1966 issue of *Product Engineering* picked up on the story and gave it credibility by declaring that change in the color of a substance when it is exposed to radiant energy, such as sunlight, is known as *photochromism*. Additional authenticity was added to the story each time it passed from one scientific journal to another. In 1967 the Pittsburgh Plate Glass Company traced the story back to its beginning and asserted that photochromic materials were first exploited by Alexander the Great and "among historians it is known as Alexander's Rag Time band." The footnote gave reference to the original spoof paragraph that was written August 5, 1961, in the *Saturday Review* Trade Winds section. The fabricated story had come full circle.

I suppose it's quite common to take what is false, whether it be political, religious, or historical, and teach it as truth. Satan, "the father of lies," is equally guilty of the opposite error. He would like for us to think that the account of his three-step rebellion in heaven isn't a historical fact at all but simply a fable like the other stories in the Bible.

We are told that Adam and Eve "were not left without a warning of the danger that threatened them. Heavenly messengers opened to them the *history of Satan's fall*" and his plot to overthrow God's government.[15] This was all transmitted to them shortly after their creation. The fact that our first parents chose to believe the serpent, rather than what God and the angels had shared with them, leads us to this question: Did our first parents truly understand and accept what they had been told about Satan's fall? We will take a look at the evidence in the next chapter.

---

[1] It has been observed that the great controversy theme dominates the writings of Ellen White, of which the five books in the Conflict of the Ages Series are its most complete and comprehensive form. In this series she unfolds the most important controversy in human history, identifies the main issues, and demonstrates their relevance for each individual.

[2] Ellen G. White, *The Great Controversy* (Mountain View, Calif.: Pacific Press Pub. Assn., 1911), p. 498.

[3] Ellen G. White, *The Desire of Ages* (Mountain View, Calif.: Pacific Press Pub. Assn., 1898), p. 57.

[4] Ellen G. White, *Testimonies for the Church* (Mountain View, Calif.: Pacific Press Pub. Assn., 1948), vol. 8, p. 290.

[5] Ellen G. White, *Patriarchs and Prophets* (Mountain View, Calif.: Pacific Press Pub. Assn., 1890), p. 37.

[6] Ellen G. White, *Thoughts From the Mount of Blessing* (Mountain View, Calif.: Pacific Press Pub. Assn., 1956), p. 109.

[7] E. G. White, *The Great Controversy*, p. 495.

[8] E. G. White, *Patriarchs and Prophets*, p. 41.

[9] John T. Anderson, *Three Angels, One Message* (Hagerstown, Md.: Review and Herald Pub. Assn., 2012), p. 191.

[10] E. G. White, *Thoughts From the Mount of Blessing*, p. 119.

[11] Ellen G. White, *The Story of Redemption* (Washington, D.C.: Review and Herald Pub. Assn., 1947), pp. 13, 14.

[12] *Ibid.*

[13] *The Seventh-day Adventist Bible Commentary* (Washington, D.C.: Review and Herald Pub. Assn., 1953-1957), Ellen G. White Comments, vol. 7, p. 972.

[14] *Ibid.*, p. 973.

[15] E. G. White, *Patriarchs and Prophets*, p. 52. (Italics supplied.)

★ 3 ★
The Controversy Renewed

Sir Walter Raleigh, born in 1552, is credited with introducing potatoes and tobacco to England. At the age of 51 he was arrested and imprisoned in the Tower of London, from 1603 to 1616. Although innocent of the charges brought against him, he was apparently thankful for those responsible for putting him there. He said it gave him the chance to write the book *History of the World*. It is believed that when he had written about 200 pages, he was interrupted by a commotion in the courtyard caused by two prisoners who were involved in a violent argument. In the midst of the fighting, Raleigh tried unsuccessfully to discover the reason for this prison squabble. He later confessed that when he failed to find out why this ruckus right under his window had occurred, he began to seriously question his attempt to explain events that had happened more than a thousand years earlier.[1]

How thankful we should be for the Bible, which "is the most ancient and the most comprehensive history that men possess. . . . Here only is given a history of our race unsullied by human pride or prejudice."[2] So what do we find? God's Word draws back the curtains, giving us a glimpse of the dawn of humankind, as well as a firsthand view of the inception of sin. With amazing accuracy and candor it reveals that the seeds of rebellion and warfare were first sown within the borders of heaven itself (Rev. 12:7). It makes known the tragedy of Lucifer's implausible revolt, with the Creator Himself becoming the first Father to experience the loss of a prodigal son—a son who never does return to his Father. When heaven's government becomes the target of an ugly angelic uprising, and God unbelievably loses one third of His heavenly family, understandably it sends shock waves throughout the universe (see 1 Cor. 4:9).

Two Rebellions Linked
Revelation 12:8, 9 is the only text in the Bible that directly links the war in heaven with the spiritual warfare that now rages on Planet Earth. Verse 8

describes the war and how the dragon and his angels "lost their place in heaven." Further explanation is carried forth in verse 9: "The great dragon was hurled down—that ancient serpent called the devil, or Satan, who leads the whole world astray. He was hurled to the earth, and his angels with him."

It would be a serious error to assume that Satan and his angels had no choice in coming to this earth after their defeat in heaven, that they were indiscriminately flung into space and they just happened to land on this planet. After being cast out of heaven, Satan held a strategy session with those who fell with him, and a cleverly laid plan was devised. It was determined that they would come to this planet, which was created very shortly after their rebellion, to set up a rival kingdom that would hopefully one day encompass the whole universe. Indeed, "Lucifer had concluded that if he could carry the angels of heaven with him in rebellion, he could carry also all the worlds."[3]

There seem to be at least two underlying reasons that Satan came to this earth: to tempt Adam and Eve and to establish his headquarters here. First of all, he was still angry over the fact that he felt snubbed with its creation. Scripture makes this clear when it says, "The devil has come down to you [the earth] in great wrath," knowing he only has a short time to carry out his vengeful designs (Rev. 12:12, RSV). When "God said to His Son, 'Let us make man in our image,' Satan was jealous of Jesus. He wished to be consulted concerning the formation of man, and because he was not, he was filled with envy, jealousy, and hatred."[4] Second, it was his scheme to get the inhabitants of this newly created planet to join him in his rebellion against God's government. He had reasons to believe that those who would remain faithful to God would one day take the place of the angels who had rebelled.

This is what Ellen White asserts: "God created man for His own glory, that after test and trial the human family might become one with the heavenly family. It was God's purpose to re-populate heaven with the human family, if they would show themselves obedient to His every word. Adam was to be tested, to see whether he would be obedient, as the loyal angels, or disobedient."[5]

Ellen White also states that Satan knew of this plan, as indicated when he hurled the following accusation against God: " 'Are these,' he says, 'the people who are to take my place in heaven and the place of the angels who united with me?' "[6] The apostle Paul provides an additional dimension to this when he states that God will give His saved people the special opportunity to "judge [the fallen] angels" (1 Cor. 6:3; cf. 2 Peter 2:4; Isa. 14:16, 17).

This is confirmed when we are informed in Isaiah 14:13 that Satan's ambition to sit on God's throne is never realized; instead, Satan is "hurled to the earth" (Rev. 12:9) at the conclusion of the war in heaven, and God ultimately offers the redeemed the privilege of sitting with Jesus on His Father's throne (Rev. 3:21).

No doubt, the divine intention to exalt the role of the redeemed in this way continues to fuel the fierce anger that Satan has for this planet, his anger toward all earthlings who are faithful to their Creator and are taken to heaven at the Second Coming. Revelation 12:17 states that to the very end he is "enraged at the woman" (symbol of the faithful). It also indicates why Satan so impassionedly detests the Sabbath—it is, after all, a special memorial of the Creation event.

The close link that exists between the rebellion in heaven and the creation of the earth, as just pointed out, suggests that these two events apparently follow each other rather closely.[7] One can only assume that old accusations and angry resentments of God's government by the defeated angelic foes are carried over from one event to the other.

In light of this background, we see that it's not a coincidence that Genesis is placed at the beginning of the biblical narrative. The opening story of the Bible is the Creator's introduction of Himself to us following heaven's rebellion. He is mentioned 26 times before human beings even come on the scene. It is the Creation that clearly reveals the heart of God—His generosity, His goodness, and His loving intentions for human beings. Every human need is lavishly provided for. Eden's first residents, amidst the luxury, beauty, and sensory delights, have no harsh or unseemly restrictions. You could not ask for a more ideal beginning. One can only agree with God that His creation was indeed "very good" (Gen. 1:31). With the very first biblical event, earth's creation, God makes evident that He is not what Lucifer and his cohorts make Him out to be (see John 8:44). Romans 1:20 makes this clear: "Since the creation of the world God's invisible qualities—his eternal power and divine nature—have been clearly seen, being understood from what has been made."

God as a person who is loving, intimate, and personal is not only portrayed in the act of creating Adam and Eve but also demonstrated in providing the Sabbath rest for them. Keep in mind God's seventh day, which was Adam and Eve's first full day, was not simply a day of rest but a special day set aside for intimate fellowship and celebration with loved ones. The Sabbath was a time for God the Creator and His creatures to commune and worship together. Setting aside the Sabbath for such a purpose was God's unique way of saying to the earth's first residents, "I love you. Let's spend some time together." God blessed and sanctified the seventh-day Sabbath with His presence before there was any mention of an anticipated human response. How sad that God's appointed day of rest at Creation has been distorted into a legalistic symbol of salvation by works. Just as Creation was not completed with natural causes, so it is that redemption is not to be completed by human works.

It is not by accident that the gracious events associated with earth's creation were undoubtedly one of God's ways to answer Satan's charges. Rather than being severe or repressive, as Satan had alleged, the Creator is very open and loving in His dealings with earthlings. Clearly, the Scripture wants our first impression of God to be a lasting one. It wants us to have a positive picture of our Maker as we maneuver our way through the sordid stories that follow in the Old Testament, stories that may at times cloud and distort the loving intentions of God.

Shortly after the Creation week came to a close and Adam and Eve were settled in their lovely Eden home, angels were sent to share with them significant details regarding a lurking, unseen enemy. What they needed to know regarding the issues at stake is especially applicable to us: we are born in a world that's already under siege by this evil one. Unlike Adam and Eve, none of us showed up as loving sons and daughters in the Father's house but rather as shameful slaves in a "far country" (Luke 15:13, NKJV). Granted, "God is love" (1 John 4:8), but like the prodigal son, we're prone to believe that the Father has not been good to us. But the truth about His infinite love has been obscured, distorted, and defaced by the graffiti of our own sin and rebellion. Our hearts and minds have been crippled with lies about true love, bombarded as we are with neurotic stories of lust and rampant covetousness that have such great appeal. From the very start we are "born sinners, even from birth [we] have lied [and have been lied to by those around us] and gone [our] own way" (Ps. 58:3, NLT). The apostle Paul declares that we arrive on this planet "gratifying the cravings of our flesh and following its desires and thoughts" (Eph. 2:3). Under such debased conditions it's imperative to know the truth about a dangerously deceptive enemy and why everything in the world is in the predicament it is—and God's plan for resolving it.

From the Very Beginning

The Bible makes it obvious that before sin entered this world, humankind only experienced life in harmony with God. There was wholehearted unity—an expression of heartfelt agreement and obedience to God's Edenic instructions. Simply put, living was all about loving, sharing, and giving. From the very beginning love was at the heart of Adam and Eve's relationship with their Creator and with each other. In such an environment there was no lack of any kind.

In the first two chapters of Genesis, God provides Adam and Eve with every physical, social, and spiritual comfort; an ideal world of gratifying tasks to perform; appetizing food to eat; aesthetic pleasures to enjoy; and the Sabbath for rest, communion, and worship. He gave them grand, ennobling purposes for their lives, guiding principles for their personal relationships, and appointed them as regal caretakers over all creation. They received specific guidelines for their work and conduct in Eden, including permission to freely eat of every tree of the garden, except the tree of the knowledge of good and evil. Denial of access to this tree served as a simple but essential test of their faith and loyalty to their Creator.

We do not know how much time elapsed between the impeccable beginning and the subtle entrance of the serpent, that beautiful creature through which Satan tempted Eve to eat the forbidden fruit. One needs only to read Genesis 3 for a few moments to encounter this baffling story—the event that changes everything. The wily serpent tempts Eve and then Adam, not with fear or intimidation, but with the thought that life isn't quite the way it should be. The serpent suggests that perhaps God, by limiting their freedom, is withholding something good from them. And what is their response? They choose to listen to the serpent that gave them nothing, and become suspicious of the One who has given them everything. Talk about twisted logic. Someone has rightly observed: sin is supremely stupid!

My father had a favorite saying that's very apropos to this situation: "Don't throw away the old bucket until you know the new one doesn't have any holes." In other words, why lose faith in God's abundant provisions and place your trust in someone who provides no evidence that he's trustworthy and credible? But that's exactly what Adam and Eve did. They chose to indulge in the forbidden fruit, hoping to experience what they thought they were missing. While living in their sought-after Shangri-la, their world turns upside down; joy and gladness dissipates into sorrow and bitterness. And if that wasn't bad enough, Adam and Eve also develop a deep-seated distrust and fear of their Creator that they just couldn't shake.

The fall of our first parents introduces a new worldview: a life perspective that is in direct conflict with the one God has given. This switch in loyalty to a twisted mind-set is earth's inauguration into the great controversy. It's essential to understand that the rebellion that now exists on earth is simply an extension of heaven's rebellion. In tempting Adam and Eve Satan entices them to come to the same conclusions, take the same steps he took, and be on the same side he was on. The spiritual warfare that now engulfs our planet is the result of their choice to join Satan's rival kingdom. In light of what was stated, this comment by Ellen White is especially significant: "In the great final conflict, Satan will employ the *same* policy, manifest the *same* spirit, and work for the *same* end, as in all preceding ages." [8]

The Controversy Renewed

A few decades ago when personalized license plates were introduced in Illinois, the Department of Motor Vehicles received more than 1,000 requests for the number 1. The state official whose job it was to approve requests lamented, "I am about to assign it to someone and disappoint a thousand others." He came up with what he thought was a great solution. He gave the number to himself. This kind of self-serving attitude can be traced all the way back to Eden. At Creation, God handed this planet over to Adam and Eve to manage in harmony with His instructions, but thinking themselves wiser than the Creator, they ruined it instead. Running a planet wisely or ruining it by mismanagement all comes down to the letter *I*. But that made all the difference. In their choice to rebel, Adam and Eve moved God aside in order to become number 1. Let's take a look at what might have led them to make such a fateful faux pas.

Three Steps Downward

We've already noted that the Bible describes three stages in the downward progression of sin: gradual, decisive, and final. These steps not only were a vestige of Satan's rebellion but also describe the fall of Eden's original occupants.

As we briefly analyze the beginning of sin on this planet, we will see how the truths of God's Word are countered by Satan's deceptions in Eden. In contrast to God's *laws*, there was introduced what could be called Satan's *flaws*. It is these flaws that the archdeceiver was determined to foist upon Adam and Eve in the garden; they were at the heart of his rebellious design to establish an earthly kingdom of evil. When Adam and Eve chose to disobey God and accept Satan's proposal, the initial sparks of that transgression have since then exploded into a worldwide conflict. The original flaws—a demonically twisted worldview—now enshroud the entire globe.

Flaw One: You Can't Trust God

The Creation event begins with "And God said . . ." In contrast, Satan's first words, spoken to Eve, are *"Did God really say* 'You must not eat from any tree in the garden'?" The tempter's innuendo that God had slapped a ban on eating from all trees in the garden quickly got her attention. What an example of subversive efficiency! The serpent never told Eve to disobey God's command. He simply called into question God's truthfulness (by denying His warning) and God's trustworthiness (by impugning His motives). Eve's choice was not "Should I or should I not eat?" but rather "Whom do I believe?" For Eve to disobey, she had to first withdraw her trust in God. It's hard to imagine a more important conversation than this exchange between Eve and the serpent, given the devastating outcome. It's been said that these two, Satan and Eve, held the first religious discussion in the Bible. It was a dysfunctional dialogue, at best.

Getting Eve to quibble and have doubts about God's initial instructions eventually led her to question the truthfulness of everything else God had said. That kind of reasoning still holds true today. As a general rule, those who question the validity of the Creation story eventually dismiss the credibility of the remainder of God's Word. Like an ever-widening ripple effect, rejection of the first miracle leads to a thumbs-down attitude regarding the miracles that follow. Those who dismiss the six-day creation also discard a universal flood, the appearance of Jesus—the Second Adam and the re-creation of a new earth.

From the very outset God reveals Himself as a loving Creator and caring provider. Throughout the Creation account God speaks—creating all things, explaining their purpose, and providing structure for their existence. In Satan's initial encounter with Eve, the evil one does not deny the Creator's existence but rather casts suspicion on His motives and character. Just as Satan disguises his real identity, he camouflages his attack by casting doubt on what God has said and done. In questioning God's instructions, Satan twists God's true intentions and maligns His goodness and generosity. He leads Eve to wonder why that particular tree was off limits, especially since it looked so good, so pleasing, and so desirable to her. If God really loved her, then why would there be *any* restrictions? Not even the extravagance of Eden convinced her that God's heart was good and honorable.[9] In intimating an erroneous worldview, Satan distorts reality by misrepresenting the character of God and casting doubt on the nature and necessity of divine law.

Every temptation that comes our way to distrust and disobey God is simply an echo of that original challenge. In the midst of our daily lives when we crave affirmation of God's unfailing love, the truthfulness of His Word, the necessity of obedience, or the surety of His promises, doubt may occur and provoke us to question, *Did God really say that?* Through perplexing world events, pain and suffering, scientific assertions, or just plain laughter, our faith is assaulted. While doubts attack us head-on, they usually come in sinister ways, cleverly disguised, appealing to the senses, and religiously attired—just as in Eden.

Perhaps one reason that Adam and Eve had such a hard time recognizing the ugliness of sin is that it came in such an alluring and cunningly attractive manner. This was the same approach Lucifer had taken earlier with the angels in heaven. His tactics could very well have been described in the paradoxical book *The Beautiful Side of Evil*, by Johanna Michaelsen.[10] No doubt about it, when evil comes in a delightful package, promising a winner's trophy, the pinnacle of success, or a higher spiritual realm, it makes it impossible to recognize it as sin. Sin can look so desirable yet be so destructive. This is a lesson we all should learn.

Although Adam and Eve were placed within an ideal environment, they were not beyond the possibility of wrongdoing. In order for love to exist, for character development to take place, their relationship with God has to be on the basis of their own free, intelligent choice (Gen. 2:16). True free will includes the freedom to experience the consequences of one's choice—bad ones as well as good ones. As a sign of this freedom, and to provide an opportunity to accept this responsibility, God places within their Eden home the *tree of life* and the *tree of the knowledge of good and evil*. For faith in God to be confirmed, it had to be tested. God is in effect telling them, "Trust Me on this one!" The issue is not so much about the forbidden fruit as it is their faith in what God said about it. In obeying the Creator, Adam and Eve would be acknowledging their humanness and recognizing the limits of their authority and the need to depend upon their Maker. They chose, however, to disbelieve and disobey.

The bottom line to all of this is very simple: the root of sin is disbelief. Jesus Himself defines sin as the refusal to believe in Him (John 16:9). The failure of Adam and Eve is their unwillingness to trust God for their needs. In their relationship with the Creator, sin is their only alternative to faith (Rom. 14:23). They're inclined, however, not to believe that they can experience true joy and happiness under the care and command of God; thus, they choose to rely upon themselves.

When we arrived on this planet we quickly discovered that we've been born on a battlefield—a world at war. Our planet has been portrayed in Scripture as the combat zone in God's universe (Rev. 12:9). As earth's inhabitants we are not merely spectators but key participants in this cosmic struggle. "The flesh desires what is contrary to the Spirit. . . . They are in conflict with each other" (Gal. 5:17). The key issue in this warfare is whether we will exercise faith in God's love and rely on His wisdom or choose unbelief and go our own way. We have two choices: faithful cooperation or competitive rivalry. Those who believe they can partake of both should remember, "No one can serve two masters. Either you will hate the one and love the other, or you will be devoted to the one and despise the other" (Matt. 6:24).

Flaw Two: Just an Idle Threat

The second fundamental truth of God's Word is that death is the lethal consequence of disobeying the Creator. God plainly warned Adam and Eve not to eat of the tree of the knowledge of good and evil, "for in the day that you eat of it you shall surely die" (Gen. 2:17, NKJV). As human beings it's essential that we realize the end results of our choices or else we are not truly free. While obedience to God sustains life, disobedience breaks the relationship with the Creator, and death occurs; but death is not an arbitrary act of malice or vengeance on God's part. It's been observed that "sin has death wrapped within itself." God is the source of life, and our existence depends on His sustaining power. When we reject His sovereignty, it means we have chosen to cut ourselves off from the wellspring of life.

From a biblical perspective, death is not an idle threat; it is a stark reality. It was God's plan for us to live forever, but death became an obtrusive intruder brought into existence by sinful rebellion. It would be fair to say that Adam and Eve did not really understand the nature of death or its implications until they saw it with their own eyes. By simply exercising faith in God and His instruction, their lack of understanding becomes irrelevant.

Satan's counterattack is found in his second statement in the garden, where he defiantly declares, "You will not certainly die" (Gen. 3:4). He wants Adam and Eve to take the second step in rebellion—the step of presumption, to create an alternative to God's life-giving instructions. In questioning God's credibility, Satan not only entices Eve to ignore God's commands but also to push aside the consequences of such a choice. Implied in Satan's declaration is the idea to always think positively: *Don't put up with laws that impose restraints or limit your freedom. Death is just an idle threat! Disregard codes of conduct that cramp your style or lead to negative thinking. You'll not regret being assertive and looking out for yourself.*

Can you imagine what it was like the next morning after the wrong choice was made, not to mention the days, weeks, and years that followed? There was no denying that death was in the air, and the loss it brought was incalculable. No doubt about it, Adam and Eve made an unbelievable discovery; they had been duped. They lost everything!

"You shall not die" is the first recorded lie in Scripture, yet most of the world's religions continue to believe the father of lies (John 8:44). The erroneous idea that humans have an immortal soul (Eze. 18:4) that lives forever reduces the resurrection to a sideshow and robs God of His mercy and restorative power. Beyond that, it gives credence to eternal torment, purgatory, reincarnation, communication with the spirit world, and other doctrines of demons (1 Tim. 4:1, NKJV). These spiritual errors from the pit of hell distort the loving character of God in so many ways. Even though Satan denies that death can ever occur with this deception, he has made sure that it has become the ugly trademark of this planet. Death has no favorites; it tolerates no exceptions.

To some, death is an illusion, merely a veil through which we pass. To others the body dies but the soul goes on to exist in another realm. There are those who view death as simply the cessation of one's earthly existence and nothing more. But there is much more. The biblical view speaks of death as humankind's "last enemy" (1 Cor. 15:26), a toxic nemesis that comes in two stages—the first and the second death. The first death is likened to a sleep (John 11:11-14; 1 Cor. 15:20) such as Adam and Eve have experienced and the rest of humankind is subject to. The ultimate "wages of sin" (Rom. 6:23) is eternal death, which Jesus went through on the cross on behalf of all the "ungodly" (Rom. 5:6). He came back to life, but those who reject Christ's death on their behalf are choosing to die the second death.

According to the Bible, sin and death come together—wrapped in the same package (Rom. 5:12). Since every person is affected, every religion has its own rationale as to why this ugly predicament exists on our planet. In search for the most plausible explanation some choose to view our first parents as stumbling out of a darkened cave, naive and ignorant; while others see them walking out of a pristine garden enlightened by their Creator. Some people believe that humans are "trousered apes," grown-up animals for which death is simply the lingering effects of an evolutionary ascent. This views humankind as weak and warlike, diseased and dying, but not sinful. On the other hand, others see the human race as "fallen sinners," people originally created by God but driven out of Paradise because of their rebellion against Him. Today we collectively endure the results of that lethal choice, but individually we have the privilege of negating that choice by opting for eternal life through the merits of Jesus (Rom. 6:23).

Flaw Three: Follow Your Heart

Here is Satan's third statement to Eve: "For God knows that when you eat from it [the tree of the knowledge of good and evil] your eyes will be opened, and you will be like God, knowing good and evil" (Gen. 3:5). The big lie sounds so exalting, so captivating, and so liberating to the human heart—the creature breaking free and becoming like the Creator—and doing it on his or her own terms. The apostle Paul refers to this twisted ideology when he talks of those who have "exchanged the truth about God for a lie" (Rom. 1:25).

Oh, to be divine, to be "like God," is a possibility that kings, popes, impostors, and common folks like us find so believable and irresistible. This declaration is the capstone, the grand climax to Satan's deceptions in Eden. If the creature gains independence from God by partaking of the forbidden fruit, will it not open the door to an experience that is akin to being like God Himself—to be all-knowing and wise? What an enticing enterprise. Lurking in this supposedly newfound freedom is sinful pride, which ultimately leads to the worst kind of slavery, slave to an egotistic tyrant we've come to know as *self*.

In taking another reflective look at the experience of Adam and Eve in the garden, there emerges an agonizing truth: the Eden story has not ended. In one way or another we all face our own Garden of Eden experience. Each of us confronts similar challenges and grapples with all kinds of reasonably attractive solutions. Like the residents of Eden, when we sidestep obedience that comes through a faith relationship with God, it means that we too have been ensnared by the three flaws.

Remember, Eve was not attracted to any old tree, only the one forbidden by God. Through the serpent's charming lies, her worldview was radically distorted. She is now enticed by that which appeals to her mind's eye—desired wisdom, delicious rewards, and a consciousness equal with that of God. How easy it is to believe a lie that caters to one's selfish desires. This marked the earthly debut of sin, serving the creature rather than the Creator (Rom. 1:25), and that's idolatry.

An expanded definition of idolatry is holding a view of God that is not in harmony with a revelation of Himself in His Word. In our desire for a god with whom we can be comfortable, it's quite feasible not to see God as He truly is but rather create a god in our own image (Isa. 40:25, 26). Usually, an image built by human hands simply reflects the imagination of the human heart. Naiveté about idolatry is like the mistake made by the residents of Troy who welcomed the Trojan horse, filled with enemy soldiers, into their city. Likewise, within the human heart there lurks a natural bias toward self-worship, a danger usually unrecognized. In reality, everything around us is a potential idol. We can make an idol of anything, especially good things. Our restless hearts tend to cling to things that reflect our own desires and aspirations and then promote them until they take God's place in our lives.

Perhaps that's why idolatry has been depicted, not so much as people's search for God, but rather their flight from Him. How significant when one considers that humanity's concept of God lies at the very core of all religions. It is what separated Israel from Baal, Ashtoreth, and Dagon—false gods steeped in pagan rites, orgies, and child sacrifices. In much more subtle ways, key differences still exist between Christianity and the non-Christian religions of today.

Back in Eden, Adam and Eve were in for a rude awakening. Their hopes for a higher, more exalted state actually resulted in a moral downfall. The spirit of defiance and self-justification promptly followed subsequent denial and cover-up of what had happened. No matter how ridiculous or ill-conceived the excuse, the competitive mind is quick to defend itself at any cost. As the Creator begins to converse with Adam and Eve, they quickly place the blame on everyone around them—accusing each other, the serpent, and even God Himself for the situation they were in. It's only natural for sinful beings to find a way out of their predicament, to find some kind of justification for what happened.

When Adam and Eve ate from the forbidden tree, their disobedience to God severed their intimate connection with Him and brought havoc into their lives. They fell from a high and holy plane to one of apprehension and fear of their Creator. In their one act of distrust and disobedience, they disconnected themselves from His rulership and became the center of their own universe. They were now driven by a newly awakened self-centeredness, an ego quickly absorbed with guilt, evasion of the truth, and a spirit of vindication.

The Bible affirms that the forbidden fruit eaten by Adam and Eve never lived up to the high billing given by the serpent, "Your eyes will be opened, and you will be like God" (Gen. 3:5). Eve had never met a snake that could carry on a conversation; thus, she was unwittingly tempted into thinking that he had transcended his creaturely limits by having eaten the forbidden fruit. So why could it not do the same for her, expand her status and make her more like God? With such thoughts floating through her head, the tree that had the forbidden fruit looked "pleasing to the eye, and also desirable" (verse 6). But the exalted state the crafty serpent had so persuasively promised them never happened. Although Eve imagined herself experiencing something new and exciting, the momentary exhilaration quickly disappeared. What actually occurs is a fall, an immediate plunge from a high and holy plane to one of depravity, embarrassment, and shame. It doesn't take long for the smitten pair to realize the awful truth—the serpent's claim of having "acquired the power of speech" by eating the banned fruit is but a sham that cleverly "concealed his own misery" and infinite loss.[11]

Since the Edenic fall, human beings continue to be infected with an inherent disdain for God's will. We are born with a mind-set that's determined to follow its own course, to go its own way (Isa. 53:6). As extended members of Adam's family, our narcissistic ways are not so much what we do; it is what we are; it is our moral state of being. In following our own hearts, like Adam and Eve, we find ourselves in a selfish rivalry with God. This is our spiritual inheritance.

---

[1] Gordon Kainer, *World Views Make a World of Difference* (Brushton, N.Y.: Teach Services, Inc., 2008), p. 75.
[2] E. G. White, *Education*, p. 173.

[3] E. G. White, *Patriarchs and Prophets*, p. 41.

[4] Ellen G. White, *Early Writings* (Washington, D.C.: Review and Herald Pub. Assn., 1882), p. 145.

[5] *The SDA Bible Commentary*, Ellen G. White Comments, vol. 1, p. 1082.

[6] E. G. White, *Testimonies*, vol. 5, p. 473.

[7] E. G. White, *The Story of Redemption*, p. 19.

[8] E. G. White, *The Great Controversy*, p. 11. (Italics supplied.)

[9] "It was distrust of God's goodness, disbelief of His word, and rejection of His authority, that made our first parents transgressors and that brought into the world a knowledge of evil" (E. G. White, *Education*, p. 25).

[10] Eugene, Oreg.: Harvest House Publishers, 1982.

[11] E. G. White, *Patriarchs and Prophets*, pp. 54, 55.

★ **4** ★

Fear and Fig Leaves

Nakedness and Fig Leaves

It is highly significant that the Bible does not initially define sin. Instead, it introduces the concept with a story. That's a good maneuver, since it's easier to relate to stories than just hearing the facts. And the story reads like this: "When the woman saw that the fruit of the tree was good for food and pleasing to the eye, and also desirable for gaining wisdom, she took some and ate it" (Gen. 3:6). Although God had earlier instructed them "not [to] eat from the tree of the knowledge of good and evil" (Gen. 2:17), she is fixated on the serpent's promise that if she eats the forbidden fruit, her eyes will be opened to that which is new and exciting.[1] She confidently expects to experience something higher and ecstatic (see Gen. 3:5, 6). With trembling hands filled with the forbidden fruit, she excitedly relates to her husband all that has occurred.[2] The next step is quick and effortless; she gave him some fruit, "and he ate" (verse 6).

After eating the forbidden fruit, "the eyes of both of them were opened." Instead of experiencing something smart and dressy, to their horror, "they realized they were naked" (verse 7). Their nakedness was a blunt and distressing indication that they had been deceived by a serpent who had mysteriously disappeared. No doubt about it, they had plunged from a high and holy sphere to one of embarrassing indecency.

They were at a loss as to how to resolve their miserable dilemma. In the search for something expedient "they sewed fig leaves together and made coverings for themselves" (verse 7). The context suggests that this decision was made rather hurriedly, that no serious thought was given to approach God for His solution. The very idea that "fig leaves" could effectively help their problem or hide it from God appears ludicrous, doesn't it? The entire episode reminds me of a little boy, as the story goes, who was looking through the big family Bible, when something fell out of it. Looking down at the floor, he saw a rather large leaf pressed between its pages. With a grin

53

on his face the boy remarked to his mother, "I think I just found Adam's underwear!"

If Eden's fig leaves were similar to what they look like today, then there's a good chance they were thick and leathery, at least three to four inches wide and six to eight inches long. Adam and Eve may have taken the stems of the leaves, braided them together around their waist and inserted the leaves so they would (conveniently) hang down. Quite likely, the fig leaves didn't provide an ample covering, but they were easily accessible, a quick and simple solution. It was the natural thing to do in light of their nakedness and awful sense of shame and guilt. Do you think that we would have responded any differently? Definitely not!

Fig leaves are not simply an Adam and Eve thing. It is instinctively etched in our minds as well. The world, our church, our schools, and each of us individually have untold ways we can circumspectly cover up our sin. This can readily be done with dressy attire, physical fitness, a promotion, a winning record, or perhaps a well-developed knack of rationalizing. It may also involve spiritual activities, such as acts of worship, religious pageantry, or adherence to certain religious rules or formalities. It's been observed that there's nothing more appealing to a self-centered person than his or her own ideas or solutions. While you may not agree, you can be sure that apart from God's provision, each of us is prone to wear some kind of designer "fig-leaf" garment. As life would have it, it usually comes with a one-size-fits-all guarantee. How often we smugly ridicule Adam and Eve for hiding behind a patchwork of fig leaves, while at the same time we're busy conniving ways to cover up our own sin and brokenness.

Let's not forget that all of us are born bruised, bloody, and totally naked, which is exactly the condition of Adam and Eve at the time of their fall in Eden. This means that all human beings require a redemptive or atoning covering that will take care of their spiritual dilemma, but we are totally unprepared or unable to do anything of the sort.

It reminds me of a story I heard several years ago about a textile factory at which certain instructions had been posted in the workroom for all to see. They read, "If your threads get tangled, send for the foreman." One day an employee got her threads all turned and twisted out of shape, and she promptly tried to straighten them out on her own. With things going from bad to worse, she finally sent for the foreman. When he arrived, he looked it over and asked, "Have you been trying to untangle these threads yourself?" When she admitted that she had, he asked, "Why didn't you send for me according to the instructions?"

"I did my best," she responded.

"My dear lady," the foreman replied, "remember that doing your best is sending for me."

After the forbidden fruit had twisted their lives out of shape, why didn't Adam and Eve send for their Creator? Genesis records that when God voluntarily entered the garden at the end of the day, they were overwhelmed with fear. In reality, He was the last person they wanted to see. They were very uncertain as to what He would say or do. Just hearing Him walk "in the garden in the cool of the day" caused them to instinctively take cover "among the trees of the garden" (verse 8). Can you blame them? The Creator's simple instructions were still indelibly impressed on their minds: if you eat from the forbidden tree, "you will surely die." But beyond that, at their deepest level, and almost imperceptibly, fearful dread had replaced loving veneration for their Creator.

As they foolishly hid among garden foliage, God, in a gentle and gracious manner, sought to converse with them regarding their disobedience. I like the way Calvin Rock describes it: "He is a God who comes looking. It was the 'plight,' not the 'plea,' of the first pair that occasioned His presence. He was looking while they were hiding, looking even though they wished not to be found."[3] With calmness, compassion, and candor God enlightened the guilty pair as to the gravity of what they had done and the urgency of a right solution. Perhaps we'll have a more realistic idea of what may have happened in the garden if we keep in mind that Adam and Eve could have been 10 to 12 feet tall.[4] This would have enabled them easily to run 40 to 50 miles per hour. And since Eden could have been as large as any state in the United States (we tend to have such a scrawny view of this immense garden), this first hide-and-seek episode could have been much more of an adventure than any of us could ever imagine.

As Adam and Eve attempted to resolve their accelerating predicament on their own, it quickly became the focal point of the Edenic saga. To their dismay, they grudgingly admitted that covering themselves with hastily prepared fig-leaf garments didn't solve anything. Granted, fig leaves may have been conveniently large and readily available, but probably itchy, irritating, and downright embarrassing. Quite likely, they served only as constant reminders of the pain, guilt, and shame their choices had already brought them.

To better understand this whole episode, we need to see it in light of the following context. From the outset it was God's desire to have an intimate bond with the human family. In the divinely prescribed arrangement, relationships governed by loving obedience were to be the key to all earthly fulfillment and prosperity. Thus, when Genesis recounts the dramatic shift in the relationship between Adam and Eve and their Creator, it immediately gets our attention. When sin bursts upon the scene and selfishness replaces love it has an obvious, destructive effect on all connections and kinship. It creates havoc and disorder, twisting and distorting God's original design.

Alienation from God instills in humans all kinds of negative emotions, such as guilt, shame, fear, defensiveness, and distrust. This becomes decidedly apparent when God enters the garden, only to discover that the inhabitants were nowhere to be found. No longer coming to greet Him with open arms, to talk with Him and enjoy the beauty and pleasures of the garden, they've now hidden themselves "from the Lord God among the trees of the garden" (verse 8). This suggests that they found refuge in the garden, rather than with its owner. Were not Adam and Eve created to be close to God, to walk and commune with Him (Amos 3:3)? Walking with Him means living in His presence, going His way, learning to see the world through His eyes, and getting to know His character so that unshakable trust would be developed. By loving God first and foremost, they were to learn how to love and serve others.

After Adam and Eve ate the forbidden fruit, it became obvious that they failed to discern the real nature and full extent of their problem. They are unaware that a large ocean now separated them from their Creator. They were oblivious to their need of confession, repentance, and forgiveness—thus none was forthcoming. They did not recognize that an underlying rivalry now existed between them, as well as between themselves and God. Sin not only distorted their vision but also blinded them to the damage it caused. This is made evident by their stilted reaction to God's presence, as well as their doltish decision to hide behind the fig-leaf garments they made for themselves. The makeshift cover-up revealed a total misconception of their problem and its solution, a fact still very much apparent in today's world.

Messed-up Minds

It is significant that even though Adam and Eve valiantly tried to cover their nakedness and shame with fig leaves, they still found it necessary to hide "among the trees of the garden" when they heard God approaching. All their efforts proved to be of no help. Case in point: Rather than welcoming Him with open arms, they now viewed God as an uninvited intruder. Their response to the Creator's questions "Who told you that you were naked? Have you eaten from the tree that I commanded you not to eat from?" is telling. Readily exposing their newly scarred natures as self-absorbed and competitive, "the man said, 'The woman you put here with me—she gave me some fruit from the tree, and I ate it.' Then the Lord God said to the woman, 'What is this you have done?' The woman said, 'The serpent deceived me, and I ate'" (Gen. 3:11-13).[5] Sin not only changed their outward appearance but also messed up their minds. It brought alienation to all of their essential relationships. It distorted their thoughts about God, about each other, about themselves, and about the rest of creation. In their discourse with the Creator, we see neither of them backing down; in this awkward confrontation, they are determined to come out as winners.

As the story progresses, it becomes apparent that the spirit of loving cooperation is replaced by a self-serving, combative spirit. A self-justifying attitude prevails; no apology is given, and no remorse is shown. All that occurs is finger-pointing. How quickly these once-loving partners turn into quarreling rivals, how readily they are contemptuous of God's questions. By getting them to eat of the forbidden fruit, God's archenemy has successfully passed on to Adam and Eve his own vindictive, competitive disposition. The description of Satan's initial approach via a "cunning" or "crafty" serpent literally means being sharp and clever in a selfish way (see verse 1, NIV, TEV).

Defiance and a spirit of looking out for themselves promptly follow the subsequent denial and cover-up as to what had happened. No matter how ridiculous or ill-conceived their excuses, their sin-damaged minds are quick to defend themselves at any cost. This is the way rationalization works in all of us.

A Deposed Royalty
Most people, regardless of their spiritual orientation, have a nagging feeling that something has gone very wrong with the human race. Everything suggests that we're not the people we were meant to be. While there is general agreement regarding the moral condition of our world, there is no consensus as to the reason. Some contend that it is primarily the result of

our evolutionary environment; others hold that it's probably the result of some kind of inbred inner flaw or maybe something in between.

When wrestling with these kinds of issues, human reason is adversely debilitated and skewed by its own sordid imagination, self-interest, and pride. Aware of the confusion and our inability to objectively sort out truth from error, God does not leave us groping in darkness. While the answer isn't handed to us with our birth certificate, it is through divine revelation that God helps us to understand *when, where, why,* and by *whom* the wrong turn was taken. If it weren't for the Bible, we wouldn't have the slightest clue as to why the world is in such an unbelievably hopeless mess.

The Creator is amazingly forthright regarding the nature of evil and its outbreak on Planet Earth. In the Genesis account, the Fall of human beings is candidly presented in the context of their creation in the image of God—that they were the crowning act of Creation. From this perspective, Christians come to recognize not only the high level on which the biblical account places human beings at the outset but also the low level to which sin has taken them. At times we hear a great deal about original sin but perhaps not enough about original glory. Too often we overlook that the dignity as well as the depravity of humankind are intricate parts of the biblical perspective. God's Word is very candid about these two extremes. We are at the same time the glory and the garbage of the universe. Quite graphic, but accurate!

Our heights of goodness and the depths of our evilness often puzzle humans. It haunts our songs, our poetry, and our art. It stalks our relationships, and it troubles our religions and philosophies. But the Creation, as well as the Fall of Adam and Eve, best explains the paradox of the human condition—we were created in God's image—Adam was a "crowned king in Eden,"[6] yet we've been morally decimated by sin. The human race started out holy, innocent, and pure, but in presumptuous pride, it chose to become its own center and withdrew from God's sovereign rule. Such a belief leaves us with the conclusion that earth's inhabitants give evidence of being both royal and rundown. Clearly, they possess the wretchedness of a deposed king who's searching for a lost throne . . . a throne that is beyond human grasp but available through divine grace.[7]

Let's return to the Fall in Eden. "When the woman saw that the fruit of the tree was good for food and pleasing to the eye, and also desirable for gaining wisdom, she took some and ate it. She also gave some to her husband, who was with her, and he ate it" (verse 6). Considering the devastating effect of their sin, the question naturally arises, How could such disaster spring forth from such a small infraction? The answer lies in what the act represented—not the act itself. By this one deed of distrust and independence they withdrew from God's rulership and placed themselves at the center of their own universe (see Rom. 5:16-19).

One key accessory consequence of Adam and Eve's choice was that it transferred not only them but also the entire human race into Satan's rival kingdom. With humanity's roots polluted by sin, every member of the human family arrives separated from God and sinful in nature (see Ps. 51:5), "dead in trespasses and sins" and by "nature children of wrath" (Eph. 2:1, 3, NKJV).

At birth, self is already seated on the throne. Being the very essence of selfishness, it craves for itself the highest place—the position and power of God. *Displacing God is the sin that is the source for all other sins.* Any attempt by the Creator to gain for Himself His rightful position as supreme ruler in the human sphere is met by a declaration of war by the self-centered. Self is not about to hand over the scepter to a rival power that it views with suspicion, fear, and animosity. Starting out in the kingdom where self reigns means that we are by nature *I*-centered, since self-seeking is the "very principle of Satan's kingdom." [8]

It is obvious that all of us begin life with hearts—the control centers of our lives—that are self-serving and rebellious. Sin never has to be taught; it needs no training or practice; it comes naturally for all of us. It includes everything we say or do that is not in harmony with God's law of love (see 1 John 3:4). Since Adam and Eve's fall, all of us live east of Eden, eyewitnesses of the garden's closed and securely guarded gate (see Gen. 3:24). As one scholar put it, "Where there is history . . . there is sin." [9] After Eden, human history clearly confirms that "wickedness is part of man's nature from the time he is born. His inclinations are toward self as soon as he comes out from his mother's womb" (Ps. 58:3, Clear Word). Sin is an evil force that deviously twists human nature into something inhuman. Even more, it creates an addiction for evil and blinds us to our spiritual rivalry with God and one another.

Garments of Skin

In their frazzled state of mind, it appears, Adam and Eve could not sense the seriousness of their offense. It's as if they couldn't grasp the fact that they faced a death sentence for their rebellion against their Creator. Or maybe it was just a desperate attempt to ignore or explain away what they had done. After all, could God really be upset with their mere sampling of the forbidden fruit?

In a spirit of defiance and self-justification, they quickly proceeded to place the blame on everyone around them for their ugly situation. It was only natural for them to seek justification, to come up with some kind of plausible or credible rationale for what they had done. Sinful beings are so constituted that it's imperative for them to find a way out of their predicament, to find some kind of justification that comes from either God or themselves.

There is a vast difference, however, between God's justification of the sinner and the sinner's justification of his or her sin.[10] In the former there is admission of guilt, repentance of wrongdoing, and a reception of God's pardoning grace. In the latter, as in the case of Adam and Eve, sinners defend their ways, look for a scapegoat, hoping to rationalize away the guilt. Putting it in today's vernacular, they cut and paste, make themselves look good by shifting the blame or negating their failure. Eden's story line teaches an important lesson that still holds true for all of us: self-justification is a powerful instinct. The Laodicean church is especially singled out for this innate inclination. Though depicted by God as "wretched, pitiful, poor, blind and naked," Laodicea triumphantly boasts, "I am rich; I have acquired wealth and do not need a thing" (Rev. 3:17).

Thankfully, the story of Adam and Eve's fall into sin is not all bad news. The offer of divine redemption—a gift from God, received by the sinner through faith—is introduced (see Rom. 6:23). However, Adam and Eve face an enormous dilemma. They lacked understanding as to what had happened and what could be rightfully done about it. Consequently, an initial lesson the Creator had to teach Adam and Eve after their fall was that the solution to their problem came from somewhere entirely outside of themselves.[11] There is nothing inherently good within them or in their environment that can bring them back to their acceptance with God. In their relationship with God, they do not become approved, adequate, or acceptable. This can only be received as a gift by faith in God's declaration as to what He has already accomplished for them in Christ.

This truth also applies to us. In order to understand why the solution is limited to divine grace, we too need to grasp the full extent of the sin problem. Unfortunately, many are sidetracked one way or another by a sentiment that first became popular in the 1970s: "I'm OK, you're OK, and that's OK." But this pop psychology didn't work for Adam and Eve, and it doesn't work in our day. Since things are not OK, it's imperative that we understand the underlying nature of sin and the all-encompassing scope of its destructive effects.

As we dig further into the Eden story, we quickly sense that the biblical focus is on relationships—at first whole and harmonious, then splintered and broken by sin. This fracture is the root cause of most of the conflicts between good and evil on our planet. At this point we need to clarify Adam's relationship with the entire human race. As the first man, Adam was humankind's legal representative, our lawful standard bearer. Since all humans were still in him, it meant that in Adam's fall the whole human race plunged into sin along with him. In Adam's choice to separate himself from God, all humankind suffered the same consequences. As head of the human race, he took all of us from the domain of God's government and placed us under the dominion of an evil, corrupt system. We discover at birth that we have already eaten from the forbidden fruit. Thus every human being is born under the legal condemnation of having broken God's law. Romans 5:18 states, "One trespass resulted in condemnation for all people."

In addition to this, Adam was also the moral head of the human race. Hence, it's only natural that every child since that time has been captivated by the same self-seeking spirit that took control of Adam's life (see 1 Cor. 15:22). Obviously, sin is not only tyrannical in its power; it's sweeping in its coverage. What we're saying is this: Adam and Eve have passed on to us—the entire human family—their sinful, fallen nature; a spirit of war against God had replaced loving cooperation with Him. The apostle Paul put it this way: "The mind governed by the flesh is hostile to God; it does not submit to God's law" (Rom. 8:7).

As already mentioned, it's quite likely that Adam and Eve did not really understand the extent of their sin, the nature of the curse, and the meaning of death. Nor did they comprehend the significance of the Creator's promise, "I will put enmity between you [the serpent] and the woman, and between your offspring and hers; he will crush your head, and you will strike his heel" (Gen. 3:15). Clifford Goldstein rightly observes that following a series of questions, "God's first declarative statement to the fallen world, then, is a condemnation of Satan; yet even in that condemnation He gives humanity the gospel. As He declares Satan's doom He proclaims humankind's hope. Despite their sin, the Lord immediately revealed to Adam and Eve the promise of redemption." [12]

In order that they might more fully grasp their predicament and the significance of His promise to them, "the Lord God made garments of skin for Adam and his wife and clothed them" (verse 21). With immense tenderness and compassion the Lord provides garments of skin for Adam and Eve and personally attires them. He replaces their woefully inadequate fig-leaf coverings with animal-skin tunics—newly prepared garments that fully clothe their exposed bodies. Let's emphasize what just took place. The garb that had been derived solely from the vine was now exchanged for that which was conceived only by death. This dramatically altered their view of things.

Adam and Eve never think about grace until God does the unthinkable: the innocent dies. Slaying a garden animal to provide "garments of skin," the Creator gives Adam and Eve their first glimpse of the horror of death. They never witnessed anything like this before. The reality of it all shocks their minds, touches their hearts, and affects every fiber of their being. While sin brings with it the tragic seeds of death, at the same time, it eventually dawns on them that they're still alive simply because of one thing—a sacrificial animal has taken their place. It is significant that the only death that takes place in Genesis 3 (where sin occurs) is the lamb from which "God made tunics of skin, and clothed them" (verse 21, NKJV). This is still hard to believe today; a substitutionary death is God's personal revelation of His mercy and grace. This has always been the good news of the gospel!

After Adam and Eve became transgressors, it was imperative for God to act. In the face of this human uprising, something had to be done. He must either allow the punishment of death to fall on sinners or bear the burden Himself. Grace impels Him to assume it, and in so doing, He upholds His law while saving the guilty. Did Adam and Eve understand that the slain substitute—the ultimate act of grace—was, in fact, a symbol of their Creator? The truth is that when the forbidden fruit touched their lips, at that moment the shadows of the cross already appeared on the horizon. Indeed, the cross of Calvary was etched in God's heart long before it was set up on a hillside outside Jerusalem.[13] But for the heartbroken pair, God Himself dying on a cross was too horrifying to comprehend, too selfless to appreciate. Nevertheless, it was a reality known and experienced by the Creator from all eternity, for He was "the Lamb who was slain from the creation of the world" (Rev. 13:8).

What they knew for certain was in His tenderheartedness God provided a replacement on their behalf. The shocking realization that their lives had been compassionately extended beyond sin's penalty brought Adam and Eve to their knees in tearful repentance and gratitude. Grace had done its work. For them, as it is for us, it is "the goodness of God [that] leads . . . to repentance" (Rom. 2:4, NKJV). What transpired in Eden—a wonderful scene of reconciliation—must take place wherever the noxious seeds of sin are found.

The Double Cure

A song well known to most Christians is the beloved hymn "Rock of Ages." The concluding words of the first stanza are profoundly true: "Let the water and the blood, from thy riven side which flowed, be of sin the double cure, cleanse me from its guilt and power." What did Augustus M. Toplady mean when he wrote that sin needs a "double cure"?

The Bible declares that sin has wrought such havoc in our lives that God alone is the solution. What exactly is this damage that only a divinely initiated "double cure" can resolve? The first problem that sin creates is God's condemnation. Sin has severed our relationship with Him, affecting our status or legal (rightful) standing before God. We enter this world "separate from Christ, excluded from citizenship in Israel . . . without hope and without God" (Eph. 2:12).

The first cure takes care of our status—our standing with God. When Adam and Eve fell into sin, they switched kingdoms. In their decision to disobey, they separated themselves from the kingdom of God and entered the kingdom of rebellion. As head of the human race, Adam was the broken link that loosed the entire planet from the sovereignty of God. Thus, unrepentant humans are separated from the Creator's rulership and are the center of their own world.

Heaven's initial prescription for sin, the first cure mentioned above, is *justification by faith*.[14] As people grow up and sense the system they are under, they can choose to remain or transfer to another. Justification is the legal transfer from the kingdom of our birth that leads to eternal death to the kingdom of God that brings eternal life (John 5:24). According to John 14:6, this transfer means that Jesus is "the way" back to God. It gives to those who have "faith in Christ" (Phil. 3:9) or have the "righteousness that is by faith" (Rom. 9:30), the assurance of salvation that God has "made [them] accepted in the Beloved" (Eph. 1:6, NKJV).

Remember that justification is not based on the holiness of the one who believes but the holiness in *whom* one believes. Despite our unworthiness, God accepts us through faith in Christ and frees us from being engrossed with our standing before God. What we have by faith eliminates our need to gain by our works.

Second, sin brings about an inner corruption that affects every aspect of life. In the wonderful story of redeeming grace, redemption takes place in an orderly fashion. Sanctification, which we have labeled the second cure, takes place within the new kingdom, within our new status. The first cure—justification or imputed righteousness[15]—takes care of our legal standing, while the second cure—sanctification or imparted righteousness—deals with moral renewal. Justification refers to Christ's substitutionary work, restoring us to God's favor; sanctification points to the transforming work of the Holy Spirit, restoring us to God's image. While justification gives a new standing to the repentant sinner, sanctification is the day-by-day development of a new character. As faith lays holds of divine forgiveness and acceptance, the Holy Spirit, who inspires that faith, initiates a new life, a loving, heartfelt response within us. Does this imply that justification automatically leads to sanctification? Not necessarily. Only Christ as our Savior and Lord can initiate redemptive restoration to bring us the full range of the benefits of His atoning, reconciling grace. When penitent sinners accept Christ as Savior from the guilt of sin, in faith they also receive Him as their transforming Lord.[16]

How thankful we should be that through God's grace we could meet sin's challenges with an all-encompassing solution: whatever sin ruins, salvation redeems and restores.

---

[1] Because of my fear and utter dislike of snakes, I find it especially difficult to understand how anyone could listen to one and believe what it has to say. Was Eve simply enamored by a snake that could speak or maybe spellbound by its rare and exceeding beauty? When temptation comes with unique characteristics or dazzling charm, it is much more enticing.

[2] E. G. White, *Patriarchs and Prophets*, 56.

[3] Calvin Rock, "The God Who Comes Looking," *Adventist Review*, Dec. 20, 2007, p. 9.

[4] "He [Adam] was more than twice as tall as men now living upon the earth. . . . Eve was not quite as tall as Adam. Her head reached a little above his shoulders" (E. G. White, *The Story of Redemption*, p. 21).

[5] This is a prototype (example) of divine judgment that will be repeated, on a larger scale, many times in the future. Although God is asking Adam and Eve questions for which He already knows the answer, He is going about His work establishing confidence that the sentence will be fair and just. (See Dan. 7:9, 10; Rev. 20:12.)

[6] *The SDA Bible Commentary,* Ellen G. White Comments, vol. 1, p. 1082.

[7] D. Groothuis, *Christian Apologetics,* pp. 418-437.

[8] E. G. White, *The Desire of Ages,* p. 436.

[9] Larry Rasmussen, ed., *Reinhold Niebuhr: Theologian of Public Life,* The Making of Modern Theology series (Minneapolis: Fortress, 1991), p. 31.

[10] The *Seventh-day Adventist Bible Dictionary* (Washington D.C.: Review and Herald Pub. Assn., 1960, 1979) defines justification as follows: "the divine act by which God declares a penitent sinner righteous, or regards him as righteous. Justification is the opposite of condemnation (Rom. 5:16). Neither term specifies character, but only standing before God. Justification is not a transformation of inherent character. . . . When God imputes righteousness to a repentant sinner He figuratively places the atonement provided by Christ and the righteousness of Christ to his credit on the books of heaven, and the sinner stands before God as if he had never sinned" (p. 635).

[11] This redemptive aspect of an *imputed* righteousness—a righteousness that is outside of us, is also difficult for many Adventists to understand and accept. (To *impute* means to *ascribe, attribute, credit, declare, reckon,* or *to put on someone else's account.* What is imputed is never an inherent or intrinsic quality.)

[12] Clifford Goldstein, "Grace and Judgment in Genesis 3," *Adventist Review,* Oct. 8, 2009.

[13] "All heaven suffered in Christ's agony; but that suffering did not begin or end with His manifestation in humanity. The cross is a revelation to our dull senses of the pain that, from its very inception, sin has brought to the heart of God" (E. G. White, *Education,* p. 263).

[14] "What is justification by faith? It is the work of God in laying the glory of man in the dust, and doing for man that which is not in his power to do for himself" (Ellen G. White, *Testimonies to Ministers and Gospel Workers* [Nampa, Idaho: Pacific Press Pub. Assn., 1962], p. 456).

[15] Imputed righteousness is Christ's righteousness—His sinless life and sacrificial death, "credited" to the penitent sinner's account.

[16] Woodrow W. Whidden II, *The Judgment and Assurance* (Hagerstown, Md.: Review and Herald Pub. Assn., 2012), pp. 75, 76.

★ 5 ★

The Ultimate Desert Storm

While I was teaching at an academy in 1973 I was given a letter from a former student who confessed that she had cheated on her book report for an English class, having written the report without having finished reading the book. She was sorry for cheating and suggested a correction be made to her grade by half a letter. I didn't think it was all that unusual until something on the top of the letter caught my attention. It was written 34 years after the incident she described had taken place. That's an agonizing price tag for a spur-of-the-moment temptation, wouldn't you say?

What exactly do we mean by *temptation*? While there are some highly theological definitions of *temptation*, I prefer a simple one: anything that entices or encourages us to do what we know is wrong or sinful. It involves a subtle form of rationalization that leads one to find an excuse to transgress. What makes a temptation so powerfully attractive varies in many ways. It can be fun, exciting, and self-satisfying, but most of the time it comes across as the ideal solution to a particular need or problem.

The Bible generally depicts temptation as having three sources: the desires of our own heart (Mark 7:20-23; James 1:14-16); the appeal of the world around us (1 John 2:15); and those that come from the enticements of the demonic realm (Eph. 6:12). These also point to the basic kinds of temptation: greed—to want what God has prohibited; lust—to desire what the world has to offer; power—to aspire to make God expendable. Beyond that, temptation doesn't give up or go away; time and again it seems to lean on the doorbell of our hearts.

Christians are seriously mistaken if they think that Christ's temptations in the wilderness were just a singular occurrence. The truth is, in telling us about this event, God is giving us a glimpse of what took place every day in Christ's life (see Luke 4:13). Beyond that, the Bible goes on to say that Jesus was "tempted in every way, just as we are—yet he did not sin" (Heb. 4:15). My students often ask how it was possible for Jesus to be tempted as

66

we are when our temptations are so different from the ones He faced. After all, aren't there unique temptations that constantly shift to fit particular people, times, or situations? First Corinthians 10:13 helps us answer this question when it says, "No temptation has overtaken you except what is common to mankind." To me, what this is saying is that we can take all of life's temptations and put them into three common categories, as suggested in 1 John 2:16. This means no matter who you are, whatever your circumstances, or when or where you've lived, there are three common kinds of temptations all of us face. This is a relatively simple explanation as to why it can be said that Jesus, as a member of the human family, was tempted "just as we are."

Ellen White adds significance to this when she states, "Many look on this conflict between Christ and Satan [in the wilderness] as having no special bearing on their life; and for them it has little interest. But *within the domain of every human heart this controversy is repeated.*" [1]

The Two Adams, Contrasted
In the great controversy theme, there is not only a definite connection between Adam and us but also an intimate link between Adam and Jesus—evidenced by the fact that Jesus is likened to the Second or "the last Adam" (1 Cor. 15:45). While Adam is connected to us in terms of our sinfulness, the link between Adam and Jesus relates to our salvation.

Notice the similarity of these two events as they're introduced in Scripture. At Creation the Spirit hovers above the waters, and ultimately God declares, "It is good," a pronouncement that includes the appearance of Adam and Eve. In short order the Creation and pronouncement are followed by the temptations in Eden and the couple's fall. Four thousand years later, in the continued drama of the great controversy, the Holy Spirit hovers above the Jordan waters and again God declares what is good: "This is my Son, whom I love; with him I am well pleased" (Matt. 3:17). This is immediately followed by the temptations in the wilderness and Christ's ultimate victory. Adam was a representative of all his posterity at Creation, and in like fashion Jesus was the representative of all human beings at Calvary. This remarkable truth is generally known as "corporate oneness."

As a teacher I often wished I had been more aware of my students' backgrounds. It would have helped me to be more effective in relating to individual needs and differences. It reminds me of a cartoon I saw of a boy sitting at his desk—portrayed as a constant irritation to his classmates and teacher. No one could figure out why he was so unruly; he had no interest in schoolwork and was constantly getting into fights. The artist proceeded to enlighten the readers by providing a glimpse of the boy's family tree. His forefathers were a motley bunch of unruly, immoral, and overtly corrupt people. What else could you expect from a boy with that kind of a gene pool? On a wider scale, isn't sinfulness in some way or another the fate of all Adam's descendants? Thus, we all face a common dilemma, the need for a life-changing transaction that redeems and saves us from a sinful inheritance.

This is exactly what God offers each of us, a "life-saving transaction." But how does it work? In the Christian worldview there is a reference to corporate oneness—all humanity linked together in a common life and shared identity. Corporate oneness implies that when Adam fell into sin, the whole human race fell with him. What a plunge that was! Since humankind is simply Adam's life multiplied, the results of his sin were passed on to us—separation from God, a sinful nature, and condemnation by the law for our sinful condition.

If the negative side of corporate oneness is that we all fall into sin because of one man, Adam, the positive side is that God likewise redeems us all in the one Man—Jesus Christ, the Second or "last Adam" (Rom. 5:12-21). Ellen White comments: "Christ is called the second Adam. In purity and holiness, connected with God and beloved by God, He began where the first Adam began. Willingly He passed over the ground where Adam fell, and redeemed Adam's failure."[2] In other words, "He vanquished Satan in the same nature over which in Eden Satan obtained the victory."[3]

The history of these two men, Adam and Christ, affects the eternal destiny of all humankind. It is in the Second Adam that the first Adam is rescued. Scripture declares, "In Adam all die" but that "in Christ all will be made alive" (1 Cor. 15:22). That's a wonderfully amazing promise, isn't it? Paul explains in Romans 5:18-20 that just as sin entered the world through the disobedience of the one man, Adam, so also righteousness entered the world through the obedience of the one man, Jesus Christ.[4] Sin is totally unfair, but in His love and mercy God brought fairness into our warfare against the evil one. Let's put it in practical terms. Adam's choice means my initial birth occurs "in sin" (Ps. 51:5, NKJV); my choice to be "born again" (John 3:3) means to place my life "in Him" (Eph. 1:7, NKJV). Simply stated, "in Christ" we pass from eternal death to eternal life (John 5:24).

Perhaps more needs to be said regarding our transfer from the family of the first Adam to that of the Last Adam. Switching from a sinful heritage to a sinless one is what the Bible calls "adoption" (Gal. 4:5, NKJV). I like the way it's expressed in Ephesians 1:5: "God decided in advance to adopt us into His own family by bringing us to Himself through Jesus Christ" (NLT) Adoption is a legal act, like justification, that leads to a mutual relationship—sanctification between the Father and His newly adopted child. The Bible explains this life-changing transaction as follows, "So in Christ Jesus you are all children of God through faith" (Gal. 3:26; see also 1 John 3:1, 2). This act of faith is made visible by baptism, which can be seen as the official adoption or transfer ceremony. Romans 6:3 describes it this way: "Don't you know that all of us who were baptized into Christ Jesus were baptized into his death?" Being baptized "into Jesus Christ" means that when He died to pay the penalty for the sins of the world, we died "in Him" and our debts were legally cleared. This becomes our reality when accepted by faith. But Paul doesn't stop there. He goes on to say, "Just as Christ was raised from the dead . . . we too may live a new life" (verse 4). Jesus, in talking with Nicodemus, also points out this reference to the inseparableness of justification and sanctification when He said to him, "unless one is born of water and the Spirit, he cannot enter the kingdom of God" (John 3:3, 5, NKJV).

As the Last Adam, Christ offers each of us the opportunity to be represented by Him over the first Adam. Ultimately, our condemnation is not based on being born sinful but for refusing to believe what God has said and done about our sinfulness. Just as the failure of the race's first representative brought humankind into disgrace, the success of the last Representative brings grace back to us. Putting it another way: as the serpent's invitation to eat brought death to humankind, so Christ's invitation to "take and eat" (Matt. 26:26) brings eternal life to those who believe and partake (see Rom. 6:23).

It's important for us to take note of not only the similarities between Adam and Eve's temptations and those of Christ but also the significant differences. While Adam and Eve were perfect in mind and body, surrounded "with the glories of Eden," Jesus was in a weakened condition, both physically and morally, and was in the midst of a barren land infested with rodents and all kinds of wild animals.

Another significant difference was that while Adam and Eve seemed to be wandering alone through the Garden of Eden, "Jesus was led by the Spirit into the wilderness" (Matt. 4:1). Joel Ingram observes, "Could it be that the reason I fail where Christ succeeded is that I enter 'deserts' of my own choosing rather than the Spirit's leading?" He goes on to say that so often "we fail the tests of life not because obedience is impossible, but because obedience is all but impossible in the places or conditions we have wandered to on our own."[5] Now let's take a look at three significant similarities.

Temptation One: Challenge the Evidence

After Jesus fasts for 40 days and 40 nights, He feels forsaken and is extremely hungry; that's when the tempter springs into action. In this confrontation Jesus beholds a heavenly being who, unbeknown to Him, is "masquerad[ing] as an angel of light" (2 Cor. 11:14). All sensory evidence suggests that a holy angel has come from the Father's presence to announce an end to the fast and that Jesus can now deliver Himself from His famished condition.[6] Nothing suggests otherwise, until the angel speaks. His words immediately expose his identity: "If you are the Son of God, tell these stones to become bread" (Matt. 4:3). While Jesus would have enjoyed refreshing food and a cold drink of water, it was not necessary to demonstrate His identity—His divine relationship with His Father—by performing a miracle. He had all the evidence He needed. He knew His identity at 12 years of age (see Luke 2:49). It was openly and decisively affirmed by God's voice at His baptism, "You are my Son" (Luke 3:22)—significantly the first recorded words of the Father to His Son! Had Jesus provided additional evidence, He would have denied what He had already been given.

The first temptation definitely raises questions about the relationship between Jesus and the Father. The key issue was not bread but, rather, His belief in God's Word. Jesus refused to yield to Satan's challenge. He chose, instead, to "live . . . by every word that comes from the mouth of God" and to ignore the words of doubt that came from the tempter's mouth (Matt. 4:4, KJV).

Despite His dire circumstances, Jesus never wavers as to who He is! Jesus chose not to doubt His intimate status with His heavenly Father, but rather to trust Him explicitly for His every need (see Matt. 7:7-11). This was the exact point of Eve's failure. In light of His trust in God, there is absolutely no reason for Jesus to heed Satan's challenges—to miraculously provide for His sustenance in order to prove who He is. Performing a miracle was something Jesus could have easily done, but under the circumstances it would have shown a lack faith—a sin (see Rom. 14:23).

As it was in the case of Jesus, so we can be sure that one of the first challenges Satan will throw our way after baptism is evidence of our relationship with God. He will tempt us to ignore, misunderstand, or take lightly our true identity, the wonderful status we now have in Jesus—children of God. When we experience conflicts, disappointments, or apparent abandonment, the temptation will be to prove our identity that we are children of God by our own merit or efforts (see Matt. 27:40). When we are in Him, and by faith have His imputed righteousness—then we too are someone in whom God is "well pleased."[7] The apostle Paul confirms this when he writes, "He [God] made us accepted in the Beloved" (Eph. 1:6, NKJV). This God-given identity, promised to us in His Word, is our assurance that we have everlasting life; it is ours by faith, never earned by anything we do.

Temptation Two: Exploit God's Promises
"Then the devil took him [Jesus] to the holy city and had him stand on the highest point of the temple. 'If you are the Son of God,' he said, 'throw yourself down. For it is written: "He will command his angels concerning you, and they will lift you up in their hands, so that you will not strike your foot against a stone"'" (Matt. 4:5, 6).

There is a significant similarity between the second temptation in Eden and the one in the wilderness. In both cases Satan quotes God. But there's a subtle catch. In Eden Satan adds a word in an effort to falsify God's earlier instructions. In the wilderness Satan quotes Psalm 91:12 and says, "They [the angels] will lift you up in their hands." He conveniently omits the basic purpose of this promise—"to guard you in all your ways" (verse 11). In both cases Satan endeavors to cunningly exploit God's promise—to get people to believe in something false that he masquerades as true.

To exploit something means to misuse, to use unfairly, or to use unjustly for one's own advantage. In quoting Scripture, Satan wants Jesus to presumptuously believe that God's presence and protective care are available with no strings attached.[8] But God's Word makes it clear that there are conditions to be met if the objective of God's promise is to be realized (see verse 9).

I often asked my students what would have happened had Jesus decided to jump from the temple pinnacle. Most of them believed that God would have protected Jesus; after all, He is God's Son. This probably reflects the view of many older Adventists as well. Though a popular response, it ignores a key teaching of the Bible: "God does not show favoritism" (Acts 10:34). Jesus knew that apart from a direct command of God, the fatal consequences would be the same for anyone who jumped from a height of 500 to 600 feet and landed on a hard surface below. Had God miraculously intervened on behalf of Jesus it would have violated the ground rules that were to be followed in the great controversy between God and Satan. In this conflict God plays by the rules, and Satan doesn't. Satan hopes you will be presumptive to break the rules as well.

Unfortunately, many Adventists mistakenly assume that they can always rely on the protective care of angels regardless of the circumstances they may have chosen for themselves. But such a belief is not in harmony with God's Word, evidenced by the fact that Jesus refused to accept Satan's offer. Yet, wanting to be an exception to the rule is a common desire of many Christians and non-Christians alike. People want to get by; they want to escape the consequences of doing something wrong, such as driving faster than the speed limit, fudging on the truth, doing something risky, watching or participating in an event that is immoral. You can be sure that when you choose to do what's wrong, "your sin will find you out" (Num. 32:23).

In her writings, Ellen White mentions scores of ways we can forfeit the protection of angels by common everyday choices.[9] She also states, "Angels of God will preserve His people while they walk in the path of duty, but there is no assurance of such protection for those who deliberately venture upon Satan's ground."[10]

In this temptation Satan has a definite objective in mind: He desires that Jesus publicly demonstrate His arrival as the Messiah with a majestic display of power and glory, fearlessly descending from the heavens with protective, attending angels. In so doing, Jesus would be giving the worshippers at the Temple a special opportunity to acknowledge and herald His coming. Jesus, however, does not accept this tempting offer to improve or improvise God's timetable. The time has not yet come for Him to descend upon Jerusalem surrounded by a heavenly host. Such magnificent pageantry would someday take place, but not until the very end of the great controversy (see Rev. 19:11-14). Until then, Jesus chooses to live in subjection to God's will as a humble, suffering servant rather than as an ostentatious, reigning king.

Jesus chose to respond to this temptation by stating, "It is also written: 'Do not put the Lord your God to the test'" (Matt. 4:7). Why did Jesus counter this temptation by quoting this biblical passage? He evidently was impressed to use what Moses had said to the Israelites when they demanded water while in the wilderness (Ex. 17:1-7). In their unbelief, the people sought to test God. What they were actually saying was "If you really are God, and you were powerful enough to bring us out of Egypt, then give us water to drink." Apparently, the only way God could satisfy their complaint to the question "Is the Lord among us or not?" (Ex. 17:7) was to provide them with water by a miracle. But they already had sufficient evidence for their faith in God's abiding presence. Nothing more was needed; that's why Jesus refused to ask His Father to save Him by a miracle for exactly the same reason.

Temptation Three: Satisfaction Without Sacrifice
"The devil took him [Jesus] to a very high mountain and showed him all the kingdoms of the world and their splendor. 'All this I will give you,' he said, 'if you will bow down and worship me'" (Matt. 4:8, 9).

In the first two temptations Satan reveals himself as truly a liar and the father of lies (see John 8:44). That was true both in Eden and in the wilderness. We should expect nothing different in the third temptation, where Satan offers Adam and Eve, as well as Jesus, an enticing shortcut.

Let's take a look at what happened in Eden. It's quite likely that the first inhabitants of the garden were made aware of God's long-range plans for them, an outlook that may have included continual advancement in opportunities, wisdom, power, and spiritual security. Hoping to excite a spirit of curiosity or perhaps ignite a desire to know more than what God had revealed, Satan tempted them by saying, "Eat the fruit from the forbidden tree, and then you will gain something that God has not yet seen fit to give you."

Ellen White expands this thought: "By partaking of this tree, he declared, they would attain to a more exalted sphere of existence and enter a broader field of knowledge. . . . He insinuated that the Lord jealously desired to withhold it from them, lest they should be exalted to equality with Himself. It was because of its wonderful properties, imparting wisdom and power, that He had prohibited them from tasting or even touching it."[11]

In eating the fruit, Adam and Eve gained nothing. They simply lost what they already had. This was precisely what Satan hoped to accomplish with Jesus.

In contrast to Adam and Eve, the future of Jesus was clearly marked out in Scripture, and from a human standpoint, it was not a pretty picture. Throughout the Old Testament, beginning with Genesis 3:15, Jesus learned that the enemy would one day "*bruise* His heel" (NKJV). Jesus saw Isaiah amplify this by saying, "He was wounded for our transgressions, He was *bruised* for our iniquities" (Isa. 53:5, NKJV). This led Jesus to "explain to his disciples that he must go to Jerusalem and suffer many things at the hands of the elders, the chief priests and teachers of the law, and that he must be killed and on the third day be raised to life" (Matt. 16:21).

As Satan endeavors in the third temptation to mislead Jesus about the means by which He would achieve His purpose here on earth, any kind of shortcut would have had a much greater appeal for Jesus than it did for Adam and Eve. Before the Savior, Satan stands like a schoolyard bully taunting a weaker boy with his stolen ball. "Do You want it back?" he asks. "I'll give it back; just bow down to me and it's Yours." But the offer is fictitious. Satan not only planned to keep the world, but from a legal standpoint, his offer was the only means by which he could obtain it. In other words, it was not an offer about giving but of taking. Had Jesus bowed in hopes of obtaining this world, by that very act He would have been giving it away. Such a gesture would have been the last legal step in Satan's hostile bid to take over this world.[12]

Satan comes to us in much the same way, tempting us to observe our weakened condition, to abandon the path of hardship and trial for the path of immediate satisfaction—what could be called "credit card" salvation. In light of our limitations, Satan says, "Bow down to me, and I will help you obtain that which you seek without sacrifice on your part."

Satan is right in saying that we can only obtain victory as we acknowledge our weakened condition, but if we follow Christ's example, we can claim victory over Satan by recalling that which is already ours. We must not bow to Satan, because there's nothing to gain from doing so.

---

[1] E. G. White, *The Desire of Ages,* p. 116. (Italics supplied.)

[2] Ellen G. White, in *Youth's Instructor,* June 2, 1898.

[3] *The SDA Bible Commentary,* Ellen G. White Comments, vol. 5, p. 1108.

[4] "As representative of the fallen race, Christ passed over the same ground on which Adam stumbled and fell. By a life of perfect obedience to God's law, Christ redeemed man from the penalty of Adam's disgraceful fall. . . . Christ will never become a party to sin. . . . He gives the sinner another chance, a second trial. He opens a way whereby the sinner can be reinstated in God's favor. Christ bears the penalty of man's transgressions, and by imparting to man His righteousness, makes it possible for man to keep God's law"

(*The SDA Bible Commentary*, Ellen G. White Comments, vol. 6, p. 1092).

⁵ Joel Thomas Ingram, "Desert Storm," *Adventist Review*, Mar. 10, 2005.

⁶ "He [Satan] came to Christ enshrouded in light, claiming to be one of the angels from the throne of God, sent upon an errand of mercy to sympathize with Him and to relieve Him of His suffering condition. . . . He also stated that he was the angel that stayed the hand of Abraham as the knife was raised to slay Isaac, and he had now come to save His life" (Ellen G. White, *Confrontation* [Washington, D.C.: Review and Herald Pub. Assn., 1971], pp. 38, 39).

⁷ "The word that was spoken to Jesus at the Jordan . . . embraces humanity. God spoke to Jesus as our representative. With all our sins and weaknesses, we are not cast aside as worthless. 'He hath made us accepted in the Beloved.' Eph. 1:6" (E. G. White, *The Desire of Ages*, p. 113).

⁸ "Often when Satan has failed of exciting distrust, he succeeds in leading us to presumption" (*ibid.*, p. 126).

⁹ One example: "If we seek the company of sinners, . . . are pleased with their coarse jests, and entertained and amused with their stories, sports, and ribaldry, the pure and holy angels remove their protection and leave us to the darkness we have chosen" (E. G. White, *Testimonies*, vol. 2, p. 222).

¹⁰ *Ibid.*, vol. 5, p. 198.

¹¹ E. G. White, *Patriarchs and Prophets*, p. 54.

¹² Ingram.

★ 6 ★
Every Direction but West

All of us are familiar with the expression "Go West, young man, go West," a quotation usually credited to American author Horace Greeley. Some contend, however, that it first appeared in the *Terre Haute Express* in an editorial written by John B. L. Soule. *The Yale Book of Quotations* (a volume generally recognized as the most comprehensive and up-to-date quotation dictionary), published in 2006, maintains that no one can be sure who first penned those words and that they "may well have been a paraphrase" of similarly stated "advice given by Greeley." [1] Whatever the case in today's vocabulary, *West* is a word that still rings with plenty of meaning and gusto.

West is also commonly used in the Bible. However, it has no special or prophetic significance in contrast to the other three directions, *north, south,* and *east.* This is especially true in the books of Daniel and Revelation.

Let's illustrate. In Daniel 11, which primarily amplifies the great controversy as outlined in chapters 2, 7, 8, and 9, there is a lengthy description of an ongoing battle between the kings of the north and kings of the south (Dan. 11:2-43). This conflict surrounds and impacts the "Glorious Land" (verse 41, NKJV; NIV: "Beautiful Land")—a reference to ancient Israel but eventually a symbol of spiritual Israel (see Dan. 8:9). It can be said that from the middle of the chapter onward, this rather protracted prophecy becomes less local and nationalistic and distinctly more spiritual and global in nature. When this worldwide warfare finally nears its close, it is indicated by these words in Daniel 11: 40: "At the time of the end . . ." The concluding scenes in verses 40-45 seem to be primarily geared around this ominous declaration: "But tidings out of the east . . . shall trouble him [king of the north]" (verse 44, KJV).

Chapters 13 and 14 of Revelation greatly expand this conflict in Daniel 11:40-45, and eventually Revelation 16 wraps it up by describing the kings of the whole world and the kings from the east engaged as bitter rivals in the battle of Armageddon (verses 12, 14). It becomes apparent that the great prophecies of Daniel and Revelation employ every direction but west in their symbolic arsenal.

The Historical Setting

In biblical times, ancient Israel was viewed as "the center of the nations" (Eze. 5:5); in other words, it was the crossroads of the world. It was surrounded by two of the world's greatest civilizations—Egypt to the south and Babylon to the north—its general direction of attack (see Jer. 1:14, 4:6, 50:41). These two warring empires frequently traveled through the land of Israel and eventually became her primary enemies. Egypt enslaved Israel for more than 200 years and disavowed the existence of the true God. Babylon held Israel captive for 70 years and demanded that their captives worship Babylonian gods. One could say the Exodus from Egypt and the Exile into Babylon are the polar events in Israel's long and colorful biblical history.

Thus, it should not come as a surprise to us that in the play and counterplay of Old Testament history, three worldviews consistently stand paramount—those held by Israel, Egypt, and Babylon. The Bible makes it evident that the two kingdoms that opposed Israel openly rejected Israel's God, each in their own unique way, as the 10 plagues (see Ex. 7-12) and the fiery furnace (see Dan. 3:8-15) so dramatically illustrate.

It is noteworthy that the conflict in which God's remnant people are involved, during the time of the end since 1798, is couched in language that is reminiscent of ancient Israel's warfare. The reason is quite obvious: Bible-believing Christians (spiritual Israel) find themselves on a similar collision course with the same two opposing worldviews. God's people have many political foes in the present world order but primarily two spiritual enemies: spiritual Egypt—the unbelieving world that denies the existence of the biblical God; and spiritual Babylon—the believing world that is the primary vehicle of religious confusion. While the followers of God are called out of both (see Ex. 20:2; Rev 18:1-5), those who reject this call have chosen to remain in one or the other. Granted, the confrontation is different today than in Bible times, but the conflict is just as real, just as intense, and just as significant.

Meaning of a Worldview

In this controversy, what worldviews do the spiritual entities of Israel, Egypt, and Babylon represent in today's world? Before we answer that question, let's define what we mean by *worldview*. In 2006 I had cataract surgery on both of my eyes. After the cataracts were removed and intraocular lenses inserted, much to my delight it brought about a whole new way of seeing. Colors were brighter, everything was more distinct, and I could once again read fine print and decipher street signs. My vision went from 20/60 to 20/20. Now, that's what a worldview is supposed to do.

A worldview, which literally means *a way of seeing*, is the determining factor as to how we think and act. It can be compared to a pair of glasses through which we attempt to see things clearly and make sense of what's out there. It's our view of the big picture. In other words, it represents our personal outlook on life, the way we perceive and interpret reality. Someone has aptly described a worldview as "the hinges on which all of our everyday thinking and doing turns."

One of the unique characteristics of human beings is that we cannot live without the kind of orientation and guidance a worldview gives. We need some sort of rationality to live by, a mental map that helps us navigate the world effectively. All of us have been at a shopping mall, ballpark, or hospital where you see a large, centrally located map that has a brightly colored star with these words: *You are here!* The map helps us to orient ourselves to get the right perspective on things.

Modern freeways can also metaphorically illustrate worldviews, with each highway representing a different worldview. Each has its own exits; each provides unique things to see and experience; but most important, each has its own destination. This rules out the popular idea that all major worldviews are headed the same direction. Such an idea doesn't work with highways when we are going to work on Monday morning, nor does it hold true regarding our spiritual perspectives. While most worldviews are similar on the surface, at their core they are distinctly unique. The reason is quite simple. *At the heart of each worldview is what it says about God*—who or what is at the bottom of everything that exists. It presents a view of the nature of ultimate reality and how everything else relates to it.

Israel: Christian Theism

Spiritual Israel, the Israel of faith (see Gal. 3:7-9), represents Christian theism, a Creator-centered worldview, although modern Judaism and Islam also claim to have a theistic (God-centered) worldview. All three religions believe there is more than the physical world, that there is a personal God who created it. They maintain that there's a radical distinction between an uncaused Creator and a caused creation. That which is created is finite. It is limited by time and space and is forever dependent upon the Creator for life and directions as to how it should be lived. On the other hand, the Creator is infinite. He is self-existing, immutable, eternal, unlimited—a holy God who sustains and governs what He has created.

Christian theism is theocentric in its outlook. Its basic assumption is divine creation, that a personal God brought the cosmos into being. His design of orderliness, unrivaled beauty, intricate interdependence, and incredible complexity in the natural world points to a personal Creator who took His time in creating the world. Theism affirms that the world's inhabitants reflect purpose and design. As creatures, people and animals are alike in that they are all subject to God's sovereign rulership. Being created in God's image, we are fearfully and wonderfully made. Humankind is distinct from the rest of creation, possessing such unique qualities as individuality and creativity, an innate sense of right and wrong, and the power to think and make intelligent choices. In addition to this is the capacity of self-awareness, responsibility, as well as the capacity to love and be loved, to worship God, and to live in fellowship with Him.

While all three theistic world religions are theocentric (God-centered), Christianity stands apart from modern Judaism and Islam in several key ways. First, it emphasizes that God, in a unique way, is both transcendent (beyond the universe) and immanent (active within the universe). Second, Christianity is uniquely *Christocentric* (Christ-centered). While the other theistic religions believe in God, the ultimate dividing line between these three religions is their view of Jesus. Only Christians believe that God came to earth in the person of Jesus Christ and that salvation is exclusively found in Him. Finally, Christianity believes that the God who created the world is triune and that the Bible stands alone as the infallible Word of God. (In the final conflict, while some in Judaism and Islam will become Christocentric, the remainder will choose the worldview of either Babylon or Egypt).

Christian theism teaches that humankind is by nature immoral: "The heart is deceitful above all things and beyond cure" (Jer. 17:9). It is equally adamant about the need for universal principles of right and wrong, measurements based on the very nature of God that stand above the world's norms or cultures. In this worldview God is the central point, the absolute standard, by which all moral judgments are based. The moral law is seen not as righteousness developed or discovered by human instrumentality but rather as delivered by

God's own hand (see Deut. 5:22). This was made known to us through His Word; all of our behavior is to be governed by this divine yardstick.

There is a definite reason for this: generally, we are not aware of the degree of selfishness at the root of our thoughts and actions. In order to discern the subtle and pervasive nature of sin, we need the spotlight of God's Word to bring to our attention the real extent of our self-serving. So it needs to be routinely emphasized that whenever sin is unrecognized, it is because God's law is unknown. God's Word is a light that exposes the contents of the heart—selfish motives, evil thoughts, lustful desires, and every secret vice (see Heb. 4:12).

How often have you walked into a room where a beam of sunlight is streaming through a window, exposing all of the dust particles in the air? Without the light you wouldn't be aware that there were tiny bits of debris floating around. In fact, at times you might prefer not knowing that you're breathing all of that stuff. Jesus said, "Light has come into the world, but" "everyone who does evil hates the light, and will not come into the light for fear that their deeds will be exposed" (John 3:19, 20). Jesus knew human nature very well, didn't He? (See John 2:25.) It's been rightly observed, "If the sinner does not first stand in the searching light of the law, he will not stand in the saving light of the cross."[2]

In my classes I often spoke of this world as the pigsty of the universe. The Bible goes one step further and calls it a "bottomless pit" (Rev. 20:3, NKJV). It is nasty and nauseating, a place that all of us would like to scrub, decontaminate, and make suitable for wholesome living. But on our own we're no match for the sin-laden scourge that has ravaged and ruined our planet and its inhabitants. For us to understand the one and only remedy God Himself stands behind, Christian theism takes us back to the initial outbreak of sin—the Garden of Eden, where the original antidote is prescribed.

Adamandeve@eden.com could have been the e-mail address of the world's first home. When things went wrong in the Edenic setting, God could have simply pressed the "delete" button on His cosmic computer, wiped the slate clean, and started over gain. But He chose not to deal with sin in that way. From the very inception of sin, God did not do away with the death penalty, nor did He require the guilty to die. Instead, the God of grace chose an innocent substitute to die in the sinner's place. In slaying an animal and covering Adam and Eve's nakedness with tunics of skin, God figuratively revealed His decision not to condone sin but to personally atone for what had been done. As already stated, a divinely prepared covering replaced the human patchwork of prickly fig leaves. Now Adam and Eve could rightfully exclaim, "For He has clothed [us] with the garments of salvation, He has covered [us] with the robe of righteousness" (Isa. 61:10, NKJV). Sin brought about a loss of clothing; redemption was God once again clothing the sinner!

In all of this, the gravity of sin and the grace of God are clearly demonstrated—for them as well as for us. Simply put, disgrace is replaced by grace—an exclusive work of God. Since "it is the blood [death] that makes atonement" for sin (Lev. 17:11), God through Jesus Christ, symbolically offers Himself as a sacrifice to die in the sinner's behalf. God takes the initiative and in love covers the repentant sinner with Christ's robe of righteousness (see Rev. 7:9, 10). As our substitute, Jesus bears the penalty that we may receive pardon. As our example, He provides righteousness for our spiritual power and growth. What a glorious advantage for those who accept God's remedy.

Egypt: Atheism

The first recorded words to come out of Egypt prior to the Exodus were extremely significant: "Who is the Lord, that I should obey him and let Israel go? I do not know the Lord and I will not let Israel go" (Ex. 5:2). From a biblical perspective, it succinctly depicted what Egypt was all about. It describes the unbelieving attitude of all humankind in its naturally sinful condition. But more specifically, Pharaoh uttered these words of disdain in response to God's request through Moses to let His people go so that they could worship Him. Beginning with the Exodus, and extending throughout the Bible, Egypt symbolizes rebellious unbelief, an arrogant rejection of Israel's God and the right to worship Him. To disbelieve in God means to believe in and worship self. That's precisely how the pharaohs of Egypt saw themselves—divine figures who alone were worthy of worship.

In the preamble of the Ten Commandments, God declares, "I am the Lord your God, who brought you out of Egypt, out of the land of slavery" (Ex. 20:2). In describing Egypt in this very abject way, God is setting the stage that's required if His people are to obey the law He is about to give them. In this opening statement God's grace precedes true obedience to His law, an axiom that applies equally to all mankind. This principle is a basic theme that flows through all Scripture—God first delivers (saves) people from slavery (sin) before asking them to obey His laws. This freedom is gained simply through faith in the supreme lawgiver.

God wants us to understand that ancient Israel was not delivered *by* obedience but *for* obedience. They were not asked to keep the law in order to be delivered from slavery but because they had been rescued from the Egyptians and were now free to obey God. This lesson is equally applicable to us today. In salvation, we, as was ancient Israel, are first rescued (justified) by faith; what follows is heartfelt obedience to God's law (sanctification). The truly obedient believer is one who has been rescued from Egyptian slavery, and it is God's intent that the believer remain free in Him.

In Hosea 11:1, God says, "Out of Egypt I called my son." While this points back to Israel's exodus from Egypt, it also points forward to the experience of Jesus. When Joseph and Mary fled with their child to Egypt, they stayed there until they heard that Herod had died. With respect to Joseph and Mary's departure out of Egypt, Matthew declares that this is "what the Lord had said through the prophet, 'Out of Egypt I called my son'" (Matt. 2:13-15). This text suggests that Jesus was compared or likened to the nation of Israel that came out of Egypt. But more than that, Jesus was also the new and true Israel. Wherever Israel failed, Jesus was successful, and for that reason salvation doesn't come from being an Israelite but rather from being in Christ. Just as God called Israel out of Egypt to be a blessing, a kingdom of light to the world, so Jesus came to be the ultimate light of salvation, the ultimate blessing.

In Daniel 11, verse 40 points to 1798, when Egypt—the king of the south—represents unbelief or atheism. This prophecy points to a striking fulfillment in the history of France, the only nation whose surviving authentic records reveal that its legislative assembly (in 1793) decreed that there was no God. In discussing the effects of the French Revolution (1789-1797), Lars P. Qualben, in his book *A History of the Christian Church,* says that this event "marked a turning point in human thinking and progress, culminating in a new worldview and in a new outlook on life." He goes on to say that the new spirit that arose "was less conscious of God and more conscious of man and his inherent powers and possibilities. Man became the measure of all things, and human reason, ratio, was enthroned as the only religious authority."[3]

History records that extensive suppression and warfare against the Bible, carried forward for centuries by Roman Catholic clerical authorities throughout Europe,[4] but especially in France, culminated in a counteraction in the late eighteenth century that we know as the French Revolution. It was in large measure the flame that highlighted an aggressively legitimate revolt against the usurped authority of the Papacy, but at the same time, it brought about another form of illegitimate authority, namely the deification of human reason. With human reason enthroned and glorified above Deity, it eventually gave rise to such philosophies as rationalism, atheism, deism, Darwinism, Marxism, scientism, and secular humanism. Each has a significant role in eliminating God's decisive role in human life; each in its own way proclaims that the modern mind (human reason) is capable of understanding what life is all about apart from divine revelation. Each accommodates the inclination to trust in the authority of human opinion. Each is a definite reflection of intellectual pride, excessive ambition, and the desire of ultimate superiority. Whereas the Papacy brought about an ignorance of divine revelation, atheism led to its rejection.

The basic premise of atheism or the philosophy of naturalism is that our universe is a closed system in which everything has a "natural" explanation. It views the material world as ultimate reality, that all that really matters is matter. It works from a human-centered position, meaning that its basic assumption is evolution. It claims that there is nothing beyond our world that we can see, touch, or measure—no supernatural realm. God, heaven, good and evil angels, anything miraculous, are all viewed as illusions, just human inventions. It sees God as nothing more than a projection of our imagination. Deity is simply the highest and best that we see in ourselves.

Naturalism is the fountain from which all godless philosophies flow, streams of thought that widely affect every aspect of our world. In other words, if human beings do not seek meaning and purpose for their lives from the Creator, they will look for it in created things. The naturalist believes that science, not the Bible, gives humankind the best shot at knowing "how things really are." In life *someone* has to be in charge, to govern, to be in authority. No one ever dispenses with this, just relocates it. From the naturalistic viewpoint, human beings are the ultimate authority. They are in charge; they decide what life is all about.

Naturalism is generally divided into several recognizable segments. While some atheists are called humanists, others are lumped together with agnostics, skeptics, or secularists. What's the difference? The skeptic says, "I doubt there is a God"; the agnostic states, "I don't know if there is a God"; the atheist boldly affirms, "I know God does not exist." Perhaps the most common form of naturalism today is the secularist who declares, "I don't care if there is a God," choosing to live as though God does not exist. Other well-known extensions of atheistic thought are materialism, relativism, empiricism, multiculturalism, and even classical Buddhism. A more recent philosophy that is characterized by its disdain of scriptural truth is postmodernism, an ideology that maintains that truth is *made* by us, not *found*. One person has cleverly summed up this hodgepodge of unbelief with this cynical comment: "Life is nothing more than a bus ride to the cemetery, with everyone fighting for the best seats." [5]

From its atheistic viewpoint, naturalism sees humankind as being basically good. As the highest of all evolved creatures, the humans find themselves in a dilemma—not of sin but simply the limitations associated with our evolutionary climb. With no Deity to turn to, human beings can only depend upon their own resources and develop their own human potential if they are to resolve the ills of their planet. After all, what options do they have when they build their worldview on the premise that there is no God? Apart from a God-given foundation, sin and salvation are not viewed as realities at all. Human beings may be victims in need of change and treatment, not rebels in need of redemption. They may be inhibited and insecure, but nothing that a large dose of self-esteem can't resolve.

Naturalism sees religion as meaningless and outdated, offering people pious illusions instead of practical solutions. But more than that, it condemns Christian theism for distracting well-meaning people from earthly concerns, prohibiting them from helping themselves, and denying them the opportunity of reaching their full potential. In its most expansive sense, the belief system symbolized by the king of the south represents the entire human race in its natural (sinful) state, having no relationship with God, which describes every person's experience at some point. The apostle Paul sums it up when he says, "The natural man does not receive the things of the Spirit of God, for they are foolishness to him, nor can he know them, because they are spiritually discerned" (1 Cor. 2:14, NKJV).

Babylon: Apostate Religion

The lengthy and rather complicated prophecy in Daniel 11 commences when God's people (in this context, ancient Israel) were situated in Palestine. To the south was a great center of civilization along the Nile River, while to the east was the other great center for several kingdoms in the region of the Euphrates River. Over time this center to the east referred to several different powers, such as Assyria, Babylon, Persia, and even segments of the Grecian dynasty. While most of these empires were located to the east, their armies had to march northwest around a large desert region and then come down and attack Jerusalem from the north (see Jer. 4:6, 50:3); thus, they are referred to as a northern enemy. The Babylonian Empire was the most significant, not only because it was one of Israel's most prominent enemies, but also because behind it was God's archenemy, Satan himself (Isa. 14:4, 12). Time and time again these powers (the kings of the north and kings of the south) engaged in war against each other and, in the process, marched through "the Glorious Land" (Dan. 11:1-39, NKJV). In all of these struggles, Israel not only suffered as a spectator but was also taken into Babylonian captivity. As the line of prophecy comes down to the Christian era (see verses 20-39), it swings away from a localized Palestinian setting to a worldwide conflict between spiritual Israel and two of her greatest religious enemies.

Zdravko Stefanovic, in his book *Daniel: Wisdom to the Wise,* states:

"The apocalyptic visions in Daniel (chapter 11) together with their interpretations portray conflicts on two levels: First, the horizontal level: Earthly power clash because of their political ambitions. Sooner or later, however, the clashes assume the second—the vertical dimension, with confrontations that are of a religious character, often stemming from an arrogant and hostile attitude toward God, His people, and His institutions, notably the sanctuary and the worship of God."[6]

Babylon, as the word implies, represents the confusion that permeates false religions in today's world. In contrast to Egypt, which represents one ideology, that of unbelief in the biblical God, the king of the north is a symbol of all false beliefs and religious systems. In the final conflict, Babylon, the king of the north, symbolizes religion in which humanity worships self under the cover of a religious (Christian) garb, while Egypt, the king of the south, points to religion in which humanity worships self beneath atheistic attire. Thus it can be said, "All inhabitants of the earth will worship the beast [the sinful creature]—all whose names have not been written in the Lamb's book of life" (Rev. 13:8). Keep in mind that Daniel and Revelation can be more readily understood if the word *beast* is generally seen as referring to the self-serving nature of humankind.

In the book of Revelation, John alludes to the eventual takeover of this planet by one evil confederacy when he declares "Babylon"—a symbol of the corrupt religious systems of the world—"has become a dwelling for demons and a haunt for every impure spirit" (Rev. 18:2). This indicates that all religions, whether in denial or defiance of the biblical Creator, will ultimately be included in that one city divided into three parts (see Rev.

16:19). God's Word reveals that in the final conflict, those who disbelieve and those who falsely believe are but one worldwide kingdom rebelling against the Creator.

One postscript is appropriate at the conclusion of this chapter. The three worldviews that have been depicted in this chapter are quite similar to the three primary worldviews that are commonly accepted in today's culture: theism, naturalism, and pantheism. The latter two declare that only one reality exists: Naturalism upholds that there is only the natural or physical world, that there is no supernatural realm. On the other hand, pantheism affirms that only a supernatural or divine realm exists. It sees God's impersonal essence and the world's essence as one and the same. This signifies that only theism posits two opposing realities—good and evil—in conflict with each other, the very heart of the great controversy.

---

[1] Fred R. Shapiro, "Who Said, 'Go West, Young Man': Quote Detective Debunks Myths," LLRX.com, *Law and Technology Resources for Legal Professionals*, Dec. 24, 2007, http://www.llrx.com/features/quotedetective.htm. (Fred R. Shapiro is also the editor of *The Yale Book of Quotations* [New Haven, Conn.: Yale University Press, 2006].)

[2] Gordon Kainer, *Faith, Hope, and Clarity: A Look at Situation Ethics and Biblical Ethics* (Mountain View, Calif.: Pacific Press Pub. Assn., 1977), p. 50.

[3] Lars P. Qualben, *A History of the Christian Church* (New York: Thomas Nelson, 1933), p. 371.

[4] Whenever this book speaks about Roman Catholicism, it is speaking about a religious system, an ecclesiastical structure and the way it functions, not about the individual members themselves.

[5] Gordon Kainer, *Worldviews and Religion* (Nampa, Idaho: Pacific Press Pub. Assn., 1998), p. 16.

[6] Zdravko Stefanovic, *Daniel: Wisdom to the Wise: Commentary on the Book of Daniel* (Nampa, Idaho: Pacific Press Pub. Assn., 2007), p. 411.

★ 7 ★

Fresh Air or Bad News

What event do you think has drawn the world's largest viewing audience? Some may say the Super Bowl, which in 2011 had a primarily American audience of 111 million. This is far from the largest. In 1969 approximately 500 million watched the first humans walk on the moon. In 1973 more than 2 billion eager fans watched the Elvis Presley concert in Hawaii, and in 1997 2.5 billion people witnessed the funeral of Princess Diana. It is assumed, and for good reason, that the largest viewing audience generally takes place during the Olympics. It is estimated that around 4.5 billion people watched the opening ceremonies of the summer Olympics in London in 2012. Now that's what I call a global crowd!

But these numbers fall far short of what happens when human history comes to a climactic close. The Bible tells us that the final conflict that plays out on the world stage will occupy the attention of every man, woman, and child. Revelation 1:7 states that at Christ's appearance "every eye will see him" (see also Rev. 16:14). The events associated with this cosmic extravaganza, which have been prerecorded for us in Daniel 11:40-12:1, have the potential of being seen by at least 7 billion people, the approximate population of our planet right now. As we study the end-times as given to us primarily in symbolic language, keep in mind what we've already learned: it's not about political or societal differences being thrashed out in a local or even a national setting; it's about a spiritual controversy that has global implications. It involves the truth about God's government.

Three Primary Adversaries
One of the most significant prophecies of the end-times in the Old Testament is Daniel 11:40-45:

"At the time of the end the king of the South shall attack him [king of the North]; and the king of the North shall come against him like a whirlwind. . . . He shall also enter the Glorious Land, and many countries shall be overthrown; but these shall escape from his hand: Edom, Moab, and the prominent people of Ammon. He shall stretch out his hand against the countries, and the land of Egypt shall not escape. . . . But news from the east and the north shall trouble him; therefore he shall go out with great fury to destroy and annihilate many. . . . Yet he shall come to his end, and no one will help him" (NKJV).

This mysterious forewarning has a climactic end that we need to understand.

The three primary adversaries in this prophecy are the king of the south, the king of the north, and the glorious land. Ellen White describes this conflict in these words: "The world is stirred with the spirit of war. The prophecy of the eleventh chapter of Daniel has nearly reached its complete fulfillment. . . . It is impossible to give any idea of the experience of the people of God who shall be alive upon the earth when celestial glory and a repetition of the persecutions of the past are blended." [1]

King of the South Response
Centuries of papal persecution, bloodshed, and extremely harsh church practices (by the king of the north) during the Dark Ages not only resulted in irreparable damages but also left behind deep spiritual scars. When it became evident that the Roman Catholic system was morally bankrupt and scandalous, many people, especially those in France, became spiritually bitter and disillusioned. The rise of an avenging movement is described in Daniel 11:40: "At the time of the end the king of the south shall attack him [king of the north]" (NKJV). "The time of the end" is generally held by Seventh-day Adventists as pointing to the close of the 1260 years, namely, the year 1798. [2] The attack that Daniel speaks about points to the papal power receiving a fatal wound (see Rev. 13:3) by an insurgent atheistic uprising (the French Revolution) that occurred at that time.

The wound Roman Catholicism suffered was both political and spiritual. It received a spiritually lethal blow when the Bible was translated into the common languages, vigorously preached by the Reformers and believed by the people until the very foundations of Roman Catholicism crumbled under the assault. This confirms the fact that the most effective weapon against spiritual wickedness is the "sword of the Spirit, which is the word of God" (Eph. 6:17).

We stated previously that the king of the south represents the forces of atheism that were ignited in Western Europe at the close of the eighteenth century. Kindled by such movements as the Renaissance, the Enlightenment, and the Age of Reason, which secularized European thought, an aggressive mood arose for political, economic, and religious change. But that which eventually brought about a legitimate revolt against a corrupt clergy turned into a wholesale attack on religion itself, lashing out against God, the Bible, and Christianity as a whole. Being especially singled out was the aggressively repressive infrastructure of Roman Catholicism, and rightfully so, it received a political wound when French General Louis Alexandre Berthier, under orders from Emperor Napoleon Bonaparte, took Pope Pius VI captive on February 10, 1798, and placed him in a French prison, where he died 18 months later. This revolt, symbolically referred to as "Sodom and Egypt" because of its connection with immorality and atheism, is also depicted in Scripture as a "beast that ascends out of the bottomless pit" (Rev. 11:8, 7, NKJV). All of this indicates that though this atheistic revolution may have been inevitable, its origin, influence, and effects were satanic nonetheless. History depicts this as a time when the legitimacy of Christianity and of the Bible were aggressively attacked and rejected (primarily because of its condemnation of people's sins). The weekly day of worship was discarded; the Bible was officially abolished and publicly burned with great fanfare, and churches were desecrated and converted into Temples of Reason. Rather than being an antidote, human reason itself became a tyrannical enemy of the people.

The fatal flaw of this revolutionary movement was that in its coup d'état against the Papacy, the creature sought to become wiser than the Creator. The uprising rejected God and the foundational constraints of His law and placed all of its hopes in human resources. It trusted in its own unguided aspirations. It became intoxicated with a sense of its own abilities and accomplishments. Divine revelation was replaced by human reason, while deism, rationalism, evolutionary notions, and secular philosophy supplanted Christian thought. This kind of divorce from the Creator, along with the rejection of the Bible as the revealed Word of God, eventually culminated in all kinds of bloodbaths, the most notable being the Reign of Terror. We have been warned that such conflict will one day be renewed and will expand to encompass the entire world.[3]

King of the North Retaliates
Daniel 11:40, 41 points out that after the king of the south springs into action and takes an oppressive stance, two significant events follow: First,

the king of the north is aroused "like a whirlwind" against the king of the south and "shall also enter the Glorious Land, and many countries shall be overthrown" (NKJV; NRSV: "tens of thousands shall fall victim"). The "tens of thousands" in the glorious land (God's church) who are "overthrown" may point to those who, in the midst of severe conflict, give up their faith, choosing to sever their relationship with God and abandon His people. On the other hand, simultaneously, multitudes will leave Babylon and accept God's invitation to unite with those who are faithful to Him.[4]

When talking about the fall of Jerusalem, as well as the final crisis, Jesus declared, "Then many will fall away, and they will betray one another and hate one another" (Matt. 24:10, NRSV). This probably refers to what we call *the shaking,* a time when "all will be shaken out who are not willing to take a bold and unyielding stand for the truth."[5]

Next, the king of the north will also "stretch out his hand . . . and the land of Egypt shall not escape" (Dan. 11:42, NKJV), suggesting that he will be defeated. This reflects the outcome of previous conflicts between the king of the north and the king of the south down through the centuries, where the king of the north consistently came out as victor. That the land of Egypt does not escape indicates that all godless movements, philosophies, or political powers already mentioned will either fall by the wayside or join ranks with the king of the north—the symbol of corrupt and apostate religions. This is also depicted several times in the book of Revelation: in the final crisis, only one enemy—Babylon—is singled out and denounced (see Rev. 14:8). In Revelation 16:19 the enemy of God is described as one "great city . . . Babylon the Great." And in Revelation 18:1-4, the final call to those who are still outside of God's redeemed family is described as "a loud voice, saying, Babylon the great is fallen, is fallen. . . . Come out of her, my people" (NKJV).

While Egypt does not escape, Edom, Moab, and Ammon will be delivered from the wrath of the king of the north. The Edomites, Moabites, and the Ammonites—while very close relatives of Israel—were nevertheless some of the most staunch enemies of God's people; but God, in His grace, has promised to save many who were once His greatest enemies. Indeed, every saved person was originally an enemy of God (Rom. 5:10). In the last days many will come out of churches and religions that once opposed the truth of God and take their place in God's glorious land, namely God's people.

The Enigma of the East

Perhaps the most conspicuous event in the end-time, indicated by the disastrous consequences, is described in these highly charged words: "But news from the east and the north shall trouble him [king of the north]; therefore he shall go out with great fury to destroy and annihilate many. . . . Yet he shall come to his end, and no one will help him" (Dan. 11:44, 45, NKJV).

The word "news" is also translated "rumors" and "reports," but none of these give the rich and full meaning that the word "tidings" does, as translated in the King James Version and the American Standard Version. Tidings indicate good news or enlightening communication. In Revelation 18:1-4 the words of the message from heaven that enlightens the whole earth just prior to its last hours are gospel tidings that invite people to turn from error to truth, from sight to faith, from self to Jesus, from Babylon to God's remnant people.

In the Bible, figurative references to the east are always associated with God (see Gen. 2:8; Matt. 2:1-3). Cyrus, the Persian king who is referred to as God's "anointed" (Isa. 45:1), came from the east and was used by God to deliver His people from Babylonian captivity (Isa. 41:2). Ezekiel 43:2 states that the glory of Israel's God came from the way of the east; the angel who came bearing the seal of God was from the east (Rev. 7:2). While east is consistently positive in the Bible, north can be either positive or negative. When combined with east, it is positive and indicates God's intervention, since north is associated with the location of God's throne (Ps. 48:1-2; Isa. 14:13, NKJV). Tidings from the east (and north) indicate a divine message! What was good news to the worshippers of God—which Ellen White describes as "celestial glory"[6]—on the flip side, troubled, frightened, and alarmed the worshippers of Babylon. As the saying goes, what is fresh air to some is bad news to others.

Why do tidings from the east, a message enthusiastically proclaimed by the saints (Rev. 18:1, 2), trouble the king of the north and cause him to "go out with great fury to destroy and annihilate many"? Powerful preaching of Christ's imminent return to rescue those who obey God's law and to wipe out the opposition infuriates the ruling powers "of the north." They are determined to put to death those who dare to preach such an incredulous message (Rev. 13:15).

This is what happened to King Herod at the first coming of Jesus. He too heard a message that troubled him: "Where is the one who has been born king of the Jews?" (Matt. 2:2). To hear that a king was coming alarmed him to no end; after all, he already occupied the throne. Wasn't everything safely under his control? (Isn't that what self relishes when it sits on the throne?) In his pride and arrogance, Herod declared war rather than step aside or step down. In his rage Herod made a decree "to destroy and annihilate many" in Bethlehem (see Matt. 2:3, 16). Obviously, what was good news for the righteous was extremely troubling to the wicked at heart. Proclamation of the everlasting gospel in the context of the three angels' messages and the announcement of the fourth angel of Revelation 18, delivered with resounding power and success, greatly angered the king of the north (the antichrist) and sent him on a final rampage of retributive violence and death (Rev. 13:15).

In Christ's great sermon on the Second Coming, He declared that when the good news (tidings) of the gospel is proclaimed "as a testimony to all nations, . . . then the end will come" (Matt. 24:14). The everlasting gospel is an unmistakable revelation of God's sovereign grace, making plain the underlying issue of the great controversy, thus serving as the ultimate, final divider of humankind. Tidings from the east are certainly a warning against (modern) Babylon and its counterfeit gospel—a gospel that centers on the creature rather than on the Creator. It has been rightly said, "From the first conflict in Genesis to the final battle in Revelation, the religions of the world are, in varying degrees, either human-centered or Christ-centered."[7] In other words, in the concluding stages of the final conflict, the inhabitants of our planet will either rely on human works or trust in divine grace for everyday solutions as well as eternal salvation.[8]

No matter how you say it, grace is a notion that definitely runs against human instinct. The reason? It is only natural for people to strive for the good life without any reference to the good news about grace. This is based on the false idea that humans have the innate capacity to be good without being spiritually alive in Christ. Grace is a difficult concept for those who are accustomed to self-reliance; they cannot comprehend that salvation comes free of charge, with no footnotes, fine print, or strings attached. Reluctant believers have an unrelenting urge to hype up any evidence that their best achievements count, that surely they can add a few stitches of their own rags of righteousness to Christ's garment of salvation.

And why is this the case? Pride naturally resists grace because grace represents a goodness that is alien to human effort. Pride basks in its own goodness, relishes its own accomplishments, and extols its own worthiness. Consequently, the good news of the gospel is not "good news" to those who believe that they are already good. It is imperative, however, to accept the gospel of grace as the only antidote for sin, no matter how much it hurts our pride. The Bible's rejection of our best efforts to save ourselves is offensive to most non-Christians. That's even true for some Christians. But grace can do its work only for those who are humble enough to submit and trust solely in Jesus.

This is precisely Roman Catholicism's problem. It proclaims a flawed gospel, one that primarily focuses on an infused or *imparted* righteousness. Since such righteousness is always a process, never a completed work in this life (in contrast to faith in an *imputed* righteousness that is based on Christ's *finished* work), its adherents are never sure they are good enough to be fully accepted by God. Many Roman Catholics simply hope that they have done more good than bad so that God will look favorably on them and reward them with salvation. Such an erroneous view of personal piety leads to a high degree of uncertainty, as well as a works-oriented mentality. This kind of misguided notion makes necessary a humanly constructed safeguard—the fires of purgatory, a place where the final dregs of sin will be removed after a person dies. In the attempt to appease God's wrath and increase one's eternal security, Roman Catholicism has also instituted such useless activities as indulgences, long pilgrimages, penance, painful scourging, worship of relics, confession to priests, and payments of large sums of money to the church. Contrary to what is often said, Roman Catholicism is not a religion of outright works but a subtle mingling of faith and good works that distorts the real essence of the gospel.

What does this mean? Roman Catholicism views the gospel as embracing both justification and sanctification—that faith and good works are equally essential to salvation (as also some Adventists believe). From the papal perspective, God justifies (declares righteous) only those whom He has first made righteous and obedient (sanctified). In other words, God does not pronounce a person righteous unless he or she is actually righteous. Roman Catholicism mistakenly views justification as an infusion of sanctifying grace that renders one personally acceptable to God, but that's almost always completed after one's death.

In sharp contrast, the Bible teaches that when sinners are justified, they are declared righteous by virtue of their faith in the imputed righteousness of their Representative—Jesus. As Paul says in Romans 4:5, "But to him who does not work but believes on Him who justifies the ungodly, his faith is accounted for righteousness" (NKJV). This means that they have the perfect righteousness of Jesus reckoned (imputed) to them, as if His sinless life and absolute obedience were now their very own.[9] All of this takes place at the very beginning of the Christian life and not after one's death. Through faith, Christ's history, Christ's obedience, Christ's righteousness, legally becomes our history, our obedience, and our righteousness . . . the only means by which we can be accepted by a holy and perfect God. Salvation is first of all receiving, through justification, a right *standing* with God, while right *living* (sanctification) is the outgrowth or evidence of such faith in Jesus.

Roman Catholicism denounces this as heresy, reasoning that if salvation comes solely by faith in Jesus, then why would there be any need for Christians to live righteously and be obedient? It sees justification by faith alone as a threat to the church's well-orchestrated system of forgiving sin and motivating believers to live a holy life.[10]

At the Council of Trent (1545-1563) the Roman Catholic Church spent 18 years formulating its response to the Protestant position of justification by faith alone. Canon 9 of the Council affirms: "If anyone says that . . . the sinner is justified by faith alone, meaning that nothing else is required to cooperate in order to obtain the grace of justification . . . let him be anathema" (cursed). Canon 12 states: "If anyone shall say that . . . justifying faith is nothing else than confidence in the divine mercy which remits sins for Christ's sake . . . let him be anathema."[11]

These declarations, which Roman Catholicism has never rescinded, continue to defiantly reject justification "by faith alone." In sharp contrast, Paul wrote in his Epistle to the Galatians: "I am astonished that you are so quickly deserting the one who called you to live in the grace of Christ and are turning to a different gospel—which is really no gospel at all. . . . But even if we or an angel from heaven should preach a gospel other than the one we preached to you, let them be under God's curse!" (Gal. 1:6-8). In Paul's declaration that when "you . . . attempt to be justified by law [works]; you have fallen from grace" (Gal. 5:4, NKJV), he was saying that in their law-keeping they had lost sight of Christ's vicarious (imputed) obedience. The reference *falling from grace* was evidently pointing to a subtle shift from imputed to imparted righteousness, falling from explicit faith in Christ's obedience to a reliance on one's own obedience in the work of redemption. Paul would have none of it. The gospel he gave to the Galatians is clearly stated in these words: "Know that a person is not justified by the works of the law, but by faith in Jesus Christ" (Gal. 2:16).

The Catholic doctrine that believers can achieve salvation and acceptance with God through an inner holiness, an infused righteousness that is channeled only through the sacraments of the church, is a false gospel (see Gal. 1:6-8). It stands in direct opposition to the biblical gospel, which teaches that the righteousness of Jesus is imputed directly to the trusting, repentant believer (see Rom. 4:5). The false gospel fails to comfort the troubled consciences of the weary, the wayward, and the weak. Only imputed righteousness that is received by faith in Christ's finished work provides the repentant sinner with peace (no condemnation) and the assurance of salvation.

Biblical salvation meets the challenge of sin with an all-encompassing solution: separation from God is dealt with in the person of Jesus, who connects in Himself what has been disconnected—the human and the Divine. He is the link between a holy God and fallen humanity (1 Tim. 2:5). No other priest is needed. Jesus came to restore the rift between heaven and earth, because until that is taken care of, nothing else matters.

Now, what do we mean by restoring the rift between heaven and earth? Uniting in Himself our humanity with His divinity (see Matt.1:23; Phil. 2:5-8), Jesus personally represents God to us, and at the same time He is our personal connection with God. By virtue of our faith in this unique God-man, our (severed) relationship with God is *rightfully* restored, the penalty for our rebellion against Him is *legally* canceled (forgiven), and our nature is re-created and *spiritually* empowered by the Holy Spirit. Only in Jesus Christ can that kind of reconciliation with God take place. "For if, while we were God's enemies, we were reconciled to him through the death of his Son, how much more, having been reconciled, shall we be saved through his life!" (Rom. 5:10). This affirms a vital teaching of Scripture: reconciliation is never achieved by human effort; it is received by faith in the work of Jesus. Our faith does not bring God's saving grace into being; it only confesses its existence and applies its benefits.

Although we cannot comply with the claims of God's law by a personal righteousness, we can satisfy them by faith in the vicarious righteousness of Jesus.[12] In Eden humans were acceptable in their own person. Outside of Eden they are acceptable to God only in the person of Jesus. By faith they bring to God the perfect work, the unblemished obedience of Jesus. His is the only perfection that counts with God. Faith in Jesus, our Representative, our Advocate, is not optional. It is the very heart of the Christian religion.

Roman Catholicism has usurped Christ as humankind's representative, mediator, and heavenly high priest with its own sacerdotal system. By substituting an earthly priesthood and a sacramental ministry for the heavenly ministry of Jesus, the worshipper is dependent upon human instrumentality (church sacraments) rather than a divine advocate—Jesus Christ. In so doing the Papacy desecrates the true sanctuary.

The heart of Babylon's false gospel (Roman Catholicism) is highlighted in Daniel 11:45: "And he [the king of the north] shall plant the tents of his palace between the seas and the glorious holy mountain" (NKJV). The seas symbolize the people of the earth (see Rev. 17:15), and the glorious holy mountain represents God's throne room (see Ps. 2:6). It is between the people and God's dwelling place that the king of the north defiantly sets up "the tents of his palace" to occupy the place where only Jesus can sit as the "one Mediator between God and men" (1 Tim. 2:5, NKJV).

Zdravko Stefanovic, citing C. Mervyn Maxwell's *God Cares: The Message of Daniel for You and Your Family*, describes it this way: "The 'beautiful holy mountain' appears as a metaphor for the Jerusalem temple, which, in turn, symbolizes the location of God's dwelling, which is the heavenly sanctuary. The control of the holy mountain symbolizes 'the encroachment of the king of the north on the prerogatives of Christ's sanctuary ministry.'" [13]

There are several other places in the Bible where this sacrilegious act is described. Daniel 8:11 says: "He [the little horn] even exalted himself as high as the Prince of the host; and by him the daily sacrifices were taken away, and the place of His sanctuary was cast down" (NKJV). In symbolic language this is saying that Roman Catholicism has magnified its power to where it claims equality with Christ. [14] The apostle Paul puts it like this: "He will oppose and will exalt himself over everything that is called God or is worshiped, so that he sets himself up in God's temple, proclaiming himself to be God" (2 Thess. 2:4). It should also be noted that the Papacy's outright determination to take away the daily sacrifices of the sanctuary (the death of the lamb on behalf of the sinner) reveals its repudiation of the sanctuary teaching of justification by faith alone in Jesus.

In Daniel 11:31 we read that the king of the north "shall defile the sanctuary fortress; then they shall take away the daily sacrifices, and place there the abomination of desolation" (NKJV; NIV: "the abomination that causes desolation"). In Matthew 24, when Jesus speaks of "the end" (verse

14), He calls special attention to the "abomination that causes desolation" that will be "standing in the holy place" (verse 15). Here Jesus is pointing to the desolating, idolatrous king of the north who, during the Dark Ages and in the final conflict, leads people away from Jesus' priestly ministry and deprives them of their rightful access to the "prince of the covenant" (Dan. 11:22, NKJV).

Doom and Deliverance

The closing words of Daniel 11:44, 45 tell us that Babylon, the king of the north, "will set out in a great rage to destroy. . . . Yet he will come to his end, and no one will help him." The word "destroy" literally means "to sentence to death on religious grounds." This horrendous event is amplified in Revelation 13:15, which says that the second, or land, beast—a symbol of the United States—will be given "power to give breath to the image of the first beast, so that the image could speak and cause all who refused to worship the image to be killed." It's hard to believe that such atrocity will someday take place in our land, but when Protestant America begins to speak "like a dragon" (Rev. 13:11), the dragon's rage on account of "those who keep the commandments of God" (Rev. 12:17, NKJV) will then be fully vented.

Though the final events in Daniel 11 are indeed calamitous, this prophecy doesn't end there, thankfully, but extends into chapter 12. Here we find this reassuring promise: "At that time Michael, the great prince who protects your people, will arise. There will be a time of distress such as has not happened from the beginning of nations. . . . But at that time your people—everyone whose name is found written in the book—will be delivered" (Dan. 12:1).

We need to briefly unpack these encouraging verses. Michael, who Seventh-day Adventists believe is Jesus—the one whose human name is Jesus Christ and His celestial name is Michael—is not simply standing up as a victorious king. It is generally believed that the setting for this event is not military but judicial (see Isa. 3:13; 50:8; Eze. 44:24). Judges usually sit (see Dan. 7:26) during legal proceedings, and at the conclusion they would arise to announce the verdict. When Michael stands up, His posture signals the close of the pre-Advent judgment, and the verdict of eternal life is pronounced on the righteous. Although His role as the mediator of His people is concluded, nevertheless, when the great "time of trouble" erupts, Michael, the one who delivered His people in the judgment, now promises anew that everyone whose name was not blotted out of "the book" will again be delivered (Dan. 12:1). The longest prophecy of Scripture concludes with a wonderfully reassuring commitment on God's part.

Ellen White explains the meaning of deliverance a little more fully:

"I saw a covering that God was drawing over His people to protect them in the time of trouble; and every soul that was decided on the truth and was pure in heart was to be covered with the covering of the Almighty." [15]

"As dangers surround them, and despair seizes upon the soul, they must depend solely upon the *merits of the atonement*. . . . None will ever perish while they do this." [16]

"If you would stand through the time of trouble, you must know Christ, and appropriate the gift of His righteousness, which He *imputes* to the repentant sinner." [17]

The Great Controversy

It should be obvious from our study thus far that the great controversy theme is an ever-present highlight of the Old Testament, especially in the prophecies of Daniel, and later amplified in the book of Revelation. It affirms what God Himself declares: "For the Lord has a controversy with the nations" (Jer. 25:31, NKJV). In the worldviews of Egypt and Babylon, and all the religions and ideologies that flow out of them, the great controversy theme is either nonexistent, incomplete, or distorted.

The Koran, for example, the holy book of the Muslims, claimed to have been "revealed to Mohammed by the Angel Gabriel," [18] states that the reason for Satan's rebellion was that when Allah commanded the angels to "'prostrate yourselves before Adam,' they all prostrated themselves except Satan, who in his pride refused and became an unbeliever" (Sura 2:34; 18:50). Such an account of Satan's fall is totally foreign to the Bible's description as to why the great controversy erupted in heaven. This discrepancy makes the supposed identity of the angel highly suspect.

The apostle Paul warns that even if "an angel from heaven" speaks a message that is not in agreement with what the Bible teaches, "let him be accursed" (Gal. 1:8, NKJV). Clearly, only from divine revelation can we receive the truth about the nature of the enemy and what his ultimate objectives are in his warfare against God. An examination of all of the world's non-Christian religions, as well as popular ideologies of unbelief, readily reveals only erroneous beliefs about Satan, ignorance of sin and salvation, and unawareness or misunderstanding of the great controversy. It's essential, then, to conclude with this affirmation: only the Bible clearly establishes the reality of Satan, openly exposes his methods of attack and warfare, and reveals the means by which he can be defeated.

[1] E. G. White, *Testimonies,* vol. 9, pp. 14-16.

[2] See E. G. White, *The Great Controversy,* p. 356.

[3] Regarding the final conflict, Ellen White makes this prediction: "The spirit of unrest, of riot and bloodshed; the world-wide dissemination of the same teachings that led to the French Revolution—all are tending to involve *the whole world* in a struggle similar to that which convulsed France" (E. G. White, *Education,* p. 228; italics supplied).

[4] See E. G. White, *Testimonies for the Church,* vol. 1, p. 182.

[5] E. G. White, *Early Writings,* p. 50.

[6] E. G. White, *The Great Controversy,* p. 314.

[7] G. Kainer, *World Views Make a World of Difference,* p. 161.

[8] Grace is God's lovingkindness, forgiveness, and mercy given to the undeserving. It is His attitude toward sinners wherein He freely provides for their salvation.

[9] "Every soul may say: 'By His [Christ's] perfect obedience He has satisfied the claims of the law, and my only hope is found in looking to Him as my substitute and surety, who *obeyed the law perfectly for me.* By faith in His merits I am free from condemnation of the law. . . . I am complete in Him who brings in everlasting righteousness. He presents me to God in the spotless garment of which no thread was woven by any human agent'" (Ellen G. White, *Selected Messages* [Washington, D.C.: Review and Herald Pub. Assn., 1958], book 1, p. 396).

[10] While Seventh-day Adventists wrestle with the same question, their concern regarding the role of the church in all of this is very different from that of Roman Catholicism and would probably take another book to explain.

[11] Council of Trent, *The Canons and Decrees of the Council of Trent: With a Supplement, Containing the Condemnations of the Early Reformers, and Other Matters Relating to the Council,* trans. Theodore Alois Buckley (London: George Routledge and Co., 1851), quoted in Mark Gstohl, "Council of Trent on Justification," *Theological Perspectives of the Reformation,* 2004, http://www.reformationhappens.com/works/trent-justification.

[12] "Christ has made a way of escape for us. . . . He lived a sinless life. He died for us, and now offers to take our sins and give us His righteousness. If you give yourself to Him, and accept Him as your Saviour, then, sinful as your life may have been, for His sake you are accounted righteous. Christ's character stands in place of your character, and you are accepted before God just as if you had not sinned" (Ellen G. White, *Steps to Christ* [Mountain View, Calif.: Pacific Press Pub. Assn., 1956], p. 62).

[13] Mervyn C. Maxwell, *God Cares: The Message of Daniel for You and Your Family* (Nampa, Idaho: Pacific Press Pub. Assn., 1981), vol. 1, quoted in Z. Stefanovic, *Daniel,* p. 420.

[14] It might also be said that it is blasphemous to claim that it is possible to live a sinless life *just as Jesus did,* an assertion that some Seventh-day Adventists make.

[15] E. G. White, *Early Writings,* p. 43.

[16] E. G. White, *Patriarchs and Prophets,* p. 203. (Italics supplied.)

[17] E. G. White, *Selected Messages,* book 1, p. 363. (Italics supplied.)

[18] "Introduction," *The Koran,* trans. N. J. Dawood (Harmondsworth, Middlesex, England: Penguin Books, 1956), p. 9.

★ 8 ★
The Gospel Comes First

I n the editorial section of the March/April 2012 issue of *Adventist Today*, J. David Newman writes: "A pastor arrived at his new congregation and soon convinced the church board to change the sign and add a cross. A few weeks later a fellow Rotary Club member at one of their meetings approached the pastor. 'I really like your new sign,' he said. 'That cross makes it so clear. I could never figure out what the three bugs were that you had on it before.' He was referring to the three angels." [1]

This rather comical conversation confirms what I have suspected all along: most people aren't that familiar with the symbols or the message of the three angels. Quite a number of years ago an experienced Bible teacher at an academy confided in me that one day his son in elementary school came home with this innocent request: "Dad, today our teacher talked about the three angels' messages, and it didn't make much sense. Can you tell me in a simple way what they're all about?" My teacher friend confessed that this was probably the most difficult task he had ever faced as a Bible teacher. I suppose many of us can readily relate to that.

Despite the challenge, there's a good chance we would still maintain that the three angels' messages are significant and are an exclusive feature of the Seventh-day Adventist Church. In fact, this well-known motif is perhaps the most ready expression of our identity, our mission, and our heritage of what our church is all about. It symbolizes the very heart of the unique contribution we have been divinely commissioned to give to the world. All of this became a long-awaited reality at the "time of the end," the beginning of the nineteenth century when the book of Daniel was unsealed (see Dan. 12:4) by the understanding and proclamation of the three angels' messages.

This is the way these messages read:

"Then I saw another angel flying in the midst of heaven, having the everlasting gospel to preach to those who dwell on the earth—to every nation, tribe, tongue, and people—saying with a loud voice, 'Fear God and give glory to Him, for the hour of His judgment has come; and worship Him who made heaven and earth, the sea and springs of water.' And another angel followed, saying, 'Babylon is fallen, is fallen, that great city, because she has made all nations drink of the wine of the wrath of her fornication.' Then a third angel followed them, saying with a loud voice, 'If anyone worships the beast and his image, and receives his mark on his forehead or on his hand, he himself shall also drink of the wine of the wrath of God, which is poured out full strength. . . .' Here is the patience [quiet strength] of the saints; here are those who keep the commandments of God and the faith of Jesus" (Rev. 14:6-12, NKJV).

I came across an article in the *Adventist Review* in which Nathan Brown asks the question "Why do angels come in threes?" He asks this question in light of the fact that even though angels are an important factor throughout the book of Revelation, why are these three angels "introduced together, with three specific messages that fit together?"[2] He discusses the possibility that it might reflect a literary device known as trebling; however, I would suggest that the three angels are in reality God's response to the three temptations in Eden (and those Jesus faced in the wilderness). In other words, just as the temptations are linked together in one story, the same holds true for the three angels' messages. But more than that, the three temptations that represent the work of the demonic must be seen as being in direct opposition to the three messages that are angelic. These two story lines clearly represent the opposing sides of the great controversy in all of its stages as they wind their way through the pages of Scripture.

This can be illustrated as follows: the first temptation in Eden is designed to create *doubt*. Satan's first recorded words to the human pair—his first message—were intended to cause Eve to distrust God's wisdom, to doubt and to become confused concerning the explicit command He had previously given to her. Thus, the first angel proclaims the antidote—the utter necessity of faith in what God says.

The second temptation focuses on *presumption*, the false idea that there is no lethal consequence if one disbelieves or disobeys God. Fittingly, then, the second angel declares that those who defiantly choose to disobey God are fallen and will suffer the consequences of that choice.

The third temptation involves the supreme *exaltation* of self—to be "like God." For this reason the third angel adamantly warns against the worship of the beast (creature).

Revelation uses angels to symbolize human beings doing a heavenly work—proclaiming God's last-day message to the world. The original meaning of the word "angel" is "messenger," and the first thing that comes to mind is that they are extraordinary, above and beyond this world, and superior in nature and quality. This should give us a clue as to the estimate God places on this special movement of the last days. Ellen White says, "The fact that an angel is said to be the herald of this warning [first angel's message] is significant. By the purity, the glory, and the power of the heavenly messenger, divine wisdom has been pleased to represent the *exalted* character of the work to be accomplished." [3]

The First Angel

The first angel symbolizes God's end-time people and immediately draws our attention to its key component—"the everlasting gospel" that is to be proclaimed "to every nation, tribe, tongue, and people" (Rev. 14:6, NKJV). This message, delivered just prior to the Second Coming, is evidenced by the words that immediately follow the third angel: "Then I looked, and behold, a white cloud, and on the cloud sat one like the Son of Man, having on His head a golden crown, and in His hand a sharp sickle. . . . And the earth was reaped" (verses 14, 16, NKJV).

The book of Revelation identifies three key aspects of the last awakening movement at the end of time: the messenger—the *first angel*; the message— the *everlasting gospel*; and the recipient of the message—*those who dwell on the earth*. The word "dwell" is significant in that it alludes to those whose spiritual outlook is shortsighted, who have a mental perspective that regards this life as being all there is. For these people, "the earth" is their permanent home, the ultimate abiding place.[4] How appropriate, then, is Paul's advice, "Set your mind on things above, not on things on the earth" (Col. 3:2, NKJV).

While the first angel has much to proclaim to the world, we should note that none of it precedes the giving of the gospel, and for good reason. If people are not led to first accept the new covenant promise of salvation in Jesus, then all that follows doesn't really matter. The Bible is clear on this point: there is no redemption apart from the name of Jesus (see Acts 4:12; John 14:6; Rom. 10:9). What makes the scenario of the first angel's message so unusual is God's announcement that His people will proclaim the gospel. Doesn't Christ's great commission to His followers already include this directive? "And this gospel of the kingdom will be preached in the whole world as a testimony to all nations, and then the end will come" (Matt. 24:14).

Down through the ages, the most disheartening failure of the church has been the denigrating and withholding of the gospel from itself and thus from the world. Commentaries on church history abound with the unbelievable tragedy of a gospel that's been hidden away, blatantly shunted, ignored, and in some cases utterly despised. In departing from the gospel, the church turned to secular power, which led to the development of the Papacy. How did such a transition affect the giving of the gospel to the world? An answer that first comes to mind is relatively simple: if the church is to be faithful in proclaiming the gospel to the world, it must first understand, accept, and apply the gospel to itself. It is a rule of life that it is impossible to give others what you yourself do not have (see Acts 4:13). This is evident in that the first angel's message identifies the true worshippers of God by their relation to the everlasting gospel. Once the gospel is accepted and internalized by believers, there will be a driving desire on their part to share its saving message with a world that's dying without it (see Jer. 20:9).

The gospel as God's merciful gift of salvation received "by grace . . . through faith" (Eph. 2:8) is mentioned only once in Revelation: in connection with the first angel's message. If the gospel is to be relevant and applicable to the times in which we live, it must be presented within the framework of that angel, translating it into present truth. In other words, the first angel's message takes the good news of salvation and helps twenty-first-century people apply its truths to the special needs and concerns that highlight the final conflict. The everlasting gospel of the first angel is God's last appeal to earth's inhabitants; this boldly calls for a decision to willingly trust and obey the Creator.

The adjective *everlasting* affirms that the gospel is not only unchanging but also an unchanged gospel. The fact that the gospel being preached is everlasting indicates that its foundation is in the changeless character and purposes of God. God's end-time people, represented by the three angels, will have a unique mission, but their gospel message is not unique.

This can be illustrated several ways. For example, we can go all the way back to the five "I will" statements of Satan in his declaration of rebellion against God in Isaiah 14:13, 14, and then discover that they are matched by God's five "I will" statements in His unchanging covenant of grace (see Jer. 31:31-34), as devised by the Trinity in the council of peace in eternity past (see Zech. 6:13). In this meeting, shrouded in mystery, each member of the Godhead chose to participate in some uniquely redemptive way should sin ever burst upon God's creation. Sin's remedy has always remained the same; while the earthly debut of the great controversy actuated God's eternal plan of salvation, it did not alter or reshape it in any way (see Eph. 3:9-11).

That this was the gospel first spoken to Adam and Eve is affirmed by this statement: "The message proclaimed by the angel flying in the midst of heaven is the everlasting gospel, the same gospel that was declared in Eden when God said to the serpent, 'I will put enmity between thee and the woman.' "[5]

According to Hebrews 11, it was the gospel (salvation in Christ by faith alone) that saved what seem to be the best and the worst characters—Abel, Noah, Abraham, Rahab, Samson, and Jephthah. In the New Testament it was the gospel that Jesus preached, that Paul annunciated, and that redeemed sinners such as Zacchaeus, the Samaritan woman, the thief on the cross, and the Philippian jailer. It is what seals the 144,000. While the heart of the gospel clearly focuses on the life, death, and resurrection of Jesus (see 1 Cor. 15:1-4), it is in the first angel's message that we find it uniquely packaged for the end-time.

When the everlasting gospel is proclaimed in this way, it will not be hard for believers to "fear God and give him glory" and to "worship him who made the heavens, the earth, the sea and the springs of water" (Rev. 14:7). The order of the proclamation is important—the invitation to "fear God," a mental activity, is followed by the command to "give him glory," a reference to one's words and conduct. Isn't this how the Christian life should be lived?

Revelation's exhortation to fear God and give Him glory is borrowed from Moses' appeal to Israel just before they entered the Promised Land. In his farewell address Moses declared, "Fear the Lord your God, serve him only. . . . Do not follow other gods. . . . Be sure to keep the commandments of the Lord your God" (Deut. 6:13-17). Here we see commandment-keeping as the rightful response in the worship of God. More than 3,000 years later the first angel still proclaims the need to "fear the Lord and give glory to Him" because we too are standing on the borders of the Promised Land. As God's last-day messengers, should we not expect Seventh-day Adventists to be foremost in worshipping and living for the glory of their soon-coming King?

It's important to realize that human beings are, by nature, worshipping creatures. There is a common mistaken notion that only religious people worship. Neither worship nor religion ceased when humankind rebelled against God and fell into sin. What sin did do, however, was change the focus of our worship and the purpose of our religion. Clearly, the real issue is not whether to worship but rather why and whom we worship. Our "god" is that which we regard as the highest authority and with the greatest affection. We worship and obey what we love, admire, and trust, which just might be ourselves. Worship is an expression of faith and allegiance, and it reveals whose side we are on.

The first angel's call to worship has a premise that goes all the way back to Genesis—to worship the God "who made." Those who worship the Creator make known His power and greatness by declaring that He is the one "who made the heavens, the earth, and the sea." The creatorship of God is the fundamental platform on which rests His right to reign. It is the reason He is to be revered and worshipped. "You are worthy, our Lord and God, to receive glory and honor and power, for you created all things, and by your will they were created and have their being" (Rev. 4:11). Is there any greater evidence of power than that of creating life? By alluding to the commandment that contains the phrase "For in six days the Lord made the heavens and the earth, the sea" (Ex. 20:11), the first angel confirms a Creation that was wrought over six 24-hour days and a seventh-day Sabbath that was established as its memorial.

The call to worship Him who made heaven and earth is proclaimed in contrast to the increasingly popular teaching that the Genesis story is merely folklore, a myth that reflects pagan philosophies. The timeliness of the first angel's message is revealed by the fact that the Seventh-day Adventist Church and Darwinism arose almost at the same time. Around July of 1844 Darwin completed a 189-page handwritten manuscript summarizing his evolutionary theory. Interestingly, scholars refer to it as "Darwin's 1844 sketch." Like his *Origin of Species*, which he wrote later, it proposed the development of the species through an evolutionary process over millions of years. Since many professed Christians have abandoned the Genesis story for the evolutionary notion, the first angel's message has been set in motion to meet this erroneous teaching. True believers are to find their greatest joy in praising the Creator, not only for the work He has done in the world but also for what He has done in their lives.

The Pre-Advent Judgment

What makes the first angel's message additionally relevant is its proclamation that "the hour of His judgment has come" (Rev. 14:7, NKJV).

It is this announcement that opens the way for people to understand the time, purpose, and comprehensive nature of the pre-Advent judgment that they did not discern until "the time of the end" (Dan. 12:4). Israel's worship songs had already expressed the thought that God is the Judge, since He is the Creator of all things: "For all the gods of the nations are idols, but the Lord made the heavens. . . . Say among the nations, 'The Lord reigns.' The world is firmly established, it cannot be moved; he will judge the peoples with equity. . . . He comes to judge the earth. He will judge the world in righteousness and the peoples in his faithfulness" (Ps. 96:5-13).

Revelation 14:7 played a key role in the Adventist development of the pre-Advent judgment—and how thankful we should be that this major event is given in the context of the gospel, the good news that Jesus stands in as our representative! The coming of the Son of man to the Ancient of days as our advocate is Daniel's way of emphasizing the same point (see Dan. 7:13). Such a biblical setting envelops the judgment with good news that the believer has righteousness in Jesus that will stand up under divine scrutiny. Thus, we are encouraged to "approach God's throne of grace with confidence, so that we may receive mercy and find grace to help us in our time of need" (Heb. 4:16). The first angel calls us to look away from ourselves and other people and, instead, to behold the One in whose merits we can fully trust. We are not to be preoccupied with ourselves. We are not to focus on establishing our own self-worth. We are to practice looking to Jesus to find in Him all the self-worth we will ever need. Why look within when we can look to Him?

Let's consider this. Living during the time of the pre-Advent judgment, believers need a righteousness that will allow them to "come boldly to the throne of our gracious God" and stand fearlessly before Him (Heb. 4:16, NLT). As "justified sinners" we can experience the peace and joy that God has promised if our primary focus is on the cross, where Jesus declared, "It is finished," rather than our cross, which symbolizes a never-finished, ongoing journey. Our ongoing experience in Christ, the cross that is taken up daily, is always subordinate to our faith in the completed work of Jesus. In other words, if we see character development or spiritual growth as the basis of God's acceptance of us in the judgment, then our eyes will mistakenly focus on self, rather than on our substitute, Jesus Christ.

In Daniel 7 we see a glimpse of the judgment now taking place in heaven's courtroom. In verses 9 and 10 the Ancient of days is seated on His throne; and while "ten thousand times ten thousand stood before him. The court was seated, and the books were opened." As previously mentioned, Daniel, observing these judicial proceedings, declares, "There before me was one like a son of man, coming with the clouds of heaven. He approached the Ancient of Days and was led into his presence" (verse 13). Jesus is the divine advocate (not prosecuting attorney), and believers whose names have remained in the book of life "receive the kingdom and will possess it forever," because the verdict of the judgment was made "in favor of the holy people of the Most High" (verses 18, 22).

In light of this unbelievably good news, the apostle Paul asks, "Who will bring any charge against those whom God has chosen? It is God who justifies. Who then is the one who condemns? No one. Christ Jesus, who died—more than that, who was raised to life—is at the right hand of God and is also interceding for us" (Rom. 8:33, 34). The joy of the justified is that faith alone in Jesus entitles them to receive—not achieve, earn, or merit—the kingdom forever.

Despite all of the emphasis on the good news and the verdict that's made in favor of God's people, many Seventh-day Adventists continue to believe that only those who are sinless and perfect in character will be ready to face the excruciating scrutiny of the pre-Advent judgment. Such believers will become hopelessly discouraged if they try to stand before God's perfect law apart from a divine substitute.

Such misguided error occurs for at least two reasons: First, believers forget that in the judgment, Jesus, the Son of man in Daniel 7, is their advocate and gives His kingdom to the people (verse 27). It is His perfect life, His blameless record, rather than the life of the believer, that is the turning point in the judgment. Ellen White describes it like this: "He [Jesus] presents us to the Father. . . . He pleads before God in our behalf, saying: I have taken the sinner's place. Look not upon this wayward child, but look on Me." [6]

Second, there is a misunderstanding of the Bible teaching that judgment is based on our works (see Rev. 20:12, 13). While grace-induced obedience does not have any merit or contribute in any way to our salvation, acts of genuine obedience are indeed the fruit of genuine faith. Living faith produces unmistakable evidence—visible works of righteousness for which God receives the praise (see Matt. 5:16) and that are recorded in heaven's books to be examined in the judgment. Going the second mile, God provides public evidence in support of the final decisions rendered when the cases of all are settled for eternal life or eternal death.

Perhaps it's important to provide a few more details regarding the "blameless record" that's examined in the judgment. When your personal advocate and mediator points to your record, it is not blank just because you are a forgiven sinner. Careful scrutiny reveals that Jesus has placed the record of His perfect life into your file. In Christ you have by faith the righteousness that Heaven approves, the imputed righteousness of Christ that entitles you to eternal life here and now (see John 5:24). What a marvelous thought that He is willing to substitute His righteousness for your unholy and filthy life because He loves you! The apostle highlights this glorious transaction when he writes, "God made him who had no sin to be sin for us, so that in him we might become the righteousness of God" (2 Cor. 5:21).

It is imperative that we not overlook the broader context of the pre-Advent judgment. It occurs as God's response to the Papacy's challenge in speaking "pompous words against the Most High" (Dan. 7:25, NKJV). Revelation 13:6 describes the papal power as one that would "blaspheme [defame or defile] His [God's] name" (NKJV). It's essential, therefore, that we expand our view to see that the judgment isn't simply about the people whose names are written in the book, as important as that may be. The judgment does not convene a hearing to refresh God's memory regarding our works, our ways, or our thoughts; all is known to Him, including the hidden motives that drive our actions. No doubt about it, He knows His children. In a very real sense, it is the hour of *His* judgment. The ultimate purpose of this judgment is not our salvation but the exoneration of His name (character) amidst rampant misunderstanding. For that reason God engages in a heavenly hearing for the benefit of the onlooking universe (Dan. 7:9, 10). He desires that the loyal beings on earth, in heaven, and the unfallen worlds clearly see the fairness of the Deity and the perverseness of the boastful assertions of the Papacy—which reflect Satan's own rebellious aspirations.

Rather than choosing a quick fix as the cosmic moral administrator, God has chosen the long-haul approach in dealing with the terrible dilemma and challenges of sin and its evil results. God's ultimate purpose is to gain the supportive vote of all, whether saved or lost, "that at the name of Jesus every knee should bow, in heaven and on the earth, and under the earth, . . . that Jesus Christ is Lord" (Phil. 2:10, 11). When God's loving righteousness, justice, and redeeming grace are fully revealed in the pre-Advent judgment, we will then know that the same supportive conclusions will be reached in all of the judicial tribunals that follow, the millennial (see Rev. 20:4) and the "great white throne" judgments (Rev. 20:11, 12).[7]

A False or Different Gospel

One of the most significant roles of the evil spirits in the final conflict is to promote a false gospel. As already stated, these spirits presenting a counterfeit gospel to the world are the evil counterpart of God's three angels. The apostle Paul reveals the essence of the false gospel when he writes to the Galatians that you are "deserting the one who called you to live in the grace of Christ and are turning to a different gospel" (Gal. 1: 6). What Paul is saying is that the false gospel involves their turning away from the grace of Christ, endeavoring to justify themselves "by observing the law" (Gal. 2:16). After all, who can fault obedience to the law? Their decision not to seek justification "by faith in Jesus Christ" (verse 16, NKJV) was an attempt to confer glory on themselves rather than divine grace. Woodrow W. Whidden II makes a significant point when he says, "The radical nature of the 'by faith alone' concept must surely lay in the dust any lingering thoughts of self-glorification of even the *most sanctified* of 'true believers.'"[8]

Grace is a supernatural work of God and, thus, out of harmony with the world's natural order. Like us, the Galatians had to learn that grace is totally foreign to the human way of thinking. The sinful bias of humankind instinctively rejects grace, "for the flesh desires what is contrary to the Spirit" (Gal. 5:17). It innately views grace as totally unbelievable, unexpected, and undeserved, making it highly unlikely that it (the flesh) will accept the reality that the remedy of sin is grace plus nothing.

The core issue in the final conflict is a spiritual one, indicated by the fact that in describing the battle of Armageddon, God warns His people to keep their clothes about them and not to be naked (Rev. 16:15). In the midst of battle, God desires us to be "clothed . . . with garments of salvation and arrayed . . . in a robe of his righteousness" (Isa. 61:10). All of this points back to what happened to Adam and Eve in the Garden of Eden. In Genesis 3 there are two notable contrasting statements: "They [Adam and Eve] *sewed* fig leaves together and made coverings for themselves" (verse 7) and "The Lord God *made* garments of skin . . . and clothed them" (verse 21). This was probably the world's first clothing crisis. This should serve as a key teaching tool for all of us: only one of these garments will be worn. No suggestion of a gradual or a vacillating transition. The change of garments is an unwavering transaction, reflecting the decisive nature of the gospel.

What complicates this crisis for us is that demons are deceptively adept at mingling truth with error. It is their intent that we not discern the subtleties and nuances meshed within the choices we have to make. They want us to rely, at least in some way or to some degree, on sewn fig leaves rather than depend exclusively on the garment of a slain substitute. If we put it another way, one of their aims is to get obedient followers to focus on the splashy displays of the Spirit's power in their lives rather than to glory in the all-sufficiency of the imputed righteousness of Jesus. The truth is that salvation is found objectively outside of the believer, not in some internal experience induced by signs and wonders. It looks up, not in!

In some quarters of Adventism obedience to God's law (looking within) seems to have become a perpetual theme, often at the expense of imputed righteousness that's been relegated to something secondary. It is reasoned that if imputed righteousness or justification by faith (a legal declaration) becomes our main focus, it will result in either cheap grace or some kind of legalism. But the truth is exactly the opposite. When the gift of justification is given primacy—assuring the believer of a saved status—it will, in effect, provide the right motive for sanctification, obedience that's based on a loving response to the gift of salvation already received. Justification by faith actually prevents obedience from becoming legalistic. In other words, if justification by faith does not prepare the way for loving obedience, it places an unhealthy emphasis on sanctification.

When God describes Laodicea as a church that says "I am rich, have become wealthy, and have need of nothing" (a preeminence of sanctification), He points out that they are actually, "wretched, miserable, poor, blind, and *naked*" (Rev. 3:17, NKJV). He goes on to say that their greatest need is "white garments that you may be clothed that the shame of your nakedness may not be revealed" (verse 18). This divine analysis depicts a church that is blind and fails to see the real nature of its depravity—a sinful condition that can be resolved only by being clothed with white garments. This points to justification by faith in the righteousness of Christ. Ellen White concurs: "What is it that constitutes the wretchedness, the nakedness, of those who feel rich and increased with goods? *It is the want of the righteousness of Christ.*"[9]

The impetus that comes from giving justification by faith its rightful place is clearly indicated by this statement: "The thought that the righteousness of Christ is *imputed* to us, not because of any merit on our part, but as a free gift from God, is a precious thought. The enemy of God and man is not willing that this truth should be clearly presented; for he knows that if the people receive it fully, his power will be broken." [10]

According to Revelation 14:7, the final proclamation of the everlasting gospel emphasizes the element of glory—"fear God and give him glory." God's end-time people will focus on Jesus and the work He has done rather than on themselves and their accomplishments. We glorify God when we explicitly trust Him for salvation, accept the message of justification by faith, and rest in His finished work as this scripture makes evident: "For if Abraham were justified by works, he hath whereof to glory; but not before God. For what saith the scripture? 'Abraham believed God, and it was counted unto him for righteousness.' Now to him that worketh is the reward not reckoned of grace, but of debt. But to him that worketh not, but believeth on him that justifieth the ungodly, his faith is counted for righteousness" (Rom. 4:2-5, KJV).

Giving glory to God requires decided effort to put Him first in every thought and action. However, as Jon Paulien points out, "by nature, all of us 'glory' in ourselves. We glory in the things we possess, . . . in our achievements." Paulien is right when he says that we glory in our standing with others, even in our spirituality. We glory in those we know, the successes of our family, our church, and what they have attained. "We glory in anything that makes us look better in comparison with others," he adds. Giving glory to God, then, means we have to put down our pride and joy in ourselves and to celebrate what He has done for us. Why? Because divine acceptance sought apart from Christ becomes self-exaltation. Paulien references a Scripture text that speaks to this issue: "This is what the Lord says, 'Let not the wise boast of their wisdom or the strong boast of their strength or the rich boast of their riches, but let the one who boasts boast about this: that they have the understanding to know me'" (Jer. 9:23, 24). [11]

Revelation declares that in the end-times the entire earth will be "illuminated with his [God's] glory" (Rev. 18:1, NKJV). Why does the gospel that gives God the glory receive such universal attention at that time? The world's interest in the gospel and the people who proclaim it will take a decisive upturn when the gospel is unequivocally applied to issues that have become the center of the world's attention. While that is not yet the case today, it will be at the end of time. As the two gospels move forward into the world, one of them true and faithful, the other "a carefully crafted counterfeit," the world finds itself facing a moment of final decision. People must make up their minds whether to follow the progressive and persuasive traditions of the world or the saving, but radical truths of God's Word.[12]

---

[1] J. David Newman, "The Real Mark of God's People," *Adventist Today*, March/April 2012.

[2] Nathan Brown, "Why Do Angels Come in Threes? The Three Angels' Story," *Adventist Review*, Apr. 19, 2012.

[3] E. G. White, *The Great Controversy*, p. 355. (Italics supplied.)

[4] J. T. Anderson, *Three Angels, One Message*, pp. 44, 45.

[5] E. G. White, *Selected Messages*, book 2, p. 106.

[6] E. G. White, *Thoughts From the Mount of Blessing*, p. 9.

[7] W. Whidden, *The Judgment and Assurance*, p. 41.

[8] *Ibid.*, p. 71. (Italics supplied.)

[9] Ellen G. White, *Our High Calling* (Hagerstown, Md.: Review and Herald Pub. Assn., 1961, 2000), p. 349. (Italics supplied.)

[10] E. G. White, *Gospel Workers*, p. 161.

[11] See Jon Paulien, *Armageddon at the Door* (Hagerstown, Md.: Autumn House Publishing, 2008), p. 155.

[12] *Ibid.*, pp. 160, 168.

★ 9 ★

Pride Goes Before a Fall

Humpty Dumpty sat on a wall; Humpty Dumpty had a great fall.
All the king's horses and all the king's men couldn't put Humpty together
again!

Most of us are familiar with the Humpty Dumpty nursery rhyme, but there is much we don't know about it. We have no idea who wrote it and we don't know when it was composed, although there is evidence it first appeared in 1648. It was first published around 1820. It is generally thought that Humpty Dumpty referred to an egg; others believe it was a clumsy person. In a Ripley's "Believe It or Not" column, it was suggested that it could have referred to King Richard III of England (who ruled from 1483-1485), who was humpbacked and was often defeated in battle. We are not sure of who or what Humpty Dumpty originally represented. There is, however, one thing of which we can be sure: Humpty Dumpty is a not a true story.

In contrast to this fable, the Bible tells us of a great fall that does have the ring of truth: "A second angel followed and said, 'Fallen! Fallen is Babylon the Great, which made all the nations drink the maddening wine of her adulteries'" (Rev. 14:8).

While Babylon is commonly spoken of in the Old and New Testaments, it is in the second angel's message that the word first occurs in the book of Revelation. Since Babylon no longer existed as a nation at the time Revelation was written, it is obvious it is being used as a symbol (see 1 Peter 5:13), which brings up the question What does it symbolize and what is meant by its "fall"? In answering these questions, keep in mind that the original setting of many of the symbols in the book of Revelation, including Babylon, can be traced back to Genesis. In order to understand the spiritual significance of Babylon, let's take a look at its historical background, a history that includes several stages that are nicely delineated in Scripture.[1]

113

Babylon's Beginning

According to the Old Testament, after the Flood God made a covenant with Noah's family, a promise to never again destroy the earth with a flood (see Gen. 9:8-17). The covenant was as worldwide as the Flood had been. But those who lacked confidence in this divine promise resorted to something else. That "something else" was constructing the Tower of Babel (see Gen. 11:1-9), the first stage of what became known as Babylon. Although it can't be proven, it's been said that the city of Babylon was "built on the very ruins of the ancient tower of Babel."[2]

The name *Babel* literally meant "gate of the gods." Designed to be the connection between the "here" and "hereafter," it was a bold, innovative attempt to sidestep the revealed will of God and instead come to knowledge by another way, one of their own making.[3] It was akin to constructing their own tree of knowledge and again eating of the forbidden fruit. This magnificent city and tower was built as an unforgettable memorial of humanity's disbelief in and defiance of God. More than that, these structures were designed to capture the admiration of the world and to demonstrate the self-sufficiency of its builders. Keep in mind that every generation has its own Tower of Babel.

At this point in human history, the Babel tower was probably the greatest structure the world had ever seen. Breathtaking in appearance and grandeur, its builders saw it as the ultimate solution for the preservation and safety of the world's inhabitants. God revealed His displeasure of their *united* effort by confounding their language, which effectively "*scattered them*" over the entire earth (see Gen. 11:8, 9).

It's important that we consider some significant contrasts between Noah's family and the builders of Babel. To start with, the proposals of the builders stood in direct opposition to the plans God had given Noah's family as they left the ark. After placing the rainbow in the heavens, God instructed Noah, "Go . . . abound [flourish] on the earth, and be fruitful and multiply" (Gen. 8:16, 17, NKJV). Noah's clan was not afraid of being scattered over the entire earth, because the rainbow was a perpetual reminder of God's promise to protect, bless, and provide for them, no matter where they lived on terra firma. But the Babel builders had their own self-serving, self-preserving ideas; in contrast, they declared, "*Come, let us build ourselves a city, and a tower whose top is in the heavens; let us make a name for ourselves*" (Gen. 11:4, NKJV). What the builders viewed as a sign of their greatness was in fact evidence of supreme weakness. The tower that was to be a monument to their fame instead became a memorial of their foolishness.

God's people had placed their trust in God's promise (the rainbow), while the builders of Babel attempted to save humankind by their own endeavors. The contrast could not have been more pronounced. The tower and the rainbow served the same purpose: each denoted what people had come to trust; each represented what they relied on when looking to the future. The tower exemplified their acceptance of a human proposal; the rainbow pointed to a future viewed through the eyes of God's promise.

Each of us in our own way responds to life in these two ways: we either "*Go* and make disciples" (Matt. 28:19) for the Lord as the main focus of our lives or else we call out to those around us, "*Come,* . . . let us make a name for ourselves." I suppose it could be said that life is a matter of either coming or going.

Babylon and Abraham

After a general worldwide separation (scattering) of the people had occurred, our attention is directed to a much smaller separation that involved only one family: Abraham and his clan "set out from Ur of the Chaldeans to go to Canaan" (Gen. 11:31). When Abraham left Ur, we can only assume that he might have been acquainted with the Babylonian king Hammurabi, whose heyday was also about this time. However, when leaving Babylon during its second stage—often referred to as the Neo-Babylonian or Chaldean Empire, Abraham didn't make any headlines; in fact, it's quite possible that no one even noticed. There was no splashy fanfare, no news conference, and no big announcement of any kind. This is important because Abraham's leaving the land of his origin is a symbol of our spiritual departure from the land of our birth. The Bible calls it conversion. All of us are born in the land of the lost and need to be spiritually transferred to the realm of the living (see John 5:24). And this should be done without showiness or undue publicity.

God asked Abraham to leave Ur, the capital city of the ancient Sumerian (Babylonian) Empire, while it was one of the greatest kingdoms of the world at the height of its splendor. It was prosperous largely because it was strategically situated near the Euphrates River. While Abraham and his family lived in Ur, it was already famous for its advanced knowledge in mathematics and astronomy as well as its wealthy kings. Naturally, we may wonder what Abraham and his family left behind in Ur when they departed. From what we have been able to find out, they probably turned their backs on the world's most advanced culture and storehouse of extravagant treasures. Much of this could only be ascertained by extensive excavation, generally known as an archaeological dig.

Excavations associated with archaeology have been carried on at hundreds of sites for decades in virtually every area of Bible lands, including ancient cities such as Ur. These projects have uncovered massive foundations, magnificent temples, palaces, and tombs and brought to light such objects as weapons, tools, musical instruments, works of art, and thousands of written texts. Findings like these have provided valuable illustrations of local customs and practices that are generally not made known in Scripture.

Led by Sir Leonard Woolley, archaeologists spent nearly 13 years from 1922 to 1934 excavating Ur and, in the process, unearthed evidence of a thriving community involved in a complex system of commerce. Clay documents pointed to an impressive city, one whose residents had been prosperous, wealthy, highly educated, and had developed an advanced culture. Though this ancient city had been plundered several times, they still discovered large amounts of jewels, china, crystal, elegant vessels made from precious metals, richly decorated drinking cups, bowls, and weapons made of gold. The city had paved streets with well-built two-storied houses connected to a city sewer system. Ur gave abundant evidence of its past grandeur, a center of luxury, commerce, and trade.

Archaeologists also uncovered a lavish temple complex (a ziggurat) in Ur, as well as a royal palace and regal tombs. One royal burial was accompanied by scores of servants, fully armed soldiers, "court ladies" dressed in their regalia, and a multitude of treasured objects, no doubt a gallant attempt to make sure that the deceased would have the same luxurious lifestyle in their next lifetime. Ur showed evidence of worldly greatness, extreme immorality, and total devotion to a highly sophisticated system of pagan gods. Although the city was spiritually fallen, it was not until Abraham left the city that its enemies physically destroyed it. The destruction was so complete that Ur was hidden in relative obscurity until it was excavated in modern times.

In his book *The Bible in World History* Stephen Leston writes, "Abraham lived in a very developed society. This is what makes his move from Ur to Canaan so remarkable. Abraham left Ur during its economic and political pinnacle to move to a land that was rough and undeveloped."[4]

Surely, it must not have been easy for Abraham to leave the sophistication, the learning, and the comfort of Ur. One wonders how many times the members of his well-ordered clan may have remembered with nostalgia the luxuries they had given up and questioned whether their move had been a wise one. The author of Hebrews summarizes the whole matter with these significant words: "By faith Abraham, when called to go to a place he would later receive as his inheritance, obeyed and went. . . . He lived in tents" (Heb. 11:8, 9). In fact, we never find Abraham living in anything but a tent after his departure from Ur. By faith he was always willing to live as a "stranger in a foreign country" (verse 9; also see Ex. 2:22).

God's covenant with Abraham to bless him with greatness, a land to live in, unnumbered descendants, and progenitor of the Messiah was not given to Abraham as a reward for his obedience. The Bible's stamp of approval on Abraham is not evidence of Abraham's worthiness but a revelation of God's loving goodness. Abraham had a lengthy list of accomplishments, but they were marred by mistrust and some grievous acts of wrongdoing. The righteousness that saved Abraham was not something he accomplished or attained. The Scripture says that when God presented His covenant to Abram, he "believed the Lord, and the Lord *counted him as righteous because of his faith*" (Gen. 15:6, NLT). It was this act of (imputed) grace, above all others, that set Abram apart from the residents of ancient Babylon. It has been said that God's promise of salvation has reference to the covenant in the Old Testament and the gospel in the New Testament.[5] Though their settings and descriptions may vary widely in Scripture, both represent the objective (unchanging, trustworthy, well-grounded) basis of our redemption.

God planned for Abraham to come out of Babylon and to stay out of Egypt. Yet the first act of Abraham when he arrived in Canaan was to go down to Egypt because the land was in the midst of a severe famine (Gen. 12:10). This relatively short stay in Egypt turned out to be a spiritual disaster. It was here that he, in fear, encouraged his wife, Sarah, to cover up their identity with a lie, brought a serious disease upon Pharaoh and his household, and took an Egyptian maidservant by the name of Hagar as his wife (see Gen. 12:14-20; 16:1). Once again, Egypt manifests itself as a symbol of unbelief, a lack of trust in God. Unfortunately, no matter the circumstances, it's so easy to rely on our own resources, to put our trust in what the world has to offer. As Abraham's life clearly demonstrates, such a choice always results in disastrous consequences when we do not put our trust in God.

Many years later the Israelites once again faced a similar situation. Just like Canaan appeared to Abraham, the wilderness looked like such a dreary, hopeless, God-forsaken place to the Israelites. They, too, clamored for what Egypt had to offer (Ex. 16:13; Num. 11:4-6). Yet God was there providing food (manna), water (from the rock), shelter, protection, and guidance (pillar of cloud and fire). Like Abraham, they too had to learn to trust God, to rely on His promises. It was important for the Israelites to look back and see how God had delivered them from the cruel demands of Pharaoh and how He had also blessed them by the gentle, almighty touch of His hands. They needed this kind of reflective faith in order to handle new challenges in the wilderness and in the Promised Land.

Babylon—a Spiritual Symbol

Nebuchadnezzar, the first king of the north (see Eze. 26:7) and the ruler of Babylon during stage 3, was represented by the head of gold in Daniel 2. Indeed, the golden head is an appropriate symbol of Babylon. It's been said that in the city of Babylon gold was as plentiful as dust. The phrase "Babylon the Great" (mentioned five times in the Bible) points to Nebuchadnezzar's self-glorification in Daniel 4:30: "Is not this the *great Babylon* I have built . . . by my mighty power and for the glory of my majesty?" Nebuchadnezzar ruled just over 40 years and lived nearly 70 years. Historians agree that he was a great ruler, brilliant and successful both at home and abroad. He not only ruled over the world's greatest empire but also rebuilt the city of Babylon to unbelievable power and beauty. Cuneiform lists indicate that the city had as many as 280 temples, 955 sanctuaries, and 384 street altars. The city had three huge palaces; the largest one had a throne room that was 173 feet long, 57 feet wide, and 66 feet high. He embellished the temples, not just for the gods he worshipped, but also for his own glory. His Median wife was homesick for the mountains where she had grown up, and so he built for her the hanging gardens that were to simulate the hills she was familiar with. These gardens had to be watered regularly perhaps with a built-in drip system. No wonder Nebuchadnezzar was exceedingly proud of the city he had built.

Indeed, it was his proud declaration of greatness that promptly resulted in his becoming a helpless, fallen leader. "Pride goes before destruction, a haughty spirit before a fall" (Prov. 16:18) was perhaps never more evident than with this Babylonian king. When Nebuchadnezzar felt that he was at the height of his power and glory, God withdrew His Spirit from this proud monarch, and he became like a wild beast of the field. In this beastlike condition, he ceased to be a person of strength, intelligence, and trustworthiness. This kind of mental and spiritual brokenness not only represents the spirit of modern Babylon but also points to the condition of the entire world after probation closes. At that time this planet will become like "the den . . . of every dirty and hated animal" (Rev. 18:2, CEV). It will be graphically demonstrated what humankind is actually like without the upholding presence and restraining power of God (see Acts 17:28).

As a political power Babylon appeared to have had a past of royal splendor, but in God's Word it is a spiritual symbol of unbelief, confusion, and self-sufficiency. This is especially true in the next stage, the Babylon of the Dark Ages. During this time the Roman Catholic Church dominated Christendom for 1,260 years, a time period symbolized by either 1,260 days, 42 months, or three and a half "times" (see Dan. 7:25, 12:7; Rev. 11:2, 3, 12:6, 14, 13:5). Babylon also became a symbol of religious captivity and oppression. By the time the book of Revelation was written (modern) Babylon was already a code word for a persecuting "enemy" (1 Peter 5:13). It was used to represent any entity that disbelieved or defied the God of heaven or oppressed those who were loyal to Him.

In the second angel's message, Babylon's opposition to the first angel's message—which highlights, among other things, the everlasting gospel and the sacredness of the seventh day—identifies Babylon. It should be noted that the second angel's message is given twice in Revelation: in 14:8 and in 18:1-5—in the latter the proclamation reaches a crescendo in the severity of its condemnation of Babylon's spiritual immorality and global supremacy. Some believe that the first fall of Babylon initially occurred at the falling away of the church founded by Christ and the apostles, eventually culminating in the Papacy of the Dark Ages. The second fall of Babylon is seen as pointing to the decline of the Protestant Reformation that will increasingly reflect the papal power until it no longer serves as a spokesperson for God. Others hold that the first fall has reference to the rejection of present truth as presented by the Advent movement in the early 1840s. The second fall refers to the rejection of the Advent message by nominal Christians, which ultimately results in the global apostasy that takes place during the final crisis. No matter how one interprets the fall of Babylon, both make it clear that Christendom will deteriorate morally and spiritually until it takes a totally pernicious stance in the end-times.

This leads us to the final stage, apocalyptic Babylon, a biblical symbol of the last-day confederacy of all the forces in opposition to God, the truths of His word, and His people. In Revelation 18:2-5, the warning is given that Babylon the Great "has become a dwelling for demons and a haunt for every impure spirit. . . . For all the nations have drunk the maddening wine of her adulteries [Phillips: "the wine of her passionate unfaithfulness"]. The kings of the earth committed adultery with her. . . . Then I heard another voice from heaven say: 'Come out of her, my people, so that you will not share in her sins, so that you will not receive any of her plagues; for her sins are piled up to heaven, and God has remembered her crimes.'"

The "city" of Babylon is "divided into three parts" (Rev. 16:19, NKJV). This threesome first appears in Revelation 13 as the dragon, the sea beast (verses 1-10), and the land beast (verses 11-18). While the dragon primarily represents Satan, Adventists also see him as working through spiritualism (which includes paganism, heathenism, Hinduism, and perhaps Islam); the other two beasts represent Roman Catholicism and apostate Protestant America. They reappear in Revelation 16:13 as the dragon, the beast, and the false prophet, which are discussed more fully later in this book.

Revelation 13 gives us the setting as to why the second angel proclaims his message twice: a warning that is more powerfully repeated the second time reflects an ever-deepening crisis. In this chapter (verses 1-10) the first, or sea, beast (Roman Catholicism) is described in several ways. It receives power and authority from the dragon, the whole world worships and follows it, it blasphemes God, it makes war against the saints, and it receives a deadly wound that's eventually healed. At this juncture the second, or land, beast appeared who "had two horns like a lamb, but he spoke like a dragon" (verse 11). The land beast, representing Protestant America, is first portrayed "like a lamb" with two horns—possibly symbolic of a Christian nation, but definitely a fitting symbol of a youthful nation without a crowned king or pope, where church and state are separate powers. Revelation goes on to predict that this lamblike beast will ultimately speak "like a dragon."

Though this nation may always retain its appearance as a Protestant nation, its voice—the laws that its government eventually enacts—exposes its new persona, the "image of the beast," a replica or likeness of the first beast (see verse 15). An image is not the exact thing but something so near to the original that it looks or acts the same. As the United States becomes a spokesperson for the dragon, severe and oppressive measures will be taken against those who oppose the laws that govern worship (see verses 14-17). The image of the beast is established when the United States repudiates the principles of separation of church and state and sets up a system that closely resembles the Papacy's behavior. It is this union of apostate churches with the government that enforces a prescribed form of worship. The laws that bring persecution to God's people will be acclaimed and honored, seen as God-sent solutions to society's problems. To erase all doubt, miracle-working powers will deceive the world into thinking that this spiritually bankrupt nation is actually experiencing the blessings of God. This manifestation of demonic power is so deceptive because it hides its true identity behind a Christian guise.

Although Revelation 13 is highly symbolic, its message is vivid and unmistakable. In this chapter Satan's master plan is exposed, and his final assault on God's people is made known. It is his final attempt to be the uncontested ruler of this world. The decrees of the state will endeavor to bring about worldwide unity and peace by enforcing a system of worship invented by humanity, namely, Sunday observance. "When the leading churches of the United States, uniting upon such points of doctrine as are held by them in common, shall influence the state to enforce their decrees and to sustain their institutions, then Protestant America will have formed an image of the Roman hierarchy, and the infliction of civil penalties upon dissenters will inevitably result."[6]

John T. Anderson looks at it this way: someday what Revelation 13 predicts will become a reality when so-called Christians unite to pass any religious law or amendment they think is needed. And what kind of legislation will that be? Fallen Protestantism of America will join hands with Roman Catholicism to cause the U.S. government to enact laws restricting freedom by honoring the first day of the week as a national rest day. It could very well sneak in the backdoor by posing as a "National Family Day" or a "National Worker Rest Day."[7]

Babylon greatly influences, deceives, and persecutes those who disagree or refuse to obey her corrupt and destructive decrees. The wine of Babylon, by which all the nations of the earth have been intoxicated, refers to doctrinal teachings by which the fundamental distinction between the Creator and creature, between biblical teachings and church decrees, becomes blurred in the minds of the people. The act of making all nations drink indicates the global nature of its apostasy. That Babylon makes them drink indicates the enforcement of religious laws by a church-state union that extends to all nations; thus it can be said that "the Lord has a controversy with the nations" (Jer. 25:31, NKJV). That Babylon has fallen has reference to the churches that have united with the state and thus have broken away from God's Word as their ultimate authority. As a result, the churches are as unreliable as a person reeling and falling from his or her own drunkenness. The wine of Babylon is its proposals—the global enforcement of its doctrines and decrees that it claims will bring peace to the world. Instead, these only bring the wrath of God.

Babylon: A Personal Decision

From God's perspective, there was never a time when modern Babylon was anything but fallen; it could never save; it was never redemptive. Yet, strangely enough, God finds it essential to announce to the inhabitants of the world that Babylon is fallen. In other words, from what we can see with our eyes, it doesn't appear that way to us. Like the Tower of Babel, it appears to be standing strong and tall, that it can be relied upon, that it is the solution to our problems, that it can save us no matter what our dilemma may be. But God warns the world, the church, all of us, that what may appear as strong, glorious, and ever so helpful is fallen. Though it may appear judgmental at times to present such a message, it is imperative that we judge the claims of the world's religions in light of what God says about them.

Babylon is generally thought of as representing false religions, worldly systems, or the union of church and state. It is viewed as humankind collectively depending upon political powers and human resources, holding to unbiblical worldviews, or believing in worldly philosophies. While all of this is true, the problem is that it leaves you and me too easily off the hook. In other words, we see Babylon as something out there, as primarily pointing to the sin of others. But there's something very shortsighted with that kind of reasoning. It is so easy to smugly pray as did the Pharisee, "God, I thank you that I am not like other men" (Luke 18:11). The great peril of the last days is a subtle one. False worship, not denial of worship, will be the test. It will be like the worship of Pharisees who thank God for their good works but who do not know their own depravity or the necessity of relying fully on the imputed righteousness of Jesus.

It should be clear to us that the second angel's message, to come out of Babylon, is not merely an organizational call but an individual one. It is a call to each and every one to separate from the sin that resides within their own hearts. The truth is that all of us are sinners. None of us are exempt from selfishness, pride, and self-sufficiency. This means that the message of each angel must first have personal relevance before we can effectively point to its global application. So often we're told that in order to maintain good relations, we shouldn't take everything so personally. In the case of the three angels' messages, that's exactly what needs to be done.

Keep in mind that Babylon, from the biblical point of view, primarily means confusion. In other words, if we are looking for clear-cut lines between good and evil, between biblical truth and worldly error, we will discover a lot of muddy waters, a deceptive mixture of good and evil, a large gray area where clear lines are hard to find. Let's be certain about this one thing: Babylon refers not only to personal sin that you and I struggle with but also to our choice as to how to deal with it. The good news is we are out of Babylon when we place our ultimate trust and loyalty in Christ and in His promises, rather than in ourselves.

_____

[1] It is significant that the Bible views Babylon's *fall* as a reflection of Lucifer's *fall*. Isaiah 14 begins by discussing the "king of Babylon" but then switches to Lucifer ("How you are fallen from heaven, O Lucifer, son of the morning!" [verse 12, NKJV]), implying that he is the one who inspired the Babylonian king with pride and self-seeking that led to his downfall.

[2] J. T. Anderson, *Three Angels, One Message*, p. 22.

[3] *Ibid.*, p. 129.

[4] Stephen Leston, *The Bible in World History: How History and Scripture Intersect* (Uhrichsville, Ohio: Barbour Publishing, 2011), p. 48.

[5] R. Dean Davis, "A Divine Covenant," *3ABN World*, August 2012, p. 44.

[6] E. G. White, *The Great Controversy*, p. 445.

[7] Anderson, p. 246.

★10★
The Beast: Essence of Evil

The Third Angel

A third angel followed them and said in a loud voice, 'If anyone worships the beast and its image and receives its mark on their forehead or on their hand, they, too, will drink of the wine of God's fury, which has been poured full strength into the cup of his wrath. . . .' This calls for patient endurance on the part of the people of God who keep his commands and remain faithful to Jesus" (Rev. 14:9-12).

Both chapters 13 and 14 of Revelation set the climactic stage for the third angel's message. The two opposing sides are identified in the opening line of each chapter: Chapter 13—"I saw a *beast* coming out of the sea." Chapter 14—"I looked and there . . . was the *Lamb*, standing on Mount Zion." The beast represents the spurious and those who defend "the lie"; the Lamb represents the genuine and those who defend "the truth." Chapter 13 represents idolatry and corruption and those who go along with the beast in all its ways; Chapter 14 represents the worship of God and the redeemed who follow the Lamb wherever He goes. And finally, in these rival systems of worship the beast employs *coercion*; the Lamb relies on *persuasion*.

The three angels' messages are designed to prepare humankind for the most widespread rebellion against the Creator this world has ever known. We must take note of the progression of these three messages and observe the logical relationship between them. The first invites all to believe the true gospel; the second exposes Babylon as spiritually fallen; and the third warns unbelievers of the wrath of God.

Putting it another way, the first angel *summons* all to believe the "good news" about God as Creator, Savior, and Judge; the second angel *cautions* against all apostate systems of worship; the third angel *warns* the inhabitants of the earth to reject the beast, his image, and his mark, which depict creature-centered salvation and creature-mandated religion. As we read the third angel's message, it becomes obvious that it is one of the most solemn and fearful warnings in all of Scripture. There are many, however, who cannot see these awful threats as being in line with a God who is longsuffering and forgiving. But these strongly worded warnings are necessary because they have to break through the antagonism of human pride, the intense hardness of human hearts, and the natural tendency to place one's trust in human resources. They are about eternal destinies.

Ellen G. White says this about the three angels' messages:

"The three angels of Revelation 14 are represented as flying in the midst of heaven, symbolizing the work of those who proclaim the first, second, and third angels' messages. All are linked together. The evidences of the abiding, everliving truth of these grand messages, that mean so much to the church, that have awakened such intense opposition from the religious world, are not extinct. Satan is constantly seeking to cast a shadow about these messages, so that the people of God shall not clearly discern their import, their time and place; but they live and are to exert their power upon our religious experience while time shall last."[1]

Beast—Its Meaning

First of all, it's essential to clarify the biblical use of the word "beast." For many, the symbol "beast" in Revelation connotes an openly evil and devilish power, one that readily repels and frightens us. That's what the title of the chapter implies, doesn't it? But don't forget, wasn't it a beast that Eve readily admired and took at his word in the Garden of Eden? Wasn't she deceived by the creature's impressive beauty, one that captivated her attention by speaking and dazzled her senses?[2] It was a beast that quoted Scripture and decisively trumpeted spiritual claims that led to her downfall. It was the serpent that succeeded in misleading the woman, persuading her to set aside the word of God and replace it with her own desires. Paul warns us that "just as Eve was deceived by the serpent's cunning" (2 Cor. 11:3), it should not surprise us that we too can be "led astray" by Satan's powerfully enticing and persuasive deceptions.

While there are those who believe the "beast" is something horrible, gruesome, and visibly evil, we have been shown this is not the case. When dressed up in the attire of power, spirituality, or scholarly sophistication, it is alluring and attractive not only to the worldly person but to the believer as well. If the truth be told, the beast is human nature deceptively and approvingly bedecked with a halo, rather than properly labeled as an earthly representation of hell. In the context of the great controversy, the beast is the "essence of evil," yet for the majority of people, it doesn't come across that way at all (see Rev. 13:3).

Robert Bernard Reich, an American political economist, professor, author, and political commentator who served in the administrations of presidents Gerald Ford, Jimmy Carter, and Bill Clinton, made this observation in 2004 as to what he saw as "the great conflict of the twenty-first century": "The underlying battle will be," he says, in part, "between those who believe in the primacy of the individual and those who believe that human beings owe their allegiance and identity to a higher authority; between those who give priority to life in this world and those who believe that human life is mere preparation for an existence beyond life; between those who believe in science, reason, and logic and those who believe that truth is revealed through Scripture and religious dogma." [3]

As a well-known political figure reflecting the established, secular thinking of his day, Reich confirms what the three angels' messages predicted long ago: the great controversy is between those whose focus is on the gospel and those who worship—idolize, respect, exalt, and honor—the solutions proposed by the beast. Unfortunately, humans have a natural tendency to be attracted to the creature, to be enamored, as it were, by the beauty of the beast, to be awed by human power, its accomplishments, and apparent goodness. How tragic that worldly religion so often captures people's attention with its creaturely characteristics. As the Bible makes clear, the beast of the past with all of its persuasive power and deceptive beauty (see Rev. 13:3, 4) is but a forerunner of the beast still to come, even the beast that the whole world will one day revere and worship (see verse 12).

Nebuchadnezzar's decree that all were to bow down and worship the golden image, as recorded in Daniel 3, foreshadows an ominous event of the last days: a "Babylonian" decree that once again demands all "who dwell on the earth" to worship another image, "the image of the beast" (Rev. 13:14, 15, NKJV). This image is a dramatic highlight of the controversy between the creature and the Creator (see Rom. 1:25), a fitting symbol of humankind's last-ditch effort to save the planet and its inhabitants with a worldwide religious-political bureaucracy. But our response to spiritual Babylon's appealing proposals must be the same as that of the three Hebrew youths: "We will not serve your gods or worship the image of gold you have set up" (Dan. 3:18).

Why will so many people adhere to the demands of the image of the beast in the final conflict? From a worldly, pragmatic perspective, reliance upon God's grace simply doesn't cut it. It doesn't come through as a face-saving panacea, a cure-all for the deeply profound problems that the world has to contend with. And so the call goes forth, as it did from the Babel builders of old—"Come, worship the image we have set up. . . . See its newness, its amazing feats of technological and military wizardry, and its capacity to generate prosperity. See how religion thrives, and see the wonder-working power that's produced when faith communities and government support each other." [4]

In the 1990s I served as a member of the North American Division (NAD) textbook committee, and during one of our two-week sessions, I stayed in a Best Western Inn where the cleaning ladies left a 3" x 5" placard on my desk. It read: "Save Our Planet." I appreciated the appeal to help conserve and protect the environment. But it had a glaring weakness: it pointed only to the Green movement. It gave no thought to God's grace as the underlying solution not only for everyday ills but also for the menacing crises that threaten our planet. That's the way earthly systems work: they endeavor to right the wrongs by relying on human resources, by technology, by impressive political and religious operations. This is the way it's always been done. Isn't it similar to what the Jewish people expected in Christ's day—a (kingly) Messiah who would solve their problems, overcome their enemies, and liberate them from their political foes?[5] We can be sure, whether we're dealing with the past, the present, or the future, that if the solution is not centered in Jesus and His grace, we can expect it to fail.

Ellen White warns, "But today in the religious world there are multitudes who, as they believe, are working for the establishment of the kingdom of Christ. . . . They expect Him to rule through legal enactments, enforced by human authority. . . . The establishment of such a kingdom is what the Jews desired in the days of Christ."[6]

When the image of the beast is finally set up, it gains the admiration of unbelievers, as well as many believers, because it is seen as an ingenious masterpiece, the glorious answer to the world's political, social, economic, and spiritual ills. Indeed, those who have "refused to love the truth" will accept "a powerful delusion so that they will believe the lie" (2 Thess. 2:10, 11). Jon Paulien rightly observes, "Those who reject the gospel in its clarity will gladly receive the delusion."[7] The last thing people want to hear is that they are not able to save themselves from the life-threatening problems they face. After all, can't we achieve what we believe? Through the persuasive power of the image—the union of church and state—ultimate answers will be proclaimed and "miracles will be wrought" and "undeniable wonders will be performed." [8]

Today's society is traveling down the information superhighway at breakneck speed on a roadway glutted with technological breakthroughs and highly sophisticated networks that virtually interconnect every government, corporation, institution, and household in the world. While humanity's amazing accomplishments and united efforts are extolled and honored, in the process the Creator's solutions are not in view. The reasoning goes something like this: Seeing ourselves as intelligent, powerful, and advanced, pride takes over and asks, "Who needs God anyway for anything?" Modern humanity, in its pseudospirituality, is convinced that it is self-sufficient and can take care of itself.

While the ministry of grace chooses not to embrace the power of the state to restore sought-after morality in society, apostate religions are bent on relying on Caesar rather than Christ in their attempt to make people good, pure, and prudent. In striving for peace and national security, the spirit of the beast allures people to spurn God's grace for the grandeur of human laws and the competence of their regulations. Philip Yancey rightly observes, "It is difficult, if not impossible, to communicate the message of grace from the corridors of power." [9]

By its very nature, the government will run by the rules of the ungraceful. It is usually held together by a shared self-interest that works in antithesis to the spirit of Christianity. Government, even under the auspices of the union of church and state, can legislate morality, but it cannot redeem and transform the heart. It can enforce laws, but it cannot provide forgiveness. It can impose outward compliance but not inward compassion. It can compel right behavior, but it cannot coerce true worship. Alan J. Reinach puts it this way: "Legislated worship ought to be listed among the greatest of oxymorons, for if there is one thing the law cannot command, it is genuine worship of the Almighty." [10]

The Beast: The Personal Side

Historically speaking, the book of Revelation portrays the sea beast—a symbol of the religious system that claims for itself ultimate power "as great as the Prince of the host [Jesus]," namely, the Papacy (Dan. 8:11, ESV). This means that Roman Catholicism affirms that it has the authority like

Jesus Himself to dispense grace, change God's law, mediate for sinners, absolve sin, claim infallibility, be the sole interpreter of Scripture, as well as call for our loyalty and worship. No wonder the beast is described as one who "opened its mouth to blaspheme God" (Rev. 13:6). According to the Scriptures, one explanation of blasphemy is that someone puts himself or herself in the place of God (see John 10:33).

Is extolling such pompous claims limited or applicable to just that particular religion? In a broader sense it describes what can occur in any religion. Even more than that, it has reference to the personal struggle within every sinner's heart. Jesus declared that it's quite natural for us to point out the sins of others that we are guilty of ourselves (see Matt. 7:1-5). Martin Luther expressed it so well when he said, "I am more afraid of my own poor heart than the Pope and all his cardinals." Ellen White might have been alluding to this when she said that if we study more closely the books of Daniel and Revelation, "we may have *less to say* in some lines, in regard to the Roman power and the papacy." Perhaps, then, we may have *more to say* regarding the Papacy as the Bible's foremost example to what governs the *spirit of each and every sinner.* Ellen White goes on to say: "When we as a people understand what this book *means to us,* there will be seen among us a great revival." [11]

There are many who think that the prophecies of Revelation point primarily to the final crisis, but they apply equally to the present. In the ongoing controversy between the creature and the Creator, religion often captures people's attention with its creaturely characteristics—human solutions, outward flare, and captivating opportunities that seem so liberating and dynamic. Even as Christians, we are sometimes tempted to keep tabs on our own spiritual résumé—to gauge our spirituality by holiness within, by victories gained, by stalwart obedience, and by Spirit-impelled love for God and others. In other words, we are inclined to focus on the spiritual attainments of the *creature,* but all these are far short of the perfect righteousness of Jesus that salvation requires.

To marvel after the beast—namely, us, with all of our feats and accomplishments—is not merely a last-day event; it's an everyday reality. It's imperative, therefore, that we be careful not to focus solely on the idiosyncrasies of the beast that permeates the world. After all, sin first springs up in the heart (see Mark 7:21-23); thus, our first responsibility is to keep a close eye on what's happening in our own soul. It's been observed that it's much easier to criticize when the tyrant on the horizon is a worldly beast rather than the sin of our own heart. Keep in mind that when we rely on human solutions, strive for worldly recognition, or exult in outward display, we too have the spirit of the beast within us. Too often we're so concerned about spiritual corruption and errors around us, that we overlook our own tendency to ignore scriptural principles, make our own rules, or promote our selfish ambitions. Overcoming the beast within prepares us to gain victory over the beast without. To put it another way, a proud and self-righteous spirit is a human frailty, not just a papal fault.

The Bible is filled with examples of people who in the midst of crisis turned to someone other than God for strength, counsel, and direction. Our ways and ideas look so good because our vision is limited, our hearts filled with pride, and our nature desirous for power and praise. We tend to live for our own glory, to depend unwittingly upon our own strength and wisdom, and to rely upon our own good works for salvation. When such a self-serving spirit rules within, the natural inclination is to succumb to the pressures without and go along with the beast and his image. The three angels' messages are God's final appeal, pointing us to His abundant love, revealing the sufficiency of His grace, and renewing His promise to be with us until the very end. What more could we want?

---

[1] E. G. White, *Testimonies,* vol. 6, pp. 17, 18.

[2] "The serpent was then one of the wisest and most beautiful creatures on the earth. It had wings, and while flying through the air presented an appearance of dazzling brightness, having the color and brilliancy of burnished gold" (E. G. White, *Patriarchs and Prophets,* p. 53).

[3] Robert Reich, "The Last Word," *The American Prospect,* June 17, 2004, http://prospect.org/article/last-word-4.

[4] Douglas Morgan, "Marching to the Call of History," in *Politics and Prophecy: The Battle for Religious Liberty and the Authentic Gospel,* ed. Christa Reinach and Alan J. Reinach (Nampa, Idaho: Pacific Press Pub. Assn., 2007), p. 61.

[5] E. G. White, *Thoughts From the Mount of Blessing,* p. 79.

[6] E. G. White, *The Desire of Ages,* p. 509.

[7] Jon Paulien, *What the Bible Says About the End-Time* (Hagerstown, Md.: Review and Herald Pub. Assn., 1994), p. 99.

[8] E. G. White, *The Great Controversy,* pp. 588, 589.

[9] Philip Yancey, *What's So Amazing About Grace?* (Grand Rapids: Zondervan, 1997), p. 230.

[10] Alan J. Reinach, "The Battle for the Ten Commandments," in *Politics and Prophecy,* p. 189.

[11] E. G. White, *Testimonies to Ministers,* p. 113. (Italics supplied.)

★ 11 ★

It's All About Anger

The Wrath of God

The previous chapter ended with the question What more could we want? What some of us want, perhaps, is an answer to our questions and uneasy feelings about the wrath of God that is so vividly portrayed in the third angel's message. For some, the answer is relatively simple: this message is so solemn because it is final. Anyone who rejects it and worships the beast and his image receives the *mark* of the beast, which is the prelude to eternal doom. When each person has made the choice to receive the seal of God or the mark of the beast, probation closes and the destiny of all is fixed for eternity. The third angel concludes with the declaration that those who have the mark will "drink of the wine of the wrath of God, which is poured out full strength" (Rev. 14:10, NKJV).

For the first time in history God's judgments are poured in full strength, that is, unmixed with mercy.[1] All other warnings of divine judgment in the Bible are tempered (mellowed) by the mercy and longsuffering of God. In the ancient world those who diluted their wine with water readily understood this, but there will be no diluting in the final outpouring of punishment.

The close of probation signals the time when the people of the world will have crossed that hidden line between God's mercy and His wrath. As God withdraws His Spirit from the earth and ceases to hold in check the fierce winds of human passion and demonic rage (see Rev. 7:1-3), Satan will be allowed to have complete access to the earth (except for God's remnant), to rule this world. It should be noted that when the earth is finally free from the restraints of God's law, something Satan has always wanted, it is referred to as "a time of trouble, such as never was" (Dan. 12:1, NKJV). It is during this time that Satan so desperately wants to demonstrate that his ways are superior to God's, that his rebellion was right after all, but instead, truth wins out in an overwhelmingly convincing fashion (see Rev. 19:2).

When I taught my freshman religion classes, one of the biblical events that greatly puzzled my students was the account of Jesus cleansing the Temple in Jerusalem.[2] When Jesus found the Temple complex cluttered with "people selling cattle, sheep and doves, and others sitting at tables exchanging money," "he made a whip out of cords, and drove all from the temple courts . . . and overturned their tables" (John 2:13-15). This apparent display of anger seemed so out of character with the life of Jesus as my students generally understood it. Strangely enough, they seemed more bothered by the actions of Jesus than by the conduct of those who were driven out. They just couldn't see Jesus saying, "It's OK to get angry!" Their questions generally implied that anger is basically wrong, so how could the *sinless one* act that way?[3] What really helps us to understand the anger of Jesus is to keep in mind that His anger is against sin, not against the people themselves.

While God's anger or wrath[4] may be a difficult concept for many people, the Bible is very open about the fact that God does become angry. Can it not be said that anyone who sees the heartbreak that permeates our sinful world and does not get angry is morally bankrupt? From Genesis to Revelation, God's anger is a common fact of biblical revelation.[5] While reading the book of Ezekiel for my morning devotions I repeatedly find God making known His intense anger regarding the idol worshipping of the Israelites. Unbelievers, as well as many Christians, have an attitude very similar to that of my students: there are usually more complaints about God's anger than about the sin over which He is angry. That may be a clue as to why so many misunderstand the manifestation of God's wrath in the ultimate resolution of sin.

God's Love and Wrath

It is only logical for people to ask, "How can a God of love also be a God of wrath?" First of all, we must understand that the wrath of God and the love of God are biblically compatible. The wrath of God is just as real as the love of God; they are not in opposition to each other. Without apology, God is both a gentle lamb and a conquering lion (see Rev. 13:8; 5:5).

In the Bible, God has two characteristics that are equally affirmed. He is portrayed as being "slow to anger, abounding in love and faithfulness" yet "does not leave the guilty unpunished" (Ex. 34:6, 7; see also Num. 14:18; James 4:12; Heb. 11:30). It should be noted that John, the New Testament writer who writes more about God's love than does any other biblical author, also provides the most graphic portrayal of God's wrath—the book of Revelation. The proclamation of the wrath of God as His punishing righteousness is not in conflict with His righteous love. It is His holy resolve to destroy sin and all who cling to it. Recognition of God's fierce and decisive opposition against sin creates a new appreciation of His mercy that He extends to those deserving of His wrath. What we find is that God's love and His wrath play equally important roles in both the Old and New Testaments. How can a God who loves people not be angry at the sin that destroys them? It is precisely because of His love that His wrath exists.

Let's be clear: God's wrath does not mean He has unrestrained passion, an angry impulse, or vengefulness. God's holy wrath is free from human imperfections. So what does this mean? God's righteous indignation is entirely legitimate; it is an essential characteristic of the Almighty. Wrath is an upright and honorable expression of God's unrelenting opposition to that which destroys His creation. Even loving persons are at times filled with wrath when confronted by cruelty and injustice, not despite of, but because of, their love. If you love a person and you see someone mistreating them, or maybe they're hurting themselves, your concern for their well-being may arouse justifiable anger over what's happening.

The same applies to God. To love the good is to hate the evil that is at odds with it. God's hatred of injustice and evil is just as strong as His love of good. It's like saying that God's wrath flows from His love. From this perspective, anger is not the opposite of love; they are two sides of the same coin. God is the only person who can exhibit these apparently contradictory traits in a balance that constitutes holy love.

The antithesis of love is not wrath but apathy. God is never apathetic (see John 2:14-17). He is neither cruel to sinners nor indifferent to sin. God's wrath is not a temperamental explosion but a settled opposition to that which is wrong and evil, to that which hurts His creatures. God's wrath is a righteous reaction to all unrighteousness. He is angry with sin and rebellion because it is contrary to His very nature. The psalmist declares, "The Lord watches over all who love him, but all the wicked he will destroy" (Ps. 145:20). God defends His actions by saying, "For I take no pleasure in the death of anyone. . . . [Therefore,] repent and live" (Eze. 18:32).

When we consider serious questions about God's dealings with humankind, it is crucial to take all aspects into consideration, as Jennifer Jill Schwirzer so aptly states: "How do we obtain and keep the balance of God's love and wrath? Simply by viewing His wrath in the light that streams from the cross. When we read of the pouring out of God's wrath in the final judgment, we remember that He first poured out His love on Calvary. His wrath goes nowhere that His love hasn't gone first, and it destroys no one whom He didn't first die to save."[6]

Anger's Many Sides

Paul employs this same line of reasoning in the first chapter of Romans. He starts out writing that "in the gospel a righteousness of God is revealed" (verse 17) and then quickly follows with the statement that "the wrath of God is being revealed from heaven against all the godlessness and wickedness of people" (verse 18). With this stark contrast the apostle emphasizes the sinner's need of the gospel and, in the process, establishes its value and purpose: by faith in God's righteousness, sinners are saved from the destructive ravages of their own wickedness.

The Bible reveals God manifesting His anger in several different ways. First, His righteous indignation can be very direct; He overtly punishes or destroys the wicked in such events as the earth's inundation by the Flood, the fiery destruction of Sodom and Gomorrah, or the abrupt death of Ananias and Sapphira. Second, God can employ secondary agents. He may use His own people to destroy those who are incurably defiant and rebellious (see Deut. 31:5, 6), while at other times He allows foreign armies to conquer and destroy His people for the same reason (see Dan. 1:1, 2).

The way God quite frequently exercises His anger is described in Romans 1. Let's complete the passage that was started above: "The wrath of God is being revealed from heaven against all the godlessness and wickedness of people, who suppress the truth by their wickedness, since what may be known about God is plain to them. . . . For although they knew God, they neither glorified him as God nor gave thanks to him. . . . Therefore God gave them over in the sinful desires of their hearts" (verses 18-24). In this statement Paul portrays God's wrath as being the consequences of human beings turning away from the truth that has been available to them. He goes on to say that those who suppress the truth are thus released from God's protective care and given over to the control of their own desires (Deut. 31:16-18; Ps. 81:12; Acts 7:42). In His wisdom, God has chosen to allow the wicked to experience the results of their own sin and rebellion. This does not imply that God is just a spectator observing the destruction that's taking place (see Eze. 18:32).

The worst thing that can happen to the wicked in this life is for God to step aside and allow them to suffer the full impact of their own sinfulness.

This is the way it will be in the last days when, unsheltered by divine grace, the wicked who have chosen to be left to their own devices will no longer be sheltered by divine mediation. This final choice brings with it the final, irrevocable consequences. No doubt, it also brings tears to the eyes of a compassionate God who is touched by it all (see Heb. 4:15).

While the context of the first chapter of Romans is primarily the temporal *consequences* of sin, the effect of human rebellion in this life does not negate the reality of the ultimate *punishment* of sin. Sinners who reject God's redemptive solution in the ultimate sense are consumed in the lake of fire, depicted in the Bible as the second death. The severity of the penalty is because sin is, in reality, a crime against the supreme government, the highest authority in the universe; thus, only eternal death satisfies the just and legal verdict of the final judgment.

Anger: Our Problem

The God of the Old Testament is not a God with a short fuse; on the contrary, He is incredibly patient. The first example that comes to mind is God giving the vile and depraved antediluvians 120 years to accept Noah's gracious offer to find safety in the ark. In like fashion, God did not deal abruptly with the evil and immoral Amorites in Canaan but allowed them more than 400 years of mercy and forbearance (Gen. 15:13-16). When we consider the extreme violence of the antediluvians (Gen. 6:5, 11) and the utter depravity and cruelty of the Amorites, the real question boils down to this: How could God be so patient and longsuffering with these people? In fact, many of the Old Testament prophets express more concern about the prosperity or longevity of the wicked than their punishment or demise (Ps. 73:1-9; Hab. 1:13).

The truth is that most of us want a God who doesn't sit on His hands. We want a God without ambiguity, one who responds quickly and decisively to the evils of the world. However, this is not what we've witnessed thus far in the Old Testament. It substantiates the validity of God's revelation of Himself to Moses: "the Lord, the compassionate and gracious God, slow to anger, abounding in love and faithfulness, maintaining love to thousands, and forgiving wickedness, rebellion and sin" (Ex. 34:6, 7). What else would one expect from the God of grace?

Having faith in this kind of God also means that we accept His anger in dealing with malicious injustice and brutality as a rightful step toward bringing human violence to an equitable and just end. In other words, the only reason for prohibiting all recourse to human violence is to maintain that such undertaking is legitimate only when it comes from God. This implies that God's display of wrath throughout the Bible is a flawless expression of justice, mercy, and fair-mindedness.[7]

To disbelieve in the rightness of God's vengeance encourages people to carry out such activity on their own. The human impulse to make the guilty pay for their crimes is almost an overwhelming one, as evidenced by daily events around us. Those who take vengeance into their own hands are inevitably pulled into an endless cycle of trying to even the score, turning anger into resentment and bitterness.

How can our desire for justice be honored in a way that does not nurture our desire for personal vengeance? We must believe in the biblical concept of God's justice, that He is a better justice-maker than we are. Only He knows how to avenge justly. If we don't believe that there is a God who will eventually make all things right, we will take up the sword and be drawn into an endless whirlwind of retaliation. Only when we are sure that there's a God who will make all wrongs right and settle all accounts, do we then have the power to refrain from doing it ourselves.

On July 8, 1741, in Enfield, Connecticut, a prominent Puritan minister by the name of Jonathan Edwards preached what many considered the most famous sermon ever delivered in our country. This well-known sermon, which is 13 typed pages in length, is titled "Sinners in the Hands of an Angry God." In fiery rhetoric intended to terrify his listeners, he speaks about God dangling the sinner "over the pit of hell, much as one holds a spider or some loathsome insect over the open flames."[8] The truth is quite the opposite. What we see when God comes to earth in the person of His Son Jesus, is "God in the hands of angry sinners." Such a frame of mind can be readily traced throughout the Old Testament.

In 1989 Alden Thompson, a religion professor at Walla Walla University in Washington State, published a book titled *Who's Afraid of the Old Testament God?* I suppose the answer is most everyone, including many Christians. I have often thought that Thompson's book could have been more appropriately titled *Who's Afraid of the Old Testament People?* Wouldn't it be more reasonable to be frightened of people whose "every inclination of the thoughts of the human heart was only evil all the time" (Gen. 6:5) rather than a God who declares, "For I know the thoughts that I think toward you . . . thoughts of peace and not of evil" (Jer. 29:11, NKJV)? Why are we so prone to forget that the God we serve is slow to anger, full of mercy, and quick to forgive?

Unfortunately, there are those who see a problem with this. They think that when forgiveness is extended to someone, they in turn must forgo justice. For that reason many reject grace, failing to see that it represents the best solution—the combining of justice with mercy. While forgiveness is one of the main attributes of God's grace, it operates without jeopardizing the claims of justice. You may ask, "How is that possible?" Recognizing this as a common question, Paul stresses that God Himself has already paid the ransom—the just demands of the law—so that mercy can be lawfully extended for confessed sin.

Let's read Paul's explanation: "All have sinned and fall short of the glory of God, and all are justified [forgiven] freely by his grace through the redemption that came by Christ Jesus. God presented Christ as a sacrifice of atonement, through the shedding of his blood. He did it to demonstrate his righteousness . . . , so as to be just and the one who justifies those who have faith in Jesus" (Rom. 3:23-26). In 1 Timothy 2:6 Paul affirms that Jesus "gave himself as a ransom for all people." It's been said that the cross was raised to remind us that indeed forgiveness has a price!

In the great controversy the government of God, while extending mercy to sinners, must also act in a just and lawful (legal) manner. God's grace must be true to His justice. Thus, in a unique and undeniable way, both Christ's sinless life and His sacrificial death at Calvary are expressions of justice and mercy being carried out. These make it possible for God to extend mercy to those who believe, without compromising His justice (see Rom. 3:26). Contrary to popular sentiment, God's grace is just as much about justice as it is about mercy.

Justice Includes Supreme Penalty

God has to deal justly with those who choose Him and with those who reject Him. One needs to keep in mind that Jesus paid the penalty of all sin when He died on the cross. He bore the punishment that we deserve. He took upon Himself every curse mentioned in Eden's indictment (see Gen. 3:17-19). He sweated drops of blood that He might become our spiritual life. He experienced the pain that can give birth to our salvation. He wore the crown of thorns, taking our place as the King of sinners.

Jesus' anguished cry on the cross, "My God, my God, why have you forsaken me" (Matt. 27:46), a cry expressing (eternal) separation from God, clearly indicates that it was the "second death," the agonies of hell, that Jesus experienced for us. From this we can deduce the following: The death of Jesus provides us with a window into the nature of the punishment awaiting the lost. What does it say about the final judgment against sinners? What we see is suffering that ends in death, not one of everlasting torment. In other words, His death took place within the time limitations of that Friday. Since Jesus suffered the penalty for the sins of the whole world and accomplished it all in one day, it doesn't make any sense that those who refuse that gift and choose to pay for their own sins be required to suffer for eternity.[9] Such a mistaken notion makes God out to be a cruel tyrant who has fires hot enough to torture—but not hot enough to destroy—its victims.

People who believe in eternal hell (as well as those who don't) often overlook an important fact: Jesus does not deny hell but affirms it by His teachings and by His own death. Actually, what He says about it must be understood in light of His own death. A close examination of the Bible reveals that the descriptions Jesus gave of hell are like those He personally experienced on the cross Himself.[10] In other words, Jesus willingly tasted "death for everyone" (Heb. 2:9). He paid the ultimate price of sin, the second death (it is the "lake of fire" in Rev. 20:14). God, in the person of Jesus, endured the agonies of hell for everyone, but only those who accept Him as their Savior benefit from His atoning sacrifice. As we've already stated, those who reject Christ's death are, in effect, choosing to suffer the ultimate punishment of their sin themselves.

God's end-time people proclaim to the inhabitants of the world that unless they accept the good news of Calvary, they will drink the cup of God's wrath on their own (see Matt. 26:42), a cup Jesus already drank in their behalf (Ps. 116:13). To reject the mercy of God is to receive His wrath. Either one gives sin over to the Lord in penitence and confession, or one pays the penalty of sin with their own death. Jesus said, "For if you do not believe that I am He, you will die in your sins" (John 8:24, NKJV). It must not slip past our attention that God's final act of justice (the fires of hell) is one of divine mercy; unrepentant sinners would be utterly miserable in heaven—indeed, it would be like hell to them; thus, annihilation is the most merciful alternative that God can provide for those who are lost.[11]

---

[1] In Romans 2:5 the apostle speaks of God's condemnation of human pride: "But because of your stubbornness and your unrepentant heart, you are storing up wrath against yourself for the day of God's wrath, when his righteous judgment will be revealed."

[2] Jesus cleansed the Temple twice: at the beginning and at the close of His ministry.

Regarding these cleansings, there is evidence that the condition of the Temple at the close was worse than at the beginning.

[3] While there are many examples in the Bible of human anger that are sinful and out of place, the Bible also makes it clear that anger is not evil per se (see Matt. 5:22, NKJV; Eph. 4:26).

[4] There may be some slight differences in the usage or meaning of these two words (anger and wrath) in the Bible, but they will be used interchangeably in this chapter.

[5] See Num. 11:33; Deut. 29:27; 2 Kings 13:3; Ps. 90:7; Jer. 7:20; Rom. 1:18; Heb. 3:11; Rev. 6:17; 11:18.

[6] Jennifer Jill Schwirzer, "Compassionate Wrath," *Adventist Review*, May 30, 2002, p. 45.

[7] One could say that this culminates at the cross, where God, in the person of Jesus, chooses to suffer His own wrath against human sin in our behalf.

[8] Jonathan Edwards, "Sinners in the Hands of an Angry God," July 8, 1741, Christian Classics Ethereal Library: Bringing Christian Classic Books to Life, http://www.ccel.org/ccel/edwards/sermons.sinners.html.

[9] J. T. Anderson, *Three Angels, One Message*, p. 291.

[10] Compare Matt. 8:11, 12, 13:41, 42, 24:50, 51 with Matt. 27:33-36, 45, 46.

[11] "Heaven would be to him [the lost sinner] a place of torture; he would long to be hidden from Him who is its light, and the center of its joy. It is no arbitrary decree on the part of God that excludes the wicked from heaven: they are shut out by their own unfitness for its companionship. The glory of God would be to them a consuming fire. They would welcome destruction, that they might be hidden from the face of Him who died to redeem them" (E. G. White, *Steps to Christ*, p. 18).

★12★
Safe, Sound, and Secure

Aren't we all looking for that which is "safe, sound, and secure," which probably includes most everything? When it comes to our spiritual beliefs and commitments, very few are going to look for them in the three angels' messages. In fact, it may be the last place we go. While we may openly acknowledge that they play a key role in Adventism's doctrinal framework, their prophetic nature makes them appear impersonal, nebulous, and not very appealing or reassuring. Besides, through the years the three angels' messages may have brought us a great deal of fear and uncertainty, something we haven't forgotten. However, it's essential that we change all of that.

First of all, we must realize that any belief or practice that is not immersed in the love and justifying grace of God is bad news. Unfortunately, this happens quite often. Second, the three angels' messages play a vital role in revealing the great controversy theme, and even while pointing to beliefs over which there is dissension and uncertainty, they nevertheless reassure us of their trustworthiness and validity. In so doing, they provide the kind of security we need in times of conflict and turmoil, especially when we're buffeted "by every wind of new teaching" and by people who "try to trick us with lies so clever they sound like the truth" (Eph. 4:14, NLT).

The Sabbath Significance
The first angel concludes with these poignant words: "Worship him who made the heavens, the earth, the sea and the springs of water" (Rev. 14:7). When deploying the language of the fourth commandment, this message affirms that the one we worship is the God of Genesis who created the heavens and the earth by His word in six literal days of evenings and mornings. In doing so, it supports the rationale given in the Old Testament for the significance of the seventh-day Sabbath (see Ex. 20:11). The one who made the heavens and the earth is also the person who rested on the seventh day and "blessed the Sabbath day and made it holy" (verse 11).

This is a decisive indictment of all those pompous claims of equality with God. The "ancient serpent" (and those who side with him) can't ever match God's feat of creation and thus are ineligible to pronounce another day holy (see Dan. 7:25). The first angel's message is a reminder that the Creation and the Sabbath day are forever linked together: Sabbathkeeping is an act of Creationkeeping.

I must confess that it doesn't take me much effort to trace my roots back to my Sabbathkeeping family; but in so doing, I have to admit that when I was a youngster at home, the Sabbath was not always my favorite day of the week. My parents seemed to have a lot of rules about keeping the Sabbath holy, although it came nowhere close to the estimated 1,521 do's and don'ts that the Pharisees had in Christ's day. Even at the present time Orthodox and most conservative Jews still have a great number of Sabbath rules. One notable example is prohibiting the use of mechanical devices to turn on any kind of electrical equipment. If they want to have heat, light, or watch television, it must be turned on before sunset on Friday or activated to come on automatically. Phones cannot be answered, nor food preparations made, and no household chores of any kind are allowed during the Sabbath hours. In Israel today some hotels install "Shabbat elevators," which on the Sabbath stop at every floor so that the occupants can avoid work by not having to push any buttons.[1]

Despite such negative baggage that Jewish Sabbathkeepers continue to hang on to, the seventh-day Sabbath, as rightly presented in the Bible, is "blessed" and "holy" (Gen. 2:3), "a delight" and "honorable" (Isa. 58:13), and the Lord's day (Mark 2:28). What impressive reasons for making the day that commemorates Creation an integral part of the three angels' messages! A key element in heaven's final message to the world is that celebratory worship on the Sabbath will be restored to its rightful place at the end of time.

Seventh-day Adventists generally look upon the Sabbath as a sign of sanctification, of being made holy (see Eze. 20:12, 20). But the Sabbath is also a sign that we have entered into God's rest and have ceased to rely upon our own works for salvation (Heb. 4:1-10). Jesus wanted the people of His day to see that Sabbath rest was very much a symbol, a foretaste, of salvation rest (see Matt. 11:28). While it is possible to make the Sabbath a symbol of legalism (salvation by works), true Sabbathkeeping should be the ideal response of Adventists to the gospel, because it is founded on the principle of rest after a finished work. Just as the writer of Genesis states, it was "on the seventh day God *finished* the work he had been doing; so on the seventh day he *rested* from all his work" (Gen. 2:2, CEV). The fact that the fourth commandment is given in two different settings in the Old Testament attests that the Sabbath not only commemorates God's rest at *Creation* (see Ex. 20:11) but also affirms God's rest (finished work) in *redemption* (see Deut. 5:15). Understanding the Sabbath in this way might be a fulfillment of Ellen White's prediction that the Sabbath will one day be preached "more fully." [2]

When believers experience saving grace within the context of the gospel, the Sabbath becomes a helpful reminder to rest from the endless struggle to measure up. [3] Since there is a tendency to contribute to one's salvation, we need a regular reminder that the first work of the Christian is to rest in what Christ has done (see John 6:28, 29). From the very beginning, the seventh day, which was Adam and Eve's first full day, the priority of rest—God's finished work—was highlighted for them in the most tangible way.

It is a given that Christians who trust in Jesus for salvation ought to cease from any endeavor to earn favor with God by their own righteousness. Unfortunately, because Sabbath worship comes under so much attack in today's world, Seventh-day Adventists may sometimes respond by defending or keeping the Sabbath for the wrong reasons. Instead of seeing the Sabbath as a sign of God's love and faithfulness to humankind, they turn it around and make human faithfulness to God the dominant theme.

This is where the first angel's message clarifies several significant issues. First of all, the Sabbath shines most brightly when seen in the light that streams from the gospel, safeguarding it from legalistic tendencies. Second, true Sabbath rest is to be carried out in response to divine creation made known in Eden and at Sinai. This affirms that salvation rest does not release us from Sabbath rest, as explicitly set forth in the fourth commandment. Finally, by making the Sabbath commandment the center of attention at the end of time—proclaimed "to every nation, tribe, tongue, and people"—it will be an ideal way to test whether people are truly loyal to the God of Scripture.

The foundational evidence that the seventh-day Sabbath plays a lead role in the three angels' messages is laid out for us in Revelation 13 and 14. In these two chapters, which serve as the backdrop for these messages, the word "worship" is cited at least eight times. In this global confrontation, while the beast and the image demand worship for themselves, the first angel summons humankind to "worship him who made heaven and earth." It follows that the third angel's solemn warning, "If any man worships the beast and his image, and receives his mark . . . he himself shall also drink of the wine of the wrath of God" (Rev. 14:9, 10, NKJV), reinforces the idea that the day of worship is at the very heart of the great controversy at the end of time.

It's apparent that the three angels ignite a worldwide clash over worship, between a decree by the image of the beast to observe a state-mandated day and a strong proclamation by the three angels in defense of the biblical Sabbath. The way people are to worship God in the final crisis is revealed by pointing them to the seventh-day Sabbath as the biblical memorial of God's creative work. It's not up to us to choose one day in seven as a day of worship; God has chosen the seventh-day Sabbath. In the final crisis, *when* we worship will be the sign as to *whom* we worship (see Eze. 20:12). In Revelation 14:12, the Bible contrasts "the saints . . . who obey God's commandments" with those who worship the beast and his image and receive his mark. It states that those who are obedient to the decrees of the beast and its image (and, by inference, worship on the first day of the week) oppose the commandment-keeping people—those who worship on the Sabbath.

Revelation signifies that the conflict between good and evil comes down to a confrontation of signs, which depict the two sides of the warfare. The subversive side is determined to put its "mark," which represents "the name of the beast or the number of its name" (Rev. 13:17), on its followers. This mark identifies the bearer in a decisive way. The other side in the conflict also has a sign. The end is put on hold, says an angel, "until we have marked the servants of our God with a seal on their foreheads (Rev. 7:2, 3, NRSV). In contrast to those who receive the beast's mark, those who receive God's seal have the name of the Lamb "and His Father's name written on their foreheads" (Rev. 14:1). The seal has been aptly described as "the pure mark of truth."[4] When all is said and done, the inhabitants of the earth will have either "the mark" of the beast or "the seal" of God, but they cannot have both.[5]

Care must be taken to identify the mark in its context, to see it as a knowledgeable choice regarding the worship of the beast and its image—a clearly defiant attitude of idolatry. In this setting, receiving the mark indicates the intentional antithesis to the worship God's people render to God. Thus, it's important that we are on guard to recognize when Sunday worship actually becomes the mark of the beast as depicted in God's Word. Ellen White indicates that the mark comes about "when Sunday observance shall be enforced by law, and the world shall be enlightened concerning the obligation of the true Sabbath."[6] When the Sabbath becomes "the great test of loyalty,"[7] that is, when Sunday worship become a national law, then anyone who knowingly violates the seventh-day Sabbath will receive the mark of the beast and, consequently, be eternally lost.

A Message in Verity

As we ponder the inner thrust of the three angels' messages, we are bound to raise an important question: How do they provide assurance and security to the obedient believer? Perhaps the best answer to that question was given approximately 125 years ago by Ellen White: "Several have written to me, inquiring if the message of justification by faith is the third angel's message, and I answered, 'It is the third angel's message in verity.'"[8] This means that justification by faith, which is the basis for the believer's assurance, is not simply a preamble or an introduction to the third angel's message; it is its very heart and soul. Merriam-Webster defines *verity* as something "fundamental and inevitably true."

According to the *Seventh-day Adventist Encyclopedia*, "the third angel's message" was "taught as not only climaxing but also *including the threefold message*."[9] This means that *justification by faith* is not confined to the first angel's message, where the "everlasting gospel" is proclaimed. Nor is it simply a fundamental truth that has been obscured by the apostate religions described as "fallen" in the second angel's message. By the time we get to the third angel's message, it's tempting to think that we have moved beyond justification by faith and into much more burning issues, such as the beast, the mark, the image, and the importance of obedience to God's laws. This is not the case. Justification by faith plays a significant role in all three angels' messages.

Since this is the case, it's essential to understand what justification by faith actually means and signifies. The Bible states that we are saved (justified) by grace alone (Rom. 3:24, 28), but this teaching is anathema to Roman Catholicism and even troubling to some Seventh-day Adventists. Their concern: "What about obedience?" In other words, why strive to be what God wants us to be when He accepts us just as we are?

How one answers this question stems back to one's understanding of the gospel. As stated earlier, Roman Catholicism views the gospel as embracing both justification and sanctification in a decided but erroneous way. From their perspective God justifies (declares righteous) only those whom He has made righteous and obedient (sanctified)—enabling the believer to merit the blessings of justification. This means that personal obedience (inner holiness) plays a meritorious role in salvation, without which no one is worthy or deserving of God's acceptance. While such a belief may ease the fear regarding the necessity of obedience, it does so at the expense of the assurance of salvation. More important, it's unbiblical!

So what does the Bible teach? According to Romans 3:23-28, Jesus came to this world and, through His death, took the penalty and punishment of all sin upon Himself. In God's desire to be just, He declares that repentant sinners are righteous, not on the basis of their own record, but on the basis of their faith in the perfect record of their substitute. Justification by faith provides that at every stage of our lives the entire past is covered by Jesus' perfect life and God looks at us as if we have never sinned. This great exchange is God's grace and mercy at its highest.

These verses in Romans 3 tell us that the gospel has reference to justification by faith alone, a declarative act in which God imputes (credits) the righteousness of Christ to unworthy but believing sinners. This means that when sinners are justified, they are declared righteous simply on the basis of their faith in the righteousness of Jesus—His perfect life and death alone have merit.[10] As previously stated, redemption is, first of all, receiving a right standing (status) with God, while right living (obedience) is, without fail, the outgrowth or evidence of such faith in Jesus. But Roman Catholicism denounces this as heresy.[11]

There are some Adventists who side with Roman Catholics in backing away from the idea that in justification both Christ's death and His obedient life are imputed to us.[12] They are fearful that this implies that we do not have to obey the law, since it has already been kept for us. For them, only Christ's death is imputed in justification, while only Christ's life is imparted in sanctification. However, we must not make obedience a prerequisite for salvation in order to maintain the importance of commandment keeping.

Rightly understood, justification does not depreciate sanctification (obedience); rather, it provides the appropriate motive—namely, love—for obedience.[13] You see, the primary value of obedience (good works) is that it's an expression of gratitude as an act of service or a personal testimony. It has also been perceptively suggested, "Sanctification helps us to appreciate the privileges of our justification."[14] Admittedly, God is pleased, even glorified, with the good that is done by believers—works of faith (see Titus 3:8; Matt. 5:16), but they do not have justifying merit, even when done in faith. The most dedicated followers of Jesus, or true believers, need to be reminded that not only their sins but also even their best deeds and attributes need to be atoned for. As Whidden, referencing Ellen White, says, this means that their worship, adoration, contrition, and "Holy Spirit-induced fruits of genuine obedience . . . are all in need of the cleansing effects of the justifying 'drops of the blood of Christ.'"[15] We are justified by faith in Christ's righteousness alone, for only Christ's righteous life truly satisfies the law's highest demands.

While we must be cognizant of the emphasis Scripture correctly places on the importance of obeying God's law, we must eliminate obedience to God's law as a contributor to salvation. While the Holy Spirit graciously provides the strength we need to obey all of God's commandments, we never gain merit or acceptance with God or are justified by our sanctification. Genuine obedience is basically the appropriate response of those who have already received salvation as a free gift. True commandment keeping occurs only when our actions flow out of a heartfelt love for God and others. Otherwise, it is merely outward imitation.[16]

Running like a scarlet thread through both the Old and New Testaments is the glorious truth of salvation by substitution.[17] Beginning with the first recorded death—the slain animal in the Garden of Eden, then the ram caught in the thicket, the blood on the doorposts, the brazen serpent on the pole, the prophecies of Jesus in Isaiah 53, the repentant thief on the cross, and culminating in the great multitude in Revelation who "washed their robes . . . in the blood of the Lamb"—all have shed the radiance of the gospel across the pages of God's Word. If this is the central truth of justification, it means, as Ellen White affirms, that those who accept the three angels' messages will always need the substitution of Christ's righteous life to make them acceptable to God. No matter how all-embracing our obedience and commandment keeping may be, as saved sinners we will never reach a point in this life where we can stand before God without the merits of our Savior. This is precisely the reason that justification by faith "is the third angel's message in verity." Our final hope of assurance and security rests in Jesus Christ alone.

Assurance of Salvation

There are a number of approaches to claiming assurance. Let's list briefly some of them before we discuss them in greater detail. The most common one is that we are accepted by God when we live the best life we can. Others take this view to a much higher level by declaring that assurance can be received only by living a perfect life with God's help—like the final generation. A more biblical approach is based on Romans 8:16, which states, "The Spirit himself testifies with our spirit that we are God's children." In this text acceptance with God is evidenced by an inner testimony, a Christ-centered life, and by manifestations of the fruit of the Spirit. Another view of assurance is that it has an objective basis—a premise that is fully dependent upon God's covenantal promise to the believer in Jesus.

Dependence on a promise reminds me of a little girl who asked her father, "Daddy, do all fairy tales begin with 'Once upon a time'?" He replied, "No, there is a whole series of fairy tales that begin with 'If elected, I promise.'" Although this story may evoke a smile, it has a serious side: the oft-broken promises of the politician are very much like the broken promises of the old covenant Christian. The old covenant is our promise to hold on to God's hand; the new covenant is His promise to hold on to ours. He says, "For I am the Lord your God who takes hold of your right hand" (Isa. 41:13) and "No one can snatch them out of my Father's hand" (John 10:29).

Unfortunately, such assurance of salvation is something many Adventists, young and old alike, do not feel comfortable claiming for themselves. When I was an academy Bible teacher, I asked the senior students in my classes to fill out a questionnaire in which students were asked to read two statements and choose the one they deemed to be true; the two statements read as follows:

(a) That which makes me acceptable to God and *worthy of salvation* is a clean heart that comes through the work of the Holy Spirit.

(b) That which makes me acceptable to God and *receptive of salvation* is confession of my sin and faith in Christ's finished work of atonement.

In making their choice, the students consistently chose (a) rather than (b). This was also true of academy leaders and church members who filled out the questionnaire. They generally reasoned that it didn't seem right not to choose obedience and a clean heart. While they knew that these were key elements in sanctification and essential in Christian growth, they were unaware that only the flawless righteousness of Jesus imputed to them by faith is the basis for assurance.

Before we continue, let's be sure we agree that the Bible offers us the assurance of salvation: Jesus said, "Most assuredly, I say to you, he who believes in Me *has* everlasting life" (John 6:47, NKJV). "And this is the testimony: that God has given us eternal life, and this life is in His Son. He who has the Son has life; he who does not have the Son of God does not have life" (1 John 5:11, 12, NKJV).

Such assurance will be an agonizing struggle for those who focus on whether the Holy Spirit has made them completely righteous (perfect) in God's sight, thus focusing on gaining His acceptance. Some mistakenly feel that they must see more holiness in their lives in order to have more confidence for the tests that are ahead. But such a belief does not beckon them to enter the Most Holy Place with "confidence" or "boldness" (Heb. 10:19) to face the pre-Advent judgment. It will not allow them to be certain that they are ready for the judgment if acquittal depends on the measure of their sanctification. The sad truth is that many Seventh-day Adventists still believe that imparted righteousness (sanctification) will enable the believer to keep the law perfectly to meet the judgment's scrutiny. This misunderstanding of the basis for assurance will keep them from seeing the judgment as a welcome event. Only Jesus was perfectly sinless; thus, as our substitute He fully meets the law's just demands.[18] The believer's security is based on the historical certainty of the gospel, because it reflects the absolute certainty of Christ's finished work (see John 19:30).

God's people will never attain unqualified sinless perfection where there's no longer a need for the justifying merits of Jesus. Just as God's people are to rely fully in the perfect righteousness of their divine Advocate during the pre-Advent judgment, so their only hope in the great time of trouble will continue to be in the imputed righteousness (merits) of Jesus. Despite what some may allege, this view does not minimize God-given power to overcome sin. It simply recognizes that human perfection in this life is always relative; our perfection is never absolute, the kind that qualifies one for salvation. How thankful we should be that the pre-Advent judgment is couched in the good news that we have righteousness in Jesus, which will stand in the judgment. To believe otherwise is to fall imperceptibly from faith in Jesus' good works into a trust of one's own (imparted) righteousness.

While I believe that assurance of salvation is the work of the Holy Spirit testifying with my spirit that I am a child of God, in order to avoid misinterpreting this passage, we need to expand our understanding of the Spirit's work. It is He that purifies the heart, heals the wounds of the soul, and creates spiritual life within the believer. The Holy Spirit has also been described as the one who convicts of sin, righteousness, and judgment (John 16:8-11), the great comforter (John 14:16), as well as the ever-present teacher who "will teach you all things and will remind you of everything I have said to you" (verse 26). It is the Holy Spirit who impresses our minds of God's covenant promises and to place our trust in Him, the one and only Promise Keeper. The fact that I am a child of God is not based on a subjective feeling regarding His presence in my life but my faith in the absolute reliability of God's objective promises (see Heb. 8:6).

In the new covenant God promises that we are His people and He is our God, that He forgives our evil ways and remembers our sins no more; and then through the Holy Spirit, our commitment to Him is internalized—His law is written on our hearts (Jer. 31:33, 34; Heb. 8:10-12). One could say this takes place when the *lawgiver* on the throne becomes the *lawkeeper* in our heart.

Keep in mind that the law written in our hearts, as wonderful as it may be, is not what ultimately fulfills the terms of the covenant of grace. Grace is never a reference to something we do. When Jesus "came into the world, He said: '. . . I have come . . . to do Your will, O God!'" (Heb. 10:5-7, NKJV). God's response to His Son was "This is my Son, . . . with him I am well pleased" (Matt. 3:17). Only "in Him" are we pleasing to God. Only His life of perfect obedience fulfills the new covenant and is the basis of our salvation. Apart from the merits of Jesus, even the law written on our hearts—which, at best, is sketchy obedience—has no redemptive value. We cannot expect eternal life from anything we are doing or have ever accomplished. We do not contribute to it, because it is always a gift of grace: "The gift of God is eternal life in Christ Jesus our Lord" (Rom. 6:23).

It is the Holy Spirit who reminds us that in the council of peace in eternity past, Jesus covenanted to save sinners by taking their place and fulfilling their obligations (see Zech. 6:13). Out of love and compassion, Jesus willingly came as the Second Adam and passed over the ground where the first Adam fell.[19] He walked down the very road where the first human beings had foolishly adopted the serpent's point of view. As the victorious new head of the human race, Jesus reversed (legally and morally) Adam's failure . . . in our behalf. God's Word reveals to us that just as we were ruined by our first representative, Adam, without having anything to do with it, so we have been redeemed through our second representative, Jesus, without any meritorious contribution on our part.

Jesus, as the Second Adam, through His perfect life and atoning death, has put the whole world in a new position before the Father, one that offers everyone the opportunity to be spared the condemnation that sin brings. "For if, by the trespass of the one man, death reigned through that one man, how much more will those who receive God's abundant provision of grace and of the gift of righteousness reign in life through the one man, Jesus Christ" (Rom. 5:17). Because God acted decisively in Jesus, salvation is now a certainty for those who accept this provision. It assures them of God's redeeming love and His profound desire for a personal relationship with all who believe in Him.

True believers in Jesus will see, as it were, both sides of the coin: as they appreciate the beauty of Christ's holiness, in contrast they see their own sinfulness.[20] As they grasp the far-reaching nature of God's law, they in turn realize how far they are from reflecting that standard. When they see that they cannot do business with the Almighty on the basis of their own merit, it causes them to flee to Calvary for mercy and forgiveness; it motivates them to cling to their only hope—a divine Advocate who represents them before the Father. The more clearly they see the righteousness that Jesus offers them, the more aware they are that salvation depends not upon their own goodness but on God's infinite grace. Indeed, there is no higher status a person can obtain than that which is received at the foot of the cross. As one writer so aptly expressed it: "If I am saved, it won't be my fault!"[21]

In order to grasp the nature of grace and its work, we must be diligent in "rightly dividing" the Word of God (as well as Ellen White's writings). Biblical grace is the essence of the gospel and, when rightly understood, it points exclusively and continuously to Jesus. It is wholly a gift from God; nevertheless, it's essential that we discern the different roles it plays in our lives—saving grace, justifying grace that redeems, and enabling grace—a sanctifying grace that initiates growth.

Simply put, justification looks back to the finished work of God in Christ Jesus and declares, "You are complete in Him" (Col. 2:10, NKJV). Sanctification points to the present work of God through the Holy Spirit and says, "Not . . . already perfect" (Phil. 3:12, ESV). Justification is to rest in God's finished work, while sanctification is to work with God in perfecting one's character. Some time ago I was driving through the city in which I lived, and I noticed a sign near a construction site with these words: Watch Out—Men at Work. Doesn't that accurately describe the Christian life—a construction site where hard work and changes are always taking place?

While we must deny any kind of separation between justification and sanctification, a serious problem occurs if we fail to affirm the distinction and the irreversible order between the two. They have different roles, two different meanings: one is the means of salvation, the other the result; one is legal and, in a sense, outside of us, the other subjective, personal, and intrinsic to us. Justification has been rightfully described as the root of our salvation, while sanctification has been likened to the fruit. In everyday life not only the fruit but also the root must get our attention and appreciation.

It is important for us to see that the complete sufficiency of justifying grace never denies the need for sanctifying grace, which is victory over sin throughout one's lifetime. There is no such thing as justification unaccompanied by sanctification. It is the new position one receives in justification that opens up the way for the potential blessings of sanctification. This involves a lifelong response of surrender to God's love and rulership. It leads to the purifying of our behavior as well as our motives. It is turning away from our own agenda, laying aside our selfish striving for worldly success and fulfillment.

It may appear that since believers live in enemy-occupied territory, the Christian life is nothing more than "a battle and a march." The young girl who tearfully confessed during an academy Week of Prayer, "I want to give my heart to God, but I'm afraid I won't have another fun day in my life," reflects such mentality. Thankfully that's not the whole story. As in the human realm, when people fall in love, everything changes. The moments spent together, the plans that are made, even the most difficult tasks, now become exciting adventures. Everything is transformed with new meaning, energized with gratitude and purpose.

Whidden would have us keep in mind that all of the blessings of salvation—the joys of justification, as well as continual conviction of sin, repentance, confession in sanctification—come as part of a package. Thus, when a penitent sinner receives Christ by faith, the Savior comes to the needy convert as the sole source of all His saving benefits. Faith in Christ is a " 'package' deal": you receive Him by faith and, in so doing, are open to all the other perks of His grace.[22]

For this reason Seventh-day Adventists should be foremost in lifting up Jesus before the world, glorying in His saving merits, His mercy, His righteousness, His enabling power. Because He is our all, we must personalize grace—proclaim a *person*, not merely a message. There can be no real adoration, worship, and praise apart from Jesus. He is the wellspring of everything gracious and desirable. "Hanging upon the cross Christ was the gospel. . . . This is our message, our argument, our doctrine, our warning to the impenitent, our encouragement for the sorrowing, the hope for every believer." [23] The grace of Jesus alone brings justification, and justification alone brings salvation.

When we are *"justified through faith, we have peace with God* through our Lord Jesus Christ" (Rom. 5:1). Don't miss the apostle's point. The believer's security (peace) comes through justification by faith, being forgiven, being legally declared righteous in God's sight. This peace that leads to victorious living is clearly taught in Christ's healing miracles (Matt. 9:1-8; Mark 2:1-12), where forgiveness of sin is pronounced before the healed are asked to take up their bed and walk.

In like fashion, Jesus did not ask His disciples to "take up their cross" and follow Him until they first acknowledged the primacy of Him taking His cross and dying for their sin (Matt. 16:21-26). Similarly, we are not to lug our cross to Calvary in hopes that our best endeavors will bring us acceptance and saving merit with God. While sanctification demonstrates the presence of saving faith (James 2:17-26), it has no meritorious function in our salvation. True discipleship means carrying our cross from Calvary in grateful response to Christ's all-sufficient atonement in our behalf. It's been rightly observed, "Before you run the race, make sure you're grounded in grace."

---

[1] P. Yancey, *What's So Amazing About Grace?* p. 200.

[2] E. G. White, *Early Writings*, p. 33.

[3] It should be noted that the wicked—those who worship the beast and receive its mark—are described in Revelation 14:11 as having "no rest, day or night."

[4] E. G. White, *Testimonies*, vol. 3, p. 267.

[5] Sigve K. Tonstad, *The Lost Meaning of the Seventh Day* (Berrien Springs, Mich.: Andrews University Press, 2009), p. 462.

[6] E. G. White, *The Great Controversy*, p. 449.

[7] *Ibid.*, p. 605.

[8] Ellen G. White, in *Review and Herald*, Apr. 1, 1890.

[9] *Seventh-day Adventist Encyclopedia* (Washington, D.C.: Review and Herald Pub. Assn., 1996), vol. 11, p. 774. (Italics supplied.)

[10] "He lived a sinless life so that by His substitutionary life of righteousness and His sacrificial death on our behalf, He might 'redeem those under law' (those still held accountable to a perfect standard of righteousness but condemned for having failed to achieve it), 'that we might receive full rights of sons' (Gal. 4:5)" (Skip MacCarty, *In Granite or Ingrained: What the Old and New Covenants Reveal About the Gospel, the Law, and the Sabbath* [Berrien Springs, Mich.: Andrews University Press, 2007], p. 277).

[11] The reason that some Seventh-day Adventists disagree with this belief and de-

risively label it as "new theology" is for an entirely different reason than that given by Roman Catholicism. To discuss it fully would require another book!

[12] "Some of us [Seventh-day Adventists] are teaching a disguised Roman Catholic theology of salvation" (J. David Newman, "'I, If I Be Lifted Up From the Earth': An Open Letter From the Editor of *Ministry* to the General Conference President," *Ministry,* October 1992, p. 6).

[13] "The experience of justification and its deliverance from the guilt of sin forms the essential legal framework or key motivational launching pad for any experience of character change (sanctification)" (Woodrow Whidden, "The Essence of Christian Character," Mar. 21, 2010, Sabbath School Commentary, *Spectrum,* http://spectrum-magazine.org/article/sabbath-school/2010/03/21/essence-christian-character).

[14] W. Whidden, *The Judgment and Assurance,* p. 82.

[15] *Ibid.,* p. 71. Note: Whidden references Ellen White's statement in *Selected Messages,* book 1, p. 344: "The religious services, the prayers, the praise, the penitent confession of sin ascend from true believers as incense to the heavenly sanctuary, but passing through the corrupt channels of humanity, they are so defiled that unless purified by blood, they can never be of value with God. . . . All incense from earthly tabernacles must be moist with the cleansing drops of the blood of Christ."

[16] George R. Knight, *The Apocalyptic Vision and the Neutering of Adventism* (Hagerstown, Md.: Review and Herald Pub. Assn., 2008), p. 48.

[17] In his book *The Cross of Christ,* John R. W. Stott pens this provocative insight: "The concept of substitution may be said, then, to lie at the heart of both sin and salvation. For the essence of sin is man substituting himself for God, while the essence of salvation is God substituting himself for man. Man asserts himself against God and puts himself where only God deserves to be; God sacrifices himself for man and puts himself where only man deserves to be. Man claims prerogatives which belong to God alone; God accepts penalties which belong to man alone" ([Downers Grove, Ill.: InterVarsity Press, 1986], p. 160).

[18] "He [Jesus] is a perfect and holy example, given for us to imitate. *We cannot equal the Pattern;* but we shall not be approved of God if we do not copy it and, according to the ability God has given, resemble it" (E. G. White, *Testimonies,* vol. 2, p. 549; italics supplied).

[19] "Christ came to earth, taking humanity and standing as man's representative, to show in the controversy with Satan that man, *as God created him,* connected with the Father and the Son, could obey every divine requirement" (Ellen G. White, in *Selected Messages,* book 1, p. 253; italics supplied).

[20] "The closer you come to Jesus, the more faulty you will appear in your own eyes" (E. G. White, *Steps to Christ,* p. 64). In contrast, this means that the farther you drift from Jesus, the more perfect you will appear in your own eyes, the more foggy will be your opinion of sin.

[21] J. R. Spangler, "Justification, Perfection, and the Real Gospel," editorial, *Ministry: International Journal for Pastors,* June 1988, https://www.ministrymagazine.org/archive/1988/06/justification-perfection-and-the-real-gospel.

[22] Whidden, *The Judgment and Assurance,* p. 75.

[23] *The SDA Bible Commentary,* Ellen G. White Comments, vol. 6, p. 1113.

★13★
From Adam to Armageddon

The sixth angel poured out his bowl on the great river Euphrates, and its water was dried up to prepare the way for the kings of the East. Then I saw three impure spirits that looked like frogs; they came out of the mouth of the dragon, out of the mouth of the beast and out of the mouth of the false prophet. They are demonic spirits that perform signs, and they go out to the kings of the whole world, to gather them for the battle on the great day of God Almighty. . . . Blessed is the one who stays awake and remains clothed, so as not to go naked. . . . Then they gathered the kings together to the place that in Hebrew is called Armageddon" (Rev. 16:12-16).

This passage of Scripture is filled with controversy, mystery, and intrigue. No wonder hundreds of books have been written in an attempt to explain it. Our first focus will be on a short phrase that is clearly and simply stated and should immediately catch our attention: "I saw three impure [evil] spirits." In connecting the spiritual dots between Adam and Armageddon, from Genesis to Revelation, we see the underlying theme—the great controversy—that is carried forth by a significant series of threes: the three temptations in Eden, the three temptations in the wilderness, the three angels' messages, and, finally, the three evil spirits.

Sigve K. Tonstad's comment is apropos: "Genesis and Revelation are not mere bookends. Creation in Genesis and the new creation in Revelation belong together, enhancing and clarifying each other."[1] What occurs in between, like the series of threes mentioned above, is not truly understood apart from their beginning and ending.

As we take a closer look at these "in between" scenarios, we not only discern a constant manifestation of evil, but, more important, we also discover a continual, richer revelation of God's love and saving grace. After all, the primary issue in Bible prophecy is not how clearly it paints a picture of evil but how transparent the Creator's character becomes and how we can come to know Him.

As we closely examined the three temptations of Adam and Eve, we found that they were decidedly relevant to the three temptations of Jesus. In other words, Adam and Eve's failure in Eden was remedied by Jesus' victory in the wilderness. This wondrous act of divine grace is what Paul is talking about when he says, "Just as one trespass resulted in condemnation for all people, so also one righteous act resulted in justification and life for all people" (Rom. 5:18). This statement affirms that Adam and Eve's fall in Eden and Christ's victory in the wilderness are both historical realities. Surely, a Second Adam in the Gospels has no meaning without the first Adam in Genesis.

It bears repeating that Christianity generally views humankind as linked together in a shared identity; Adam represents the whole human race (verse 12). This means that when Adam fell into sin, he took the whole human race with him. While this is the negative side of *corporate oneness*, that's only half the story. Out of love and compassion, Christ willingly came as the Second Adam and passed over the same ground where the first Adam had fallen. Since we all fell in one man, Adam, the positive side is that God in like fashion redeems us all in the one Man, Jesus Christ, the "last Adam" (verses 12-21; 1 Cor. 15:45). "For as in Adam *all die*, so in Christ all will be *made alive*" (1 Cor. 15:22). As the victorious new head of the human race, Jesus reversed Adam's failure in our behalf.

When we explore the second pair of threes, we find a similar contrast—the three angels' messages that were set into motion to expose the opposition represented by the three evil spirits. On one side we find the devil and the three unclean spirits. These spirits symbolize the wicked forces, both human and demonic, which represent the agencies through whom the evil one works. On the opposite side is God with His followers— the "three angels," which represent the people who proclaim the truths of God in the last days and, despite persecution, choose to "follow the Lamb wherever he goes" (Rev. 14:4).

What Evil Spirits Do

This subheading is a loaded statement. From what the Bible says, we live in a world infiltrated by hordes of fallen angels, namely, evil spirits, that are exceedingly active, totally engrossed in carrying out the demonic strategy that was conjured up at the time of their fall. The demonic realm includes a vast array of evil powers and authorities, demons, wicked spirits, and mighty forces of darkness (Eph. 6:12). It's scary to think that they are invisible enemies, the masters of deception, and the highest-ranking con artists in the universe. Thankfully, the book of Revelation steps in and gives us important insights to expose what the evil spirits will do in the final conflict. For this reason we ought not to ignore any of the details God gives us regarding their devious tactics.

It was already established that Revelation 13 is primarily devoted to the dragon, along with a sea beast (verses 1-10) and a land beast (verses 11-18), an alliance that is engaged in a lethal warfare against God and His remnant people. This evil threesome reappears in Revelation 16:13: "Then I saw three impure spirits that looked like frogs; they came out of the mouth of the dragon, out of the mouth of the beast and out of the mouth of the false prophet." Seventh-day Adventists have generally interpreted this spiritual coalition as a symbol of spiritualism (paganism), apostate Protestantism in America, and Roman Catholicism. These become the three parts of that great city Babylon (see Rev. 16:19), the great end-time religious confederacy.

Babylon is also referred to as "the great harlot who sits on many waters" (Rev. 17:1, NKJV), just as ancient Babylon sat securely on the river Euphrates. From the biblical perspective, the term *harlot* does not apply to secular, nonreligious individuals—those who have never professed allegiance to God. When used in a symbolic way, harlot usually refers to an entity that at one time vowed to follow God but has since slipped away from the marriage and has become involved in a life of illicit affairs—unfaithful to God and His Word. The book of Revelation also calls her the "mother of harlots" (Rev. 17:5, NKJV). This implies that there are other churches (daughters) that did not completely break away or who have drifted back to the "mother church," notably in such doctrinal teachings as the day of worship, immortality of the soul, and eternal torment.

Revelation makes a point of this when it says that from the mouths of these organizations come satanically deceptive doctrines that they wish to disseminate and promote (Rev. 13:5, 11). It is these deceptive philosophies, reinforced with miracles and supernatural phenomena (verses 13, 14) and supported by legislative assemblies (verse 15), that will rally all inhabitants—"both great and small, rich and poor, free and slave"—to unite in bitter opposition to God.

Regarding this, Ellen White warns, "The Protestants of the United States will be foremost in stretching their hands across the gulf to grasp the hand of spiritualism; they will reach over the abyss to clasp hands with the Roman power; and under the influence of this threefold union, this country will follow in the steps of Rome in trampling on the rights of conscience."[2] Though this dire warning was penned more than 100 years ago, we have no reason to believe it will not be fulfilled.

It needs to be emphasized that modern Babylon represents an end-time global confederacy of all false religions that will have a deceptively godly facade at its operational level. While it masquerades as the world's only legitimate religious community, it actually supports a worldwide religious coalition that is in opposition to God, His Word, and His people. For this reason, the Bible is consistently more concerned about apostasy (the antichrist) arising *within* the church than about attacks from without (see 1 John 2:18, 19). As Paul warns: "Even from your own number men will arise and distort the truth in order to draw away disciples after them" (Acts 20:30). John the revelator makes it clear that the final enemy of God's people is a religious one, one that makes "war against God's holy people" (Rev. 13:7) and demands that people worship the beast and its image (Rev. 13:12, 15).

The three spiritual entities that make up modern Babylon are basically global extensions of the three deceptions spoken by the serpent in Eden. Thus it comes as no surprise that modern Babylon is exposed as being demonic by the three angels' messages. The lesson is there for all to see—as the great controversy winds down in the remnant of time, Satan will employ three demonic spirits to deceive the inhabitants of the earth, just as he used three demonic deceptions to initially deceive Adam and Eve in the garden. That's why it's important for us to see Satan's successful deceptions in Eden as cunningly devised lies, spoken by a dazzling serpent (beast) who claims to have the miraculous (supernatural) power of speech (supposedly) derived from "the forbidden fruit."[3] In essence, this will all be repeated in the concluding scenes of the final conflict, a time when a beast (its image) will once again speak, demonically empowered and emboldened by "great and miraculous signs" (Rev. 13:13-15, NIrV) so that all the inhabitants of the world, except God's faithful people, will be deceived.

First Angel Versus False Prophet

The three angels of Revelation 14 proclaim a worldwide message warning "every nation, tribe, language and people" about the three demonic deceptions of Eden that have themselves become worldwide movements. Briefly summarized, the first angel's message alludes to Satan's first Edenic deception—the work carried out by the false prophet. The second angel's message warns of Satan's second deception—which is promoted by the dragon. The third angel's message denounces the fallacy of Satan's third deception—the errors trumpeted by the beast.

The primary objective of the first angel's message is to inspire faith and trust in God's eternal plans and purposes,[4] in the rightness of His laws, and in His provisions of grace as revealed in the Bible. Satan has designed to thwart all of that. His first deception, "Did God really say?" is being carried forward today in large measure by apostate (fallen) Protestantism. A false prophet represents this spiritual entity. While a prophet is a spokesperson for God, a false prophet is one who masquerades as God's mouthpiece. More precisely, a false prophet has the appearance of speaking for God but really opposes God in his or her heart. It is significant, therefore, that from the mouth of the false prophet come offensive and damaging errors such as the immortality of the soul, eternal punishment, the secret rapture, and Sunday observance, just a few examples of popular doctrines that have no basis in Scripture. These beliefs are not only blatant attacks on God's character but also a grievous onslaught on the prophetic, theological, and historical validity of God's Word.

Another example of apostate Protestantism taking the wrong side in the great controversy is their view of the antichrist that reflects either preterism (this prophetic interpretation points to events that have already taken place) or futurism (this prophetic interpretation is all about events that are yet to come). In other words, preterism maintains, "The antichrist is in the past," while futurism declares, "The antichrist is in the future."

Following the Council of Trent, two Jesuit priests, Francisco Ribera and Luis de Alcazar, in an ambitious attempt to defend the Papacy, "devised diametrically opposite systems of interpretations, both of which attempted to turn the accusing finger of prophecy away from the papacy."[5] By pushing the identity of the antichrist either back into the past or forward into the future, the Roman Church was able to counteract the Reformation's teaching that the Papacy was a manifestation of the antichrist at that time.

While the liberal wing of Protestantism has adopted Alcazar's preterism, most of American evangelicalism has gravitated to the view that the antichrist is best explained by futurism. In recent years this view was made fashionable by Tim LaHaye, an American evangelical minister, author, and speaker, with his very popular *Left Behind* series. By claiming that the antichrist is not a contemporary issue or that Roman Catholicism is no longer the biblical antichrist (for which the Bible provides ample clues), apostate Protestantism is definitely undermining its heritage from the Reformation.[6] As God's wily foe, Satan realizes that "to destroy faith in the Bible serves his purpose as well as to destroy the Bible itself. . . . And now, as in former ages, he has worked through the church to further his designs."[7]

Second Angel Versus the Dragon

As we examine the second temptation, we may find it difficult to understand how Eve could believe the serpent, a crafty creature she had never seen before, someone (she supposed) she knew nothing about nor had done anything to prove himself trustworthy. In Eve's rejection of God's warning that if she ate from the forbidden tree "you will surely die," keep in mind that the first deception set the stage for the second. Once she began to doubt God's word, it was relatively easy for Satan to deceive her into thinking that God really didn't mean what He said—that disobedience would result in death. This lie about death—that it is just a transition everyone goes through on his or her way to something better—had its birth on that fateful day when sin entered the world. That lie has grown into a worldwide error that we've come to know as spiritualism (and a host of other related falsehoods).

"Satan has long been preparing for his final effort to deceive the world. The foundation of his work was laid by the assurance given to Eve in Eden: 'Ye shall not surely die' (Gen. 3:4, KJV). . . . Little by little he has prepared the way for his masterpiece of deception in the development of spiritualism. He has not yet reached the full accomplishments of his designs; but it will be reached in the last remnant of time."[8]

Spiritualism is based on a lie—the natural immortality of the soul. Nowhere does the Bible teach that a future life is ensured because the soul is immortal; rather, the future life is entirely dependent on the resurrection of the body. Paul's argument with the Corinthians on this point is particularly striking. He singles out death, not as a welcome backdoor to a future life, but as "the last enemy" (1 Cor. 15:26) because death is simply the irrevocable cessation of human existence. When death is finally thrown into the lake of fire (Rev. 20:14), it doesn't receive a divine vote of thanks for assisting with any kind of transition. No, it is simply labeled an enemy, for since its inception it has only taken human life, never given it back to God.

Paul reaffirms that the future life depends on a Creator who can create instantaneously and out of nothing. Manifesting God's power, the dead will be resurrected "in a flash, in the twinkling of an eye" because no other way is open for those who "sleep" to be awakened and be raised "incorruptible" (1 Cor. 15:51, 52, NKJV).

The second angel's message, first proclaimed in the early 1840s and to be repeated in the end of time, is a stirring appeal to the populace to "come out of her, [Babylon] my people" (Rev. 18:4). Because most Christian churches believe in the immortality of the soul, they have inadvertently opened their doors to various forms of spiritualism. If they do not stand to be corrected, the Bible declares that this philosophy will, without fail, lead them to "become a dwelling for demons" (verse 2). Seventh-day Adventists need to be aware that they are not exempt from this warning that is ever widening in its scope. Ellen White warns, "There are many who shrink with horror from the thought of consulting spirit mediums, but who are attracted by more pleasing forms of spiritism." She then points to "Oriental religions" and to forms of spiritism that claim to "have power to heal," [9] which can include such related practices as yoga, acupuncture, and the martial arts—often defended for their "latent" health, healing, and self-defense benefits.

Francisco Gayoba, president of the Adventist University of the Philippines, in a speech to the Third International Bible Conference on June 19, 2012, alerted his listeners that spiritualism not only permeates the highly sophisticated New Age movement but also is a pervasive influence throughout Western culture, where people who call themselves "spiritual but not religious" become vulnerable to the comforts that spiritualism offers. He went on to say that spiritualism is rampant in much of Protestantism and serves as the "framework" of Roman Catholic theology with its emphasis on the soul continuing after death (that serves as the basis for indulgences, purgatory, eternal hell, masses for the dead, and veneration of Mary and the saints). He also asserted that spiritualism has totally entrenched pagan religions such as Hinduism, Buddhism, as well as folk religions because of their unbiblical views of life after death. [10]

Ellen White warned of this spiritual danger when she wrote that people who "turn from the plain teaching of Scripture and the convicting power of God's Holy Spirit are inviting the control of demons" and thus "have opened the way for spiritism." [11] (*Spiritism* is just another spelling or term for *spiritualism*.)

A survey of Adventist history reveals that shortly after the Millerites and the early Advent believers presented the second angel's message in the early 1840s, modern spiritualism came on the scene primarily through the "Rochester Rappings" (which occurred in Hydesville, New York) in 1848. When individuals, societies, or religions turn away from the truths of the Bible, they will assuredly turn to the lies and deceptions of the evil one. It is a law of life that when people close the door to spiritual light, they will inevitably open the door to darkness.

Marvin Olasky, in his article "The Return of Spiritism" in the December 14, 1992, issue of *Christianity Today*, quoting physician Thomas Nichols, points out that a massive spiritualist movement in the United States during the 1850s devastated "hundreds of churches and changed the beliefs of hundreds of thousands." Referencing and quoting author Orestes Brownson, Olasky goes on to say that by 1854 it is estimated that there were 300 spiritualist clubs in Philadelphia alone and that this spiritualistic mania affected "all classes, ministers of religion, lawyers, physicians, judges, comedians, rich and poor, learned and unlearned." He states that in 1857 the Cleveland *Plain Dealer* reported that spiritualism was "gaining ground on every side. One month ago there were not 50 believers in the city; now there are hundreds, including some of its best minds."

Throughout the country some of these "best minds" included Ralph Waldo Emerson, whose "transcendentalism fed the spiritualist movement." Harriet Beecher Stowe, whose husband, Calvin Stowe, was a spiritualist medium, was sympathetic to spiritualism in her writings, and authors such as James Greenleaf Whittier and Henry Wadsworth Longfellow "regularly attended séances." Congressmen, judges, and radical abolitionists such as William Lloyd Garrison openly supported spiritualism. Spiritualist theology reached its nineteenth-century peak on the eve of the Civil War when spiritualists were holding regular meetings and conferences in at least 3,000 different places. It's estimated that about 2 million persons out of a United States population of 30 million "espoused some spiritist beliefs or engaged in some spiritist activities."[12] This gives special impetus to the proclamation of the second angel's message that Babylon was fallen and had "become a dwelling for demons" (Rev. 18:2).

But what is the appeal that entices people to believe in or become involved with spiritualism? To start off with, studies have shown that most people who become involved in spiritualism and occult activities do so before the age of 12. With Hollywood churning out occult-focused movies at an unprecedented pace, the interest of the youth is at a fever pitch. Movies, videos, television, games, children's books, are inundated with occult themes. Sorcery, nature worship, and Wicca—the religion of witchcraft—have become the hottest topics in American youth culture today. Recent polls of Christian youth indicate that more than 55 percent dabble in some kind of occult activity, such as playing with Ouija boards, casting spells, reading astrological charts, or messing around with magick. (In contrast to *magic*, which employs sleight of hand, *magick* denotes the use of occult powers.)

Scores of books such as the popular *Harry Potter* series, marketed as entertainment for children, are actually a crash course in the occult. The spellbound readers learn about magic potions, astrology, pagan rituals, the dark force, sorcery, channeling, crystal gazing, casting spells, divination, and necromancy. Fantasy is so often an "imaginative bridge" that connects children to the dark and dangerous world of the occult and spiritualism. But more than that, it's all set forth with a "friendly face." It routinely presents evil as good, makes readers feel at home with the occult, and piques their curiosity regarding hidden powers, secret knowledge, and devices of the occult.

It could also be that spiritualism's offer of a future life without the possibility of punishment in hell is attractive to people who have fearful forebodings about the afterlife. People are eager to believe the experiences of those who claim to have died and were immersed in a radiant light of love and acceptance or have returned from a temporary but delightful sojourn in heaven.

Spiritualism can also represent a search for life after death in which everyone is inevitably happy and all religions are deemed equally good. Others may gravitate to spiritualism because there's no sense of sin and salvation; they can simply follow their natural instincts and break away from what they may call Christian superstitions. For some, spiritualism fascinates with its emphasis on the supernatural, the mysterious, and the miraculous. And for many it has special appeal because they want the privilege of conversing with loved ones who have died. Finally, human nature is always tantalized with notions that cater to self-sovereignty rather than God-sovereignty. For the defiant and the rebellious, John Milton might have said it best when he had Lucifer declare in *Paradise Lost*, "Better to reign in hell than serve in heaven."

Third Angel Versus the Beast
The third angel's message aims directly at Satan's outrageous boast to Eve

that if she ate of the forbidden fruit, "your eyes will be opened, and you will be like God, knowing good and evil" (Gen. 3:5). We know from personal experience that none of us are exempt from this selfish craving. History vividly bears out sin's mysterious power to awaken within the human heart aggressive ambitions for self-exaltation—to desire the highest place and covet the greatest power. This can happen within either religious or worldly settings. Nothing distinguishes the kingdoms of the world from the kingdom of God so clearly as their opposing views of power and control (see Mark 10:42, 43).

In its historical context, the third angel's warning deals with evil spirits "coming out of the mouth of the beast," namely, the Roman Catholic system. In the book of Daniel, the papal system is depicted as a little horn that had eyes "like the eyes of a man and a mouth speaking pompous words" (Dan. 7:8, NKJV). This description is very significant in light of Jesus' declaration "For out of the abundance of the heart the mouth speaks" (Matt. 12:34, NKJV). It indicates that at the heart of Roman Catholicism is a religion of arrogance, an organization whose beliefs and practices are primarily a display of human wisdom and authority, a power that carries forth its work from a human perspective. It views salvation through "human eyes" (Dan. 7:8, NLT); thus a flawed gospel is (pompously) proclaimed to the world. The book of Revelation states, "The beast was given a mouth to utter proud words and blasphemies" against God (Rev. 13:5, 6). This text exposes the Papacy as proudly proclaiming its own traditions and pronouncements as being equal to (or above) God's Word—an act of blasphemy (see John 10:33). The church must ever be on guard not to take center stage and usurp the work, authority, and greatness that are befitting God alone. Unfortunately, speaking *for* God can easily degenerate into speaking *as* God.

Since the beginning of the great controversy the inclination of the beast (creature) is to usurp that which belongs exclusively to the Creator. This act of treachery is one of the reasons that the third angel's message is perhaps the most frightful and ominous warning found in Scripture. It also reveals God's reaction to the extremely brutal and lethal actions of the beast and its image against His people. Their merciless edict that "no one [can] buy or sell" or that people will be "killed" sooner or later unless they have the mark of the beast (see Rev. 13:15-17) is explained more fully in this quotation:

"As the Sabbath has become the special point of controversy throughout Christendom, and religious and secular authorities have combined to enforce the observance of the Sunday, the persistent refusal of a small minority to yield to the popular demand will make them objects of universal execration. It will be urged that the few who stand in opposition to an institution of the church and a law of the state ought not to be tolerated; that it is better for them to suffer than for whole nations to be thrown into confusion and lawlessness. This same argument eighteen hundred years ago was brought against Christ by the 'rulers of the people.' 'It is expedient for us,' said the wily Caiaphas, 'that one man should die for the people, and that the whole nation perish not' (John 11:50, KJV). This argument will appear conclusive; and a decree will finally be issued against those who hallow the Sabbath of the fourth commandment, denouncing them as deserving of the severest punishment and giving the people liberty, after a certain time, to put them to death. Romanism in the Old World and apostate Protestantism in the New will pursue a similar course toward those who honor all the divine precepts." [13]

This explains why such threatening proclamations in the third angel's message come from a God who is longsuffering and forgiving. These warnings are needed to emphasize what Jesus said to His disciples, "On the earth, nations will be in anguish and perplexity. . . . People will faint from terror, apprehensive of what is coming on the world" (Luke 21:25, 26). The warnings are also necessary to wake us up to our self-centeredness, our bias toward self-worship, and our reliance on the things around us. When this kind of spirit rules within, the natural inclination is to succumb to external pressures and go along with the decree to worship the beast and his image.

A word of caution is needed here: It is so easy to focus on the dire threats of the third angel and fail to give ample credence to the very positive side of this message, "Here is the patience [quiet strength] of the saints; here are those who keep the commandments of God and the faith of Jesus" (Rev. 14:12, NKJV). What wonderful assurance that God's remnant people will be victorious in the final conflict. There are two ways that we can understand the last phrase in the above verse. Some translations emphasize that the saints will have the faith *of* Jesus, the same faith that Jesus had (NKJV, ASV), while others interpret it as the saints having faith *in* Jesus or remaining faithful *to* Jesus (NIV, NLT, NASB, CEV). What they all have in common is that the end-time people will keep the commandments because of their faith.

Ellen White makes a couple of comments that jibe very nicely with her earlier comment that justification by faith is the heart of the third angel's message:

"The time of test is just upon us, for the loud cry of the third angel has already begun in the revelation of the *righteousness of Christ,* the sin-pardoning Redeemer." [14]

"The message of *Christ's righteousness* is to sound from one end of the earth to the other to prepare the way of the Lord. This is the glory of God, which closes the work of the third angel." [15]

The outcome of the great controversy for each of us will be determined by the choice we make regarding the key issue in the final conflict—our faith in Jesus. It will sum up whom we trust, whom we love, and whom we worship and serve. For those whose decision still hangs in the balance, the three angels' messages are God's final appeal, pointing to the trustworthiness of His Word, revealing the sufficiency of His grace, and reassuring that His sovereign love is eternal and unchanging.

---

[1] S. K. Tonstad, *The Lost Meaning of the Seventh Day,* p. 404.

[2] E. G. White, *The Great Controversy,* p. 588.

[3] E. G. White, *Patriarchs and Prophets,* p. 54.

[4] The reason there is so little faith in the Bible is "because it reproves and condemns sin" (E. G. White, *The Great Controversy,* p. 526).

[5] Donald Ernest Mansell, *Open Secrets of the Antichrist: Has the Beast of Prophecy Identified Itself?* (Nampa, Idaho: Pacific Press Pub. Assn., 2002), p. 25.

[6] J. T. Anderson, *Three Angels, One Message,* p. 241.

[7] E. G. White, *The Great Controversy,* p. 586.

[8] *Ibid.,* p. 561.

[9] Ellen G. White, *Prophets and Kings* (Mountain View, Calif.: Pacific Press Pub. Assn., 1917), pp. 210, 211.

[10] Quoted in Mark A. Kellner, "Battle Against Spiritualism Far From Over, Adventist Theologian Says," *Adventist Review,* July 19, 2012, p. 12, http://www.adventistreview. org/article/5461/archives/issue-2012-1516/16-cn-international-bible-conference-opens-in-israel/16-cn-battle-against-spiritualism-far-from-over-adventist-theologian-says.

[11] E. G. White, *The Desire of Ages,* p. 258.

[12] Marvin Olasky, "The Return of Spiritism: Seeing How the Church Triumphed Over the New Age Movement of the 1850s Can Help Us in the 1990s," *Christianity Today,* Dec. 14, 1992, pp. 20, 21.

[13] E. G. White, *The Great Controversy,* pp. 615, 616.

[14] *The SDA Bible Commentary,* Ellen G. White Comments, vol. 7, p. 984. (Italics supplied.)

[15] E. G. White, *Testimonies,* vol. 6, p. 19. (Italics supplied.)

★ 14 ★
Delightful—but Demonic

Armageddon: What It's All About

Armageddon! Now here's a word that most people not only find baffling and mystifying but also a little scary. It tends to conjure up all kinds of speculative notions about a cataclysmic battle that brings the world as we know it to an end. During most of the time between 1844 and 1950, Seventh-day Adventists believed that Armageddon would primarily involve political warfare. Our understanding of truth is ongoing; thus, the church's present view of Armageddon as a religious struggle has a much stronger biblical foundation.

While you're probably aware that Armageddon is a biblical word, what may surprise you is that it's mentioned only once in the entire Bible—in Revelation 16:16. The text has a rather puzzling twist when it says that Armageddon is "the place that in Hebrew is called Armageddon"—but such a word can't be found anywhere in the original Hebrew Old Testament. It's significant that in the book of Revelation, the Hebrew spelling of Armageddon is *Har-ma-ged-on*, a word that is often seen as referring to Mount Megiddo. Since there is no such mountain in the valley of Megiddo, it only creates a more perplexing dilemma. How often God's story confuses before it clarifies, perplexes before it persuades.

Nevertheless, there is general agreement that the last movements in the history of this rebellious planet are indicated by the *symbolic* name of Armageddon. The meaning of the word, as evident in the variety of positions scholars take, is not conclusive, except that all possible derivations of the word point to the general meaning of "gathering" or "assembly." There is also agreement that *har,* the first syllable of Armageddon, is the word for "mount"[1] or "mountain" in the Hebrew language.

One position supported by many scholars is that the meaning of Armageddon is "Mount of Megiddo," often seen as a symbol of Mount Carmel. This is where the Old Testament encounter between Elijah and the prophets of Baal took place—the climactic battle between Israel's God and Baal (see 1 Kings 18:19, 20). Just as this mount was known for the assembling of the prophets of Baal in a confrontation with Elijah, the same holds true for Armageddon.

Since our world has been steadily growing into a global village, the assembling of the kings of the earth in the final conflict (Rev. 16:14) is not necessarily a physical gathering of the world's armies to one particular location but rather a situation in which all of the world's leaders will participate. It is primarily a meeting of the minds of the world's heads of state, a global agreement—being of one mind (see Rev. 17:13, 14). This is indicated by the fact that Revelation does not say that "the kings of the whole world" are going to battle one another but rather that it is a time when they are gathered together to have one last rendezvous with "God Almighty" (Rev. 16:14). As the decree to worship the beast and his image is enforced upon everyone, so is the battle that follows.

At the same time, in the supernatural realm often hidden from our view, a battle rages between two universal entities, each employing angels to persuade human beings to be on their side of the conflict. Armageddon is the conclusion of this warfare that has been going on ever since Satan came to this world and deceived Adam and Eve into becoming enemies of God. As descendants of Adam's fallen family, we are all participants in this struggle. A concise description of this conflict is given in 2 Corinthians 10:3, 4: "For though we live in the world, we do not wage war as the world does. The weapons we fight with are not the weapons of the world. On the contrary, they have divine power to demolish strongholds. We demolish arguments and every pretension that sets itself up against the knowledge of God."

Paul's admonition is significant in light of the fact that the political arena too often competes with God's Word as to what holds center stage in our lives. Politics makes a lot of noise; it gets the majority of people to watch and admire powerful nations, important elections, and significant people. Because it gets the applause and the votes, there's a real danger that it also gets our time; we focus too much on what really doesn't amount to anything. Remember God's viewpoint: "The nations [with their vast armies and political leaders] are like a drop in a bucket; they are regarded as dust on the scales" (Isa. 40:15).

Unfortunately, American Christians are often deeply polarized as to which political party or leader gets their support (loyalty), even though in the final conflict, "the kings of the whole world" appear to be united in opposition to God's Word and those who obey it. It is especially important that our ultimate loyalty be decisively cast with God's kingdom and the saving truths of the gospel, not with any particular leader or political party. Thoughtful Christians should never elevate the everyday operations of politics, even if it is American democracy, to supreme value. As God's remnant people we must not pattern our thinking after the philosophies of this world—where earthly ideas of love, allegiance, and solutions do not reflect biblical criteria.

The sixth plague describes the gathering of the kings of the world by the three evil spirits (Rev. 16:13, 14); this is the demonic counterpart to the gathering call of the three angels (Rev. 14:6-11), which unites the followers of the Lamb. The battle of Armageddon is the climax of the spiritual warfare over worship outlined in Revelation 13 and 14, a conflict that brings every human being in the world to a final decision.

This reminds me of heartily singing as a child in Sabbath school what now seems to be a very inappropriate tune for Sabbath morning worship: "I'm too young to march in the infantry, ride in the cavalry, shoot the artillery. I'm too young to fly o'er the enemy, but I'm in the Lord's army."

Is it any wonder that so many of us grew up viewing Armageddon as some kind of military conflict? Jon Paulien suggests that from a biblical perspective, the battle of Armageddon is definitely not about aircraft missiles, rocket launchers, and battlefield artillery, as is so commonly believed in evangelical Christian circles today. The Bible is primarily a book about God and His conflict with evil. Its main concern is not with political happenings—even dismissing cataclysmic events such as two world wars with such short, general phrases as "wars and rumors of wars." Armageddon is all about a spiritual struggle for the thoughts, the loyalty, and the worship of every human being on earth. This means that "our decisions and actions matter a great deal in the ultimate scheme of things," says Paulien. In the mundane battles we have with our thoughts, feelings, and actions, don't forget that we are preparing for bigger battles to come. The greatest warfare for the Christian is the struggle for the mind—one that focuses either on immediate needs or on eternal priorities. "The battle of Armageddon is about intellectual, emotional, and spiritual allegiance." [2]

Clearly, Armageddon is not a worldwide, political conflict between the East and the West, or between Israel and anti-Semitic forces, but a spiritual struggle between "the kings of the whole world" and the "kings from the east." And, who are these *kings from the east*? Revelation 5:9 states that

Christ has taken the redeemed "out of every tribe and tongue and people and nation" and has "made [them] *kings* and priests to our God" (NKJV). The "kings of the east" are none other than Christ and His followers in the final battle of earth's history. The phrase "kings of the east" represents God's united community of His people. The term has essentially the same meaning as the remnant, the 144,000, and the great multitude (see Rev. 7:4, 9, 12:17).

As already mentioned, figurative references to the east in the Bible are always associated with God and divine deliverance. After sinning, Adam and Eve worshipped God at the east gate of the Garden of Eden; the wilderness sanctuary, Solomon's temple, and all the worshippers faced east. The tribe of Judah into which Jesus was born was camped on the east side. In the act of delivering His people, God caused an east wind to blow the locusts into Egypt; an east wind blew open a path through the Red Sea. In the deliverance of the Jewish people from captivity in Babylon, God brought about the rescue by calling Cyrus from the east (Isa. 41:2, 46:11). Prophecy had pronounced Babylon's doom a century and a half before it occurred, even identifying Cyrus by name as being the instrument God would use to accomplish His purpose, as well as the means by which he would gain entrance into the city (see Isa. 45:1, 2). And just as the waters of the Euphrates were dried up so that Cyrus and his allies could overthrow Babylon, so the symbolic drying up of the Euphrates prepares the way for the ultimate victory of Christ and His people over the forces of Babylon. Let's do a little more searching for further details of this significant event.

Babylon and the Euphrates

The use of these two symbols suggests that a comparison is being made between the fall of modern Babylon and the overthrow of ancient Babylon. Ancient Babylon was generally regarded as a city that would never fall, and there were good reasons for this. Nebuchadnezzar surrounded the city with an inner double wall and an outer double wall. (Some excavations indicate that there were actually six interlocking walls.) The inner walls were 12 feet and 22 feet wide, and were surrounded by a moat, while the outer walls were 24 feet and 26 feet wide. Their dismantled condition makes it difficult to ascertain their height. The interior portion of the inner walls was employed as vaults for storage. It is contended that these vaults contained enough food and supplies to withstand a siege of several years. No wonder Belshazzar simply reveled in partying and feasting (see

Dan. 5:1-4) with thousands of his high-ranking officers the very night the Medes and Persians surrounded the city.

The colors of all of the protective structure were spectacular. The outer walls were made of glazed yellow brick, its gates were a dazzling sky blue, while the gates within the city were rose and white in color. The city was built on the river Euphrates, which flowed diagonally under the city walls and through the city itself. A water-filled moat that surrounded the city provided its inhabitants with more than enough protection from any enemy attacks. It prevented any aggressors from getting close enough to scale the walls or to batter them down. The city's strength and security—in fact, its very existence—depended on the waters upon which it sat.

Cyrus and the allied kings of the Medes and Persians (Jer. 50:41, 51:11, 28) came to Babylon as the predicted "kings of the east" to fulfill God's purpose. Led by Cyrus, the attacking army conquered the city in 538 B.C. by temporarily diverting the water into other channels. The "dried-up" riverbed allowed the Medes and Persians to gain entrance into the city and overthrow it without a major battle (Isa. 44:27, 28). As predicted by Scripture, with the fall of Babylon, the Jewish captives were delivered from their Babylonian oppressors (Isa. 45:1) and permitted to return to Jerusalem and their homeland.

Ancient Babylon's counterpart, modern Babylon, is likewise portrayed as a "prostitute, who sits by many waters" (Rev. 17:1), and in the sixth plague the waters of the Euphrates are dried up (Rev. 16:12). Revelation 17:15 explains, "The waters you saw, where the prostitute sits, are peoples, multitudes, nations and languages." Modern Babylon's power and security are dependent upon the nations and state-governed religions that support it. During the final conflict these enemies of God will eventually self-destruct (see 2 Chron. 20:22, 23; Zech. 14:12, 13; Rev. 17:15, 16). Consequently, modern Babylon, as its ancient counterpart, will find her river of support "dried up." Like Cyrus' overthrow of ancient Babylon and the deliverance of God's people from captivity, in a spiritual sense, Jesus repeats this during the plagues and at the Second Coming.

We must accept the "anointed" role of Cyrus—a type of Christ—if we are to understand the spiritual, worldwide fall of modern Babylon. In the book of Revelation, Babylon represents the great enemy of Christ and His church. In the time of the end, both Babylon and (spiritual) Israel will be universal, their territorial scope worldwide. Thus, the gospel is sent out "to every nation, tribe, language and people (Rev. 14:6), while at the same time, Babylon is accused of making "all the nations drink the maddening wine of her adulteries" (verse 8).

In harmony with this worldwide stage, Babylon's river, the Euphrates, is also worldwide: "The waters you saw, where the prostitute sits, are peoples, multitudes, nations and languages" (Rev. 17:15). God's judgment of modern Babylon is set in motion when the political rulers and the earth's nations suddenly become aware of God's condemnation of Babylon and withdraw (dry up) their support from Babylon. Such understanding moves us away from the common but mistaken notion that Armageddon, Babylon, and the kings of the east are restricted to a local (geographical) setting rather than present in a worldwide context.

Modern Babylon, a confederacy of the earth's religions, is a global alliance. While the pope is generally viewed as the head of such a confederacy, we see Babylon as much more expansive than that. This unusual union of the world's most powerful religious institutions will occur out of a need to coordinate all spiritual efforts in dealing with critical, global challenges. These may include environmental, natural, and economic disaster, the breakdown of law and order (terrorism and crime), as well as spiritual opposition on the part of the true followers of God.

Christians in the United States are increasingly taking the position that catastrophes, terrorist attacks, and natural disasters are divine punishments for the neglect of the law. (It would be more accurate to say that these disasters are the consequences of neglecting God's law.) Because of these views, they will come to believe that a worldwide movement that combines the best of all religions is the only way to bring the human race back to divine approval. In the attempt to save America, they will emphasize the need to return to God's law, even resort to legislation, if necessary, to compel people to worship God—on the first day of the week.

As a general rule, people are quite willing to accept coercive government measures when they perceive a breakdown of law and order. Submitting to restrictive authority seems a small price to pay in order to deal with crime and terrorism. When external measures are employed, such as the union of churches with political powers to bring about peace and moral renewal, you can be sure that it will stifle true spiritual revival, which comes only through the proclamation of the gospel. Alan J. Reinach has a chapter in his book titled "The Battle for the Gospel," in which he contends, "The real battle is for the gospel of Jesus Christ. . . . Politics has become the new gospel. Many Christian leaders are out to 'save America' through political means." He goes on to say, "Christians are first and foremost 'ambassadors for Christ' and serve the interests of the King and His kingdom. . . . Christians don't make the greatest impact on society by pursuing political power but by obtaining genuine spiritual power."[3]

Ellen White projects a situation in which worldwide chaos leads to an extensive drive for security and strong government. In her scenario people will come to believe that one of the measures for restoring order is a renewed commitment to Sunday observance. Those who worship on Sabbath will be perceived as enemies of earthly law and order, supporters of the very chaos that society now seeks to avoid. Society will denounce them as being in rebellion against legitimately constituted authority. The general populace will agree that it would be better to eliminate the dissenters than to allow the world to fall back into chaos.[4]

As we can see, the great battle at the end of history is not so much the movements of great armies and political powers; it is fought more at a personal level. This is because the principle of Babylon is self-centered living and counting on human resources, something that entices all of us. Whenever we are tempted to extol our accomplishments, to put ourselves ahead of others in our daily life, we are on a small scale taking the wrong side in the cosmic conflict. The most dangerous Babylon of all is the one whose spirit lurks in our own hearts.

The Mount Carmel Showdown

As Babylon suffers more and more from natural and moral breakdown, it will increasingly rely on a variety of tactics: the persuasive eloquence of evil spirits to gather all the nations to Babylon's side; the deceptive, spectacular display of miracles on "Mount Carmel" and a counterfeit Second Coming; and, when all else fails, threats and coercion. Since God's people refuse to conform to the requirements of the global confederacy, they will be perceived as a critical threat, a despicable nuisance, and will ultimately be singled out for destruction. Let's take a look at these events in a more detailed way.

In preparation for the plagues and the battle of Armageddon, the forces of heaven and hell make one last attempt to win the world to their side. According to Revelation 18:1-4, a mighty angel comes down from heaven with great power and authority, lighting up the entire earth with its splendor. This represents the greatest outpouring of the Holy Spirit the world has ever seen—the "latter rain." In a loud voice the angel warns that Babylon has "fallen" and "has become a dwelling for demons and a haunt for every impure spirit." It pleads with earth's inhabitants to "come out of her, my people, so that you will not share in her sins, so that you will not receive any of her plagues." This mighty call, known as "the loud cry," brings about the final gathering of all true worshippers from within Babylon, which, in turn, becomes the remnant in preparation for the seal of God.

Just before the earth is lit with heaven's glory, the forces of hell will launch a preemptive attack. Lighting up the skies with demonic brightness, the "spirits of demons" will cause "fire to come down from heaven to the earth" (Rev. 13:13) as well as perform "all kinds of counterfeit power and signs and miracles" (2 Thess. 2:9, NLT). This grand finale is illustrated by the term *Armageddon*, which has the meaning "Mountain of Megiddo." There is no mountain in the world by the name of Megiddo. However, there is a mountain nearby where the ancient city of Megiddo once stood, namely, Mount Carmel.

On that occasion Elijah's prayer brought down fire from heaven that consumed the "burnt offering, and the wood and the stones and the dust, and it licked up the water that was in the trench" to prove that Israel's God was the true God (1 Kings 18:38, NKJV). The book of Revelation implies, then, that the Mount Carmel experience will be repeated in the final conflict. Once again a showdown will take place between God and a devious counterfeit.

What is frighteningly different and deceptive about earth's final showdown is that the fire that is once again brought down is not done by God but by demonic powers, the three evil spirits. As fire flashes forth from the heavens, it falls on the altar of Baal. This spectacular, fiery (counterfeit) display is carried out by a religion patterned after Jezebel's arrangement, in which the prophets of Baal ate "at Jezebel's table" (verse 19), an obvious reference to the union of church and state (see Rev. 13:13, 14). Some interpret this cosmic inferno, not as literal fire, but as symbolic of a false "spirit-filled" revival that will precede the genuine loud cry (see Rev. 18:2). Everything that the world sees, hears, and feels will forcefully suggest that the counterfeit is true. The truths of Scripture, imbued in our hearts by the Holy Spirit, will be the only safeguard for the people of God.

At some point in time probation will close for everyone on earth. This is indicated in Daniel 12:1 when Michael (Christ) stands up. In Revelation 15:8, it is described as a time when smoke fills the heavenly temple and no one enters it until the plagues have done their work. The close of probation is not an arbitrary decree on God's part but rather a time when everyone on earth has reached an enlightened, settled acceptance of one of the two worldwide gospels. It points to a time when God's people, through the outpouring of the Holy Spirit (see Acts 3:19; Rev. 7:3), have reached full maturity, a state of loyalty to God from which they will never turn back. Ellen White probably describes such an event when she speaks about a time when people will have settled "into the truth, both intellectually and spiritually, so they cannot be moved." [5]

One evidence of the close of probation, the dramatic occasion when the world ultimately divides into two distinct groups—those who receive the mark of the beast and those graced with the seal of the living God—is Revelation 22:11: "He who is unjust, let him be unjust still; . . . he who is righteous, let him be righteous still" (NKJV). This text clearly describes a day when every person will either be in an "unjust" or a "righteous" condition, an *irreversible* choice that is fixed for eternity. [6]

Granted, Seventh-day Adventists believe that our world will someday end with a division between the faithful who are saved and the unbelievers who are lost that is never personally annulled or revoked. But the fact that there will be no more changing of sides one day is already falling into place in your life right now; it does not occur with one major choice at some future time but is the accumulation of a lifetime of seemingly small choices. I say "seemingly" because it's been observed that life doesn't involve small choices; they just look that way at the time. Every action, in some way, is made on account of either the right side or the wrong side. Quite often what appears at first glance to be something incidental or irrelevant can turn out to be a life-changing event. The truth is that it's these kinds of moments that make us who we are. It is through small things that our characters are formed, that destinies are determined. I wholeheartedly agree with Sherlock Holmes's observation, "The little things are infinitely the most important."

The Role of Demons

It's been wisely observed: For the truly faithful, no miracle is necessary; for those who defiantly doubt, no miracle is sufficient.

Today many Christians do not realize that the stories of Creation and the Fall of humanity, as recorded in Genesis, are not given simply to reveal how our first parents came into existence and that they fell into sin.

These stories also make known *how* Adam and Eve fell and thus serve as a purposeful reminder to future generations of Satan's subtle temptations and the methods he employs. It is for us to see that these temptations (in Eden) are only the beginning of a cleverly devised plan to deceive and control all of humankind. Satan's strategy is to involve this planet in his ultimate ambition to overthrow the highest administration in the universe—God's government.

In any warfare, it is not enough to know that you have an enemy. Information concerning his whereabouts, his strength, and his methods of attack is vital before successful planning and proper preparations can be made. Satan knows that, and so "it is his policy to conceal himself and his manner of working. There is nothing that the great deceiver fears so much as that we shall become acquainted with his devices." [7]

As we shall see, there are a great number of similarities between the temptations in Eden and the sixth plague, but one especially stands out: in both cases it is the righteous who are confronted by the demonic.

"It was by the display of supernatural power, in making the serpent his medium, that Satan caused the fall of Adam and Eve in Eden. Before the close of time he will work still greater wonders. So far as his power extends, he will perform actual miracles. Says the Scripture: 'He . . . deceiveth them that dwell on the earth by the means of those miracles which he had power to do,' not merely those which he pretends to do. Something more than mere impostures is brought to view in this scripture." [8]

In the New Testament the apostle Paul identifies evil angels as the behind-the-scenes recipients of misguided pagan worship. Paul pulls aside the curtain and declares, "The things which the Gentiles sacrifice they sacrifice to demons and not to God, and I do not want you to have fellowship with demons" (1 Cor. 10:20, NKJV). Christians find it difficult to assert that such religions as Buddhism, Hinduism, Shinto, and Taoism, in which offerings are brought to the temple in honor of their gods or deceased ancestors, in many respects involve demon worship.

Fellowship with demons was one of Paul's great concerns. For people to have fellowship with demons means that human beings are ignorantly holding communion with fallen angels. An example of this occurred in the Old Testament when the Israelites approached the Promised Land and their route took them through the region of Moab, just east of Canaan. The beautiful Moabite women invited (seduced) Israel to participate in their idolatrous practice of worshipping their pagan deity named Baal. Numbers

25:1, 2 describes what happened: "Now Israel . . . began to commit harlotry with the women of Moab. They [the women] invited the people [Israel] to the sacrifices of their gods, and the people ate and bowed down to their gods, so Israel was joined to Baal of Peor" (NKJV).

Now, who were these "gods"? The Moabites believed that their gods were actually their own tribal heroes who, after death, had passed over to the other side and to whom they were now offering sacrifices. The psalmist affirms this when he writes, "They [the Israelites] joined themselves also to Baal of Peor, and ate sacrifices made to the dead" (Ps. 106:28, NKJV). But David goes one step further by stating that the Israelites, by eating food offered to Moabite "gods," were, in effect, worshipping demons without realizing it. "They [the Israelites] served their [Moabite] idols [Baal of Peor], which became a snare to them. They even sacrificed their sons and their daughters to demons" (Ps. 106:36, 37, NKJV).

The Bible indicates that the very atmosphere around our planet is filled with a hostile race of beings superior in knowledge and power to us (see Eph. 6:12). They have the advantage of being invisible, and, being spiritual intelligences, they are able to understand the way human minds work and operate. While the Bible does not describe their personal appearance, we know they are usually invisible, though they may assume physical form. They are spiritual beings; they have personalities, have great intelligence (not wisdom), have super-physical strength, and can completely dominate human beings. They are hopelessly depraved. They are beyond the reach of redemption, and their doom is sealed (see 2 Peter 2:4).

Miracles: Delightful but Deceptive

It is highly significant that in Revelation, the book that provides more highlights of last-day events than any other book in the New Testament, each time the word "miracle" appears, it is associated with demons. This makes it rather obvious that in the final conflict demons will play a prominent role in deceiving the medium as well as the beholder (see Rev. 13:13, 14; 16:13, 14). It is plain to see that during the final crisis miraculous signs and wonders will not be what they seem. These end-time deceptions are also discussed in 2 Thessalonians 2:8-12 and Matthew 24:24-27.

"Many who refuse the message which the Lord sends them are seeking to find pegs on which to hang doubts, to find some excuse for rejecting the light of heaven. In the face of clear evidence they say, as did the Jews, 'Show us a miracle, and we will believe. If these messengers have the truth, why do they not heal the sick?' . . . Could their eyes be opened, they would see evil angels exulting around them and triumphing in their power to deceive them. The day is just before us when Satan will answer the demand of these doubters and present numerous miracles to confirm the faith of all those who are seeking this kind of evidence."[9]

Paul deals with this peculiar challenge in his letter to the Ephesians. First, he describes the nature of the enemy: "For we do not wrestle against flesh and blood, but against principalities, against powers, against the rulers of the darkness of this age, against spiritual hosts of wickedness in the heavenly places." He then admonishes: "Therefore [now that you better understand your foe] take up the whole armor of God that you may be able to withstand in the evil day." After listing several key parts of the armor, he concludes with this significant weapon: "And take . . . the sword of the Spirit, which is the word of God" (Eph. 6:12, 13, 17, NKJV).

Satan will unite the world against God's people by "working miracles" and gaining oppressive assistance from the "kings of the earth." The book *The Great Controversy* says that "through the agency of spiritualism, miracles will be wrought, the sick will be healed, and many undeniable wonders will be performed." It also says, "Papists, who boast of miracles as a certain sign of the true church, will be readily deceived by this wonder-working power; and Protestants, having cast away the shield of truth, will also be deluded. Papists, Protestants, and worldlings will alike . . . see in this union a grand movement for the conversion of the world and the ushering in of the long-expected millennium."[10]

Widespread Demonic Activity

In the book of Revelation John alludes to the eventual takeover of this planet by evil forces when he declares that "Babylon"—a symbol of the corrupt religious systems of the world—"has become a dwelling for demons and a haunt for every impure spirit" (Rev. 18:2). The world is presently being bombarded by a host of demonic exhibitions, such as psychic hotlines, astrology, apparitions, spiritualistic communications and healings, and a wide array of occult and pagan practices. To complicate things even more, those who hold to atheistic philosophies do not believe in the reality of the supernatural; they choose to dismiss the demonic realm as an illusion and say that all supernatural phenomena have natural explanations.

On the flip side, in today's increasingly pagan culture great masses of people seem to be captivated by anything that suggests the mystical, the miraculous, or the angelic. One reason for the overwhelming fascination with the paranormal (otherworldly) is that we cannot live in a spiritual vacuum. Driven by an intense desire to find help in untraditional ways or places, most people are not inclined to "test the spirits to see whether they are from God" (1 John 4:1). This is as deadly as eating or drinking something unknown to you without first checking the list of ingredients.

The point has already been made that when cultures or religions turn away from the truths of the Bible, they will surely turn to the lies and deceptions of the enemy. This includes a wide array of Eastern religions and occult practices, such as near-death and UFO experiences, mysticism, witchcraft, and angel encounters. The problem is not that angels are getting too much attention but how they're being presented. Generally speaking, false, unbiblical concepts are widely presented, generally the kinds that promote the deceptions of the evil one. Although all of these are especially attractive to the world, keep in mind that much of the occult and spiritualism has been specifically created to seduce Christians.[11]

This was vividly demonstrated by a video I showed to my senior religion classes several years ago. Titled "Miracles," this 15-minute news story had aired on a major television news network, and it featured a young woman's account of driving through New Mexico with her 6-year-old daughter. The story says that about the time the young child complains of severe stomach cramps, the car engine breaks down. The mother's earlier decision to seek a shortcut by driving on side roads means that they are stalled where there is scarcely any traffic. As the child's condition worsens, the mother realizes that it might be a long time before any help arrives. In her desperation, the mother prays for help, and almost immediately an elderly couple drives up and appears at the car window. After she explains her dilemma, the man proceeds to improvise a temporary replacement for the torn fan belt that is the source of her problem. While he's doing this, the woman gets into the back seat of the car and gently soothes the little girl. Before leaving, the couple provides the mother with directions to the nearest hospital.

After the child's emergency appendectomy, the father, who is stationed at a nearby army camp, comes to visit them. As they walk through the hospital lobby, they are surprised to see a picture of the elderly couple on the wall. It is then that they make a startling discovery—this couple had died 30 years earlier. The narrator of the video concludes by saying that in today's world, miracles still occur and heavenly angels continue to help people in times of need.[12]

My students struggled with the spiritual implications of this story. They knew what the Bible says about the dead, that they haven't ascended into heaven but are in the grave until the resurrection (see 1 Cor. 15:51, 52). Some reasoned that it might have been holy angels in disguise doing their work as "ministering spirits." After all, doesn't the Bible say that people may entertain "angels without knowing it" (Heb. 13:2)? I pointed out that in the spirit realm, there are only two options: the holy and demonic. Transformed into "ministers of righteousness" (2 Cor. 11:15, NKJV), demons can easily perform "displays of power through signs and wonders" (2 Thess. 2:9), often doing great acts of kindness. It is imperative, therefore, that we "test the spirits to see whether they are from God" (1 John 4:1). When placed under the light of God's Word, the story of the elderly couple fails the test because it persuades people that the dead are still alive.

It was extremely difficult for my students to label this kind, helpful, apparently loving couple as demons in disguise. After all, miracles that truly help people come from God, right? Keep in mind that Satan can cleverly impersonate whatever he wishes, as he did in Eden; he can masquerade as "an angel of light" (2 Cor. 11:14). When it serves his purpose, the prince of darkness can be a charming gentleman, even act as a loving person. But Satan is "a liar" (John 8:44), exceedingly cunning, carrying out "every kind of evil deception" (2 Thess. 2:10, NLT). He is well aware that through an act of kindness he can pave the way to deceive a massive audience into believing a lie regarding the dead. This will be repeated at the end of time when Satan will perform spectacular miracles, raise the dead, and personate the second coming of Jesus. This comment by Ellen White is appropriate: "I have been shown that Satan has not been stupid and careless these many years, since his fall, but has been learning. He has grown more artful. His plans are laid deeper, and are more covered with religious garment to hide their deformity." [13]

At the close of Armageddon Christ and the hosts of heaven come vaulting through the skies on the greatest rescue mission ever carried out. At that moment, "The Lord Jesus will overthrow with the breath of his mouth and destroy by the splendor of his coming" (verse 8) all the earthly enemies of God. This is greatly amplified in Revelation 19:

"I saw heaven standing open and there before me was a white horse, whose rider is called Faithful and True. With justice he judges and wages war. . . . The armies of heaven were following him, riding on white horses. . . . Coming out of his mouth is a sharp sword with which to strike down the nations. . . . Then I saw the beast and the kings of the earth and their armies gathered together to wage war against the rider on the horse and his army. But the beast was captured, and with it the false prophet who had performed the signs on its behalf. With these signs he had deluded those who had received the mark of the beast and worshiped its image. The two of them were thrown alive into the fiery lake" (verses 11-20).

New Heaven, New Earth

God's story, which culminates with the Second Coming during Armageddon, decisively shows that Christ will never forsake His people at the time of their greatest need. In the climactic conclusion of the cosmic conflict between good and evil, which extends to events on the other side of the millennium (see Isa. 24:3; Jer. 4:23-26), all the righteous are destined for deliverance, and all the evil ones are doomed for destruction. The time will come when all the accusations of Satan have been clearly answered, when all lingering issues in the great controversy have been resolved, when the story that began in Genesis finds its completion in Revelation.

In Genesis God creates "the heavens and the earth" (Gen. 1:1). In Revelation John sees "a *new* heaven and a *new* earth" (Rev. 21:1). In Genesis the created order comes under a curse (Gen. 3:17), but in Revelation "there shall be no more curse" (Rev. 22:3, NKJV). In Genesis human beings are alienated from God, running away from His presence in fear (Gen. 3:10). Revelation's view of the earth made new says, "God himself will be with them [His people] and be their God" (Rev. 21:3).

So what does this mean personally to you and me? With the end of the great controversy comes unspeakably good news: it's either translation or resurrection, and, with it, the gift of immortality and a new heaven and the new earth as our inheritance. With the eye of faith, learn to picture yourself as part of that great multitude that no one can number. With the ear of faith, learn to hear your own voice in that thunderous roar of millions of human voices from "before the throne and before the Lamb" saying, "Salvation belongs to our God, who sits on the throne, and to the Lamb" (Rev. 7:9, 10). If we already have everlasting life by faith, as Jesus says we do, then we may rightfully think of ourselves as already there. This is where we will have the unbelievable opportunity to meet the original tenants of this planet, along with unnumbered family members and loved ones. This is where all of us will walk with our loving Creator in the cool of the day. We will fellowship together, "drink from [the] fruit of the vine . . . new"

(Matt. 26:29) with our Savior, just as He promised He would do, and then feast in absolute regal style around the tree of life. Come and join us. We would love to see you there!

---

[1] In Lucifer's rebellion against God in heaven, it is significant that Lucifer is described as having an intense longing to "sit enthroned on the *mount of assembly*" (Isa. 14:13). It just might be that Armageddon not only points to the final conflict but also reflects the very first conflict in the great controversy.

[2] J. Paulien, *Armageddon at the Door*, pp. 113, 115.

[3] Alan J. Reinach, "The Battle for the Gospel," in *Politics and Prophecy*, pp. 7, 8.

[4] E. G. White, *The Great Controversy*, pp. 592, 615.

[5] *The SDA Bible Commentary*, Ellen G. White Comments, vol. 4, p. 1161.

[6] The close of probation is a time of settled convictions, not only on the part of every human being but also on the part of God Himself.

[7] E. G. White, *The Great Controversy*, p. 516.

[8] E. G. White, *Testimonies*, vol. 5, p. 698.

[9] E. G. White, *Evangelism* (Washington, D.C.: Review and Herald Pub. Assn., 1946), p. 594.

[10] E. G. White, *The Great Controversy*, p. 588.

[11] "Fearful sights of a supernatural character will soon be revealed in the heavens, in token of the power of miracle-working demons. The spirits of devils will go forth to the kings of the earth and to the whole world, to fasten them in deception, and urge them to unite with Satan in his last struggle against the government of heaven. . . . They will perform wonderful miracles of healing and will profess to have revelations from heaven contradicting the testimony of the Scriptures" (E. G. White, *The Great Controversy*, p. 624).

[12] This video was my personal recording of a news story featured on one of the major news networks (ABC, CBS, or NBC) in the late 1980s or early 1990s. It was shown on television during prime time one evening, at which time I taped it. The announcer stated that the film was a true story. Unfortunately, I have since lost my recording.

[13] Ellen G. White, *Spiritual Gifts* (Battle Creek, Mich.: James White, 1860), vol. 2, p. 277.

Let God Lead You

...to Love, Joy, and Peace

To Build a Life

Luke B. Heimann

Luke Heimann had money and success as a building contractor. What he didn't have was love, joy, or peace. So he made a deal with God: He would give the Lord 30 days to tell him why he was missing these things.

What Luke had been searching for in all the wrong places was as plain as day, once he let God reconstruct his life.

978-0-8280-2668-0

Watch this video to learn more.

AdventistBookCenter.com | 800.765.6955

Review&Herald
Spread the Word

They Didn't Believe in Jesus.

He Showed Up Anyway.

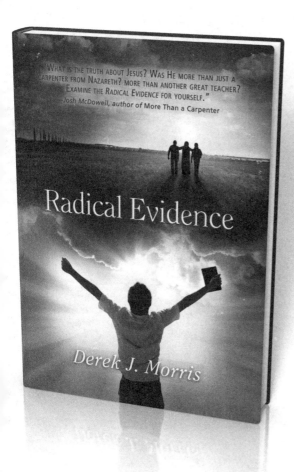

In his latest book, Derek Morris introduces you to people who have had a dramatic encounter with the Messiah they didn't believe in. There's a Shiite Muslim and an African ancestor worshipper. There's Clifford Goldstein, an atheist and obsessed novelist who found his life taking an unexpected turn.

People in Bible times also present evidence. There are the prophets who spoke of things they did not understand, but whose words came true in the gospel story.

Perhaps you have a friend who has doubts about the divinity of Jesus. Or maybe you work with a straight-up unbeliever. Invite them to read this book and see the radical evidence for a real and personal Savior.

Hardcover: 978-0-8127-0514-0.

DVD: Four presentations, approx. 28 minutes each. 978-1-936929-07-8.

--- **Other books in the Radical series you may enjoy** ---

THE RADICAL PRAYER

Hardcover
978-0-8127-0486-0

Audio CD
978-0-981712-41-3

DVD
978-0-981712-40-6

Spanish Paperback
978-8-472082-67-0

RADICAL PROTECTION

Hardcover
978-0-8127-0476-1

Audio CD
978-1-936929-01-6

DVD
978-1-936929-00-9

Trilogy Scripture Songs CD
978-1-936929-02-3

THE RADICAL TEACHINGS OF JESUS

Hardcover
978-0-8127-0498-3

Audio CD
978-0-981712-49-9

DVD
978-0-981712-42-0

Leader's Kit
978-1-932267-77-8

e and availability subject to change.

entistBookCenter.com | 800.765.6955

Review&Herald
Spread the Word

This Could Change Everything

Find transforming power for your life

Do you feel like temptations always beat you into submission? You can't seem to win a victory and wonder if you're not trying hard enough, or if God isn't holding up His end of the bargain.

In the book, *Transformation*, Jim Ayer opens up about his own experience as a serial sinner and tells how he connected with the power that God has provided to change us from the inside out.

A companion study guide, *Your Daily Journey to Transformation*, Jim and Janene Ayer take individuals or small groups on a 12-week journey toward a transformed life—a life shaped and energized by the Holy Spirit.

"Behold, I make all things new," says Jesus. See that promise fulfilled in your life today. Paperback, 978-0-8280-2711-3

Your Daily Journey to Transformation
A 12-week Study Guide
Paperback
978-0-8280-2702-1

availability subject to change.

HOP
OUR
AY

» Visit your local Adventist Book Center®
» Call toll-free 800.765.6955
» Click www.AdventistBookCenter.com

  Review&Herald®

IEW AND HERALD® PUBLISHING ASSOCIATION | SINCE 1861 | WWW.REVIEWANDHERALD.COM